PAPER MONSTERS

MATERIAL TEXTS

A complete list of books in the series
is available from the publisher.

PAPER MONSTERS

Persona and Literary Culture in Elizabethan England

Samuel Fallon

PENN

UNIVERSITY OF PENNSYLVANIA PRESS

PHILADELPHIA

Published by
University of Pennsylvania Press
Philadelphia, Pennsylvania 19104-4112
www.upenn.edu/pennpress

Printed in the United States of America on acid-free paper
1 3 5 7 9 10 8 6 4 2

Library of Congress Cataloging-in-Publication Data

Names: Fallon, Samuel, author.
Title: Paper monsters: persona and literary culture in Elizabethan England / Samuel Fallon.
Other titles: Material texts.
Description: 1st edition. | Philadelphia: University of Pennsylvania Press, [2019] | Series: Material texts | Includes bibliographical references and index.
Identifiers: LCCN 2018049428 | ISBN 9780812251296 (hardcover)
Subjects: LCSH: English literature—Early modern, 1500-1700—History and criticism. | Persona (Literature) | Characters and characteristics in literature. | Authors and readers—England—History—16th century. | Authors and readers—England—History—17th century.
Classification: LCC PR421.F35 2019 | DDC 820.9/003—dc23
LC record available at https://lccn.loc.gov/2018049428

For Anne

CONTENTS

Introduction

This book begins with the story of a strange birth. London, 1592: a young writer, fresh from the university, is down on his luck; he needs a patron and a meal. At his wit's end, he returns to the haunt of poor literary types, the churchyard of Saint Paul's, where he meets by chance the book trade's purchaser of last resort: the devil. The writer is pleased to learn that this "blind Retayler" is hungry for news from the city—he has, we understand, many interests there—and, if the writer has any scruples, he soon overcomes them. He resolves to send this new buyer a satire on the theme of the seven deadly sins: "And so," he reports, "(in short time) was this Paper-monster, *Pierce Penilesse*, begotten."[1]

The paper monster thus born was, of course, the devil's satire, the text of which follows this account of its genesis. Then, too, it was the actual book in which both satire and backstory appeared—the book written by Thomas Nashe and published by Richard Jones under the title *Pierce Penilesse His Supplication to the Diuell.* Nashe's creation, in other words, was a personified text. But it was also a textual person. For, in an ambiguity befitting a paper monster, Pierce Penilesse is the name both of the text and of its desperate young author, the charismatic protagonist who is not made but "begotten" into something curiously like life.

It did not take long for the intimation of uncanny life to be borne out. Pierce may have been conceived in the pages of Nashe's fiction, but he soon moved beyond them—and beyond Nashe's control. Praised, imitated, petitioned, and ridiculed by a series of writers and readers, Pierce took on a life of his own, as if he were a person at large in the literary world of early modern England. Nashe himself died in 1601, but even then his strange alter ego lived on. In 1604, Lucifer, the narrator of Thomas Middleton's *The Blacke Booke*, went looking for Pierce. He found him drunken and disheveled in one of London's shabbiest inns:

> I stumbled up two payre of stayres in the darke, but at last caught in mine eyes the sullen blaze of a melancholy lampe, that burnt very tragically vppon the narrow Deske o[f] a halfe Bedstead, which descryed all the pittifull Ruines throughout the whole chamber, the bare priuities of the stone-walls were hid with two pieces of painted Cloth; but so ragged and tottreb [*sic*], that one might haue seene all neuerthelesse, hanging for all the world like the two men in Chaynes between *Mile-end* & *Hackney* . . . in this unfortunate Tyring-house lay poore *Pierce* vppon a Pillow stuft with Horsemeate, the Sheetes smudged so durtily, as if they had bene stolne by night out of Saint Pulchers Church-yard when the Sexton had left a Graue open, and so laide the dead bodies wool-ward: the Couerlet was made of pieces a blacke Cloth clapt together, such as was scatterd off the railes in *Kings-Streete*, at the Queenes Funerall: vpon this miserable Beds-head, lay the old Copy of his Supplication in foule written hand which my blacke knight of the Post conueyed to Hell: which no longer I entertaynd in my hand, but with the ratling and blabbing of the papers, poore *Pierce* began to stretch and grate his Nose against the hard Pillowe.[2]

Pierce here cuts a deeply grotesque and, at the same time, a deeply compelling figure. Middleton's Lucifer seems torn between contempt and concern: he is eager to list the squalid, humiliating details of Pierce's room, and yet he seems moved by the indignity in which he finds him. Discovered as if by chance, Pierce looms for Middleton as less a fictional character than a real person. He elicits mixed feelings and mixed motives, like a real person; like a real person, he seems possessed of a will of his own. And he can surprise us, like a real person, by disappearing and going to seed.

The grotesque extremes to which Pierce was carried may have been unique, but the sense of autonomy that brought him there was not. In fact, the last decades of the sixteenth century saw a proliferation of figures like him. Philisides and Astrophil, Euphues and Martin Marprelate, Colin Clout and his cohort of shepherds, the elusive ghost of Robert Greene: it is impossible to spend much time with literature of the 1580s and 1590s without meeting these names again and again. The names identified a cast of strange literary beings: persons that fell somewhere between the poles of author and character, fiction and reality. Continually reimagined, flitting between texts, these figures lived on the terms of their seriality, and in their periodic returns they came to seem like independent agents in the real world of writing, publication, and reception. I call them *personae*, and *Paper Monsters* tells the story of their rise.

This story, as we will see, turns out to be a surprisingly complicated one. For while the persona belongs to the longer history of literary form—as a chapter in the development of practices of autofiction and self-representation or, more broadly, in the long evolution of literary character—any attempt to give an account of the persona as a form begins to lead elsewhere. This is because personae were distinctively social forms. They were fictions defined by their mobility, fictions that came to life through the writers who reclaimed them, the stationers who published them, the readers whom they enchanted. As artifacts of the networks that produced them, they bear in sedimented layers the traces of histories that we are likely to consider sociological or material rather than properly "formal": the history of the early modern literary field, for instance, or the history of what we have come to call print culture.

It is complicated, too, by the fact that personae insist on telling their own stories. They are social artifacts, but they are also reflexive ones, and their wandering paths encode the histories (in all of their eccentricity) that the literary field of Elizabethan England was beginning to tell of itself. A last example from the career of Pierce Penilesse—taken from one of Gabriel Harvey's sardonic attacks on Nashe, his longtime enemy—will illustrate the point:

> Arte did but spring in such, as Sir Iohn Cheeke, and M. Ascham: & witt budd in such, as Sir Phillip Sidney, & M. Spencer; which were but the violetes of March, or the Primeroses of May: till the one begane to sprowte in M. Robart Greene, as in a sweating Impe of the euer-greene Laurell; the other to blossome in M. Pierce Penilesse, as in the riche garden of pore Adonis: both to growe to perfection, in M. Thomas Nashe, whose prime is a haruest, whose Arte a misterie, whose witt a miracle, whose stile the onely life of the presse, and the very hart-blood of the Grape.[3]

Like Pierce himself, Harvey's potted history of English letters is hard to place. Torn between metaphors, it is also torn between pictures of literary history—between the genealogy's sense of temporal descent and garden's spatial image of a field of writers budding alongside each other. More striking, perhaps, is its divided tone: having begun with genuine praise, Harvey shifts in the blink of an eye to cutting irony, with Philip Sidney and Edmund Spenser giving way to the sprouting weeds of Harvey's nemeses, Greene and Nashe. But the passage's strangest detail may be the inclusion of Pierce, who appears alongside—or rather, in fact, *precedes*—Nashe himself. A year earlier, Nashe had begotten Pierce; now, Harvey suggests, persona begets author.

Harvey's subtle reversal marks a literary history that runs aslant those we are used to telling—a history in which the author is displaced and estranged by the figure of the persona. *Paper Monsters* takes its cue from this reversal. Rather than the authorial corpus, it mines the idiosyncratic archives left by the migratory wanderings of personae. These archives record the wide range of agents—the writers, patrons, editors, stationers, and readers—whose collective efforts lay behind the processes of literary production and reception. But they also reveal the startling agency of personae themselves: their capacity to provoke and persuade, to forge connections across space and time, to accrue prestige and earn notoriety, to win love and sympathy and (sometimes) outrage and disgust. As mobile and migratory fictions, pulled from text to text and writer to writer, personae were the forms that brought a literary culture to life. They projected presence at a moment when a widening public most demanded it, and they grounded a discourse of aesthetic value and identity when an emergent literary field most needed one. It was through its personae that late Elizabethan literary culture turned an eye on itself, and to read them is to encounter that culture in the curious vitality of its animating fictions.

Personae: A Prehistory

The concept of the persona is both an old and a new one. A Latin term for an actor's mask, *persona* marks identity as a matter of performance: to be a *dramatis persona* is to efface one identity by assuming another as a role.[4] As a device, the persona (by that name) is a more recent invention, a product of the New Criticism's fastidious separation of poetic speakers from authorial persons.[5] If the discovery of the persona, or later the implied author, ruled out naïve appeals to biography, these terms also risked anachronism, for they imposed a modern rhetorical principle on texts that make no explicit distinction between author and narrator (or "speaker," or poetic "voice").[6]

My own use of the term observes narrower limits. In early modern texts, the words *personate* and *personation* carried the force of individual specificity: they could refer to dramatic impersonation, to the adoption of false identities, or simply to the act of referring to someone by name.[7] The personae in this book are perhaps better termed personations, for they rely on the referential force of the proper name and project the narrative particularity of fictional characters. Early modern personation found a rhetorical cousin in the figure of prosopopoeia, the attribution of speech or action to an absent or imagined person.[8] In his poetic manual *The Arte of English Poesie* (1589), in fact, George Puttenham gave prosopopoeia the English name "the Counterfait in personation."[9] One could perform oneself or personify someone or something else, and Elizabethan personae drew on both possibilities, functioning at times as self-representations even as they relied for their continued survival on the narrative imagination of their readers. Here the New Critics' use of persona is instructive: for them, the device is unmistakably a method of *reading*—a way of establishing an interpretive relation to texts by imagining a particular kind of person behind them. But Pierce and Colin Clout and Philisides were not implied authors or unnamed speakers in need of critical excavation: they were right there on the surface. It was their full realization as characters, indeed, that gave them their peculiar power. Granted the specificity of narrative, the personae that occupy this book emerged as discrete and seemingly autonomous agents—and as agents capable of courting the appropriative attentions of their readers.[10]

At first blush, there was little new about such characters. Early modern writers inherited a venerable tradition of "figures of the poet," a tradition with roots in Virgil and Ovid and modern archetypes in Dante and Petrarch.[11] Such figures were typical of epic—announcing themselves in order to invoke the muses, if nothing else—but also of satire and pastoral: Virgil's Tityrus and Jacopo Sannazaro's Sincero were key sources for the shepherd alter egos of Sidney and Spenser. This tradition of poetic self-reference made its way into English verse through Geoffrey Chaucer, who inserted himself, in the opening lines of *The Canterbury Tales*, into the company of pilgrims gathered at Southwark, "redy to wenden on my pilgrimage / To Caunterbury with ful devout corage."[12] The innovation of the *Tales* was ironic humor: "Chaucer" turns out to be a delightfully incompetent poet, telling the derivative "Tale of Sir Thopas" in some of the work's crudest verse. Of course, this deflation is of a piece with the self-reflexive play that characterizes metafiction more generally: in its own way, it draws attention to and works to secure the poet's place in a literary tradition. Because of their role in shaping this tradition, poet-figures became strategies of allusive affiliation, from Dante's journey with Virgil in the *Inferno* to the Homeric resonances of John Milton's loss of sight in *Paradise Lost*. Chaucer's pilgrim quickly inspired allusive encounters of his own, encounters that canonized Chaucer even as they legitimated his readers-turned-imitators.[13] In the most well-known, Harry Bailly greets a fellow pilgrim in a Canterbury inn. "I answerde my name was Lydgate," reports the narrator, naming the work's poet as a new member of Chaucer's band and framing the poem that will follow—*The Siege of Thebes* (c. 1421–22)—as one more tale in their ongoing game of tale-telling.[14]

If one line of descent moves through winking metafictions, however, another emerges in a very different sort of figure: the unattached, authorless stock characters of the satiric tradition. Perhaps the best example is Chaucer's near-contemporary Piers Plowman, the allegorical center of William Langland's alliterative poem of the same name. *Piers Plowman*'s bitter anticlerical satire gave the poem special resonance in the reformist upheaval of the sixteenth century; in the years after Robert Crowley's 1550 print edition, numerous imitations and responses appeared, beginning in 1553 with *Pierce the Ploughman's Crede*, that centered on Piers himself.[15] These responses, unlike John Lydgate's invocation of Chaucer, did not hinge on any reference to the poet's person; rather, the plowman's appeal stemmed from his anonymity, his availability to anyone who wished to speak in his rustic, willfully marginal voice. While the attribution of *Piers Plowman* remained a matter of editorial conjecture—several manuscripts identified the poet as Robert (rather than William) Langland—Piers emerged as a character at large: a free agent with, as Sarah Kelen puts it, "his own 'authority function' separate from Langland's author-function."[16]

Chaucer the pilgrim and Piers Plowman thus mark out two competing genealogies for the late sixteenth-century persona: on the one hand, a strategy of poetic self-representation tied to a laureate tradition and, on the other, a store of stock figures, free of ties to particular authors and hence available for repeated, anonymous appropriation. It is tempting to approach personae as "fictions of authorship," in Katharine Wilson's words: as gestures of self-reference made possible (and given meaning) by the textual presence of the author.[17] For modern readers, this logic of reference may be inescapable. We grasp Stephen Dedalus as a persona, after all, inasmuch as he is a recognizable cipher for James Joyce. The personal signatures that abound in modernist and postmodern texts can thus be subsumed under the broader category of what Aaron Jaffe calls the "imprimatur": the reification at the level of form of an individuality that is unmistakably the author's.[18] Until the consolidation of the author function in modernity, however, the relation between the concept of authorship and the production of textual personae was a contingent rather than a necessary one. If, in the cases of Chaucer and Lydgate, authorial self-reference carries a claim to literary canonicity, Piers and stock characters like him make clear that personae did not depend in any simple way on authors. Personae do not simply encode something external (the mark of the author) in the body of the text, nor do they remain the property of the authors who invent them. Instead, they arise along boundaries, as characters that point beyond themselves, to a world outside of any particular text—and that, in the process, invite others to reimagine them.[19]

My aim here is not to insist on the hard and fast separation of categories that were in fact fluid. Satiric personae could be reflexive author-figures or stock characters: the nimble irony of Erasmus's *The Praise of Folly*, for instance, urges a paradoxical identification of Erasmus and Folly. In English writing in the sixteenth century, moreover, such seemingly distinct traditions as popular satire and classical pastoral substantially overlapped, a point made in different ways by Mike Rodman Jones, who traces in the rise of the plowman figure a strain of "radical pastoral," and Rachel Hile, who finds in Spenserian pastoral a new mode of "indirect satire."[20] Elizabethan personae emerged at the intersection of different forms of personation, blending character and author and straddling the putative divide between popular and literary modes.

This fluidity was already clear in the intertwined afterlives of Piers and Chaucer: early printed editions of *The Canterbury Tales* notably included a plowman text, *The Plowman's Tale* (c. 1400). Such syncretic blends flourished in what was a culturally omnivorous book trade. One characteristic form was the jestbook: an anthological collection of witty vignettes organized (at least in its later versions) around the unifying charisma of a single comic protagonist. Jestbook heroes usually were not, and did not pretend to be, the authors of their books—often they were not even their narrators, but rather the subjects of storytelling, their witty antics providing the punch line to each jest—and yet in *Merie Tales . . . by Master Skelton* (1567), in *Scoggins Iests* (c. 1540) or *Tarltons Iests* (1613) or *Kemps Nine Daies Wonder* (1600), they found their way into titles, claiming effective possession of the texts in which they appeared. The presence of John Skelton—"educated & broughte vp in Oxfoorde," as *Merie Tales* recounts, "and there . . . made a Poete Lauriat"—gives the lie to any attempt to distinguish "literary" Chaucerian metafiction from "popular" stock characters.[21] Indeed, Skelton's afterlife as an antic jester shows how readily a laureate could be claimed for popular entertainment—and how easily he could become just another fictional character. The charisma of this jestbook Skelton owes something to the irreverence of the real Skelton's poetry, but perhaps even more to the genre's fiction of extemporaneous wit.[22] It is no coincidence that the stage clowns Will Kemp and Richard Tarlton also found their way into jestbooks—a form defined, in Ian Munro's account, by its "ambiguous cultural position, balanced between performance and text, and between oral culture and print culture."[23]

Tarlton's example is particularly revealing. By some distance the most famous stage performer of his day, Tarlton found a second life as an antic performer in print. For those who had seen him in person, his appearances in jestbooks, ballads, and pamphlets—in *Tarltons Newes out of Purgatorie* (1590), for instance—would have summoned memories of the actor's voice and body, grounding his textual persona in a kinetic theatrical celebrity. If performance at some level resists translation into writing, a medium that cannot reproduce the physical experience of the stage, Tarlton's pamphlet ubiquity nonetheless shows just how eager writers and publishers were to derive textual from dramatic charisma.[24] The utility of Tarlton's name, Alexandra Halasz suggests, lay in its suggestion that pamphlets offered a kind of performative entertainment too.[25] His afterlife carried him into Henry Chettle's pamphlet *Kind-Hartes Dreame* (1592), a dialogue of ghosts that also featured Robert Greene and Pierce Penilesse. Their encounter (to which I will return in the next chapter) makes clear how much textual personation depended on an analogy to theatrical performance. Yet it also helps explain why Elizabethan personae were in the first place a literary phenomenon: their peculiar half-lives exploited text's lack of the theater's immediate, bodily presence, and they relied on the reproducibility implicit in textual circulation. On stage, Tarlton was himself; on the page, by contrast, "Tarlton" became a reimaginable persona, and a style. (So much so that Gabriel Harvey, writing in 1592, could carp at Nashe's "Tarltonizing wit."[26]) While Tarlton became a celebrity in the theater, his haunting afterlife thus depended on the (re)generative possibilities of print, the medium, as it were, through which Chettle conducts his séance of dead celebrities.

Paper Monsters

The picture that I have begun to sketch is one in which a pair of durable traditions—poetic self-reference, on the one hand, and on the other, the stock character—converge under the pressure of a shifting public culture in the latter half of the sixteenth century. One key factor in this convergence, as Tarlton's posthumous celebrity suggests, was the rise of the public theater. Another was the ongoing expansion of the English book trade.[27] The scale and the frenetic pace of the print market were widely remarked in the 1580s and 1590s, and often with dismay. "It fareth nowe a daies," fumed Nashe, "with vnlearned Idiots as it doth with she Asses, who bring foorth all their life long; euen so these brainlesse Bussards, are euery quarter bigge wyth one Pamphlet or other."[28] When William Webbe, sounding a similar note, deplored "the vncountable rabble of ryming Ballet makers, and compylers of sencelesse sonets," his anxiety pointed particularly to the growth of literary genres as a sector of the market.[29] Indeed, as Alan B. Farmer and Zachary Lesser demonstrate in their statistical analysis of the Elizabethan book trade, poetry and prose fiction alike saw their market shares increase significantly at the end of the century.[30] If reading the products of this market, as Nashe and Webbe suggest, occasioned some ambivalence, so too did writing for the diffuse consumer readerships that it supported. As John Lyly wryly observed in an epistle that prefaced his best-selling romance *Euphues. The Anatomy of Wyt* (1578), "He that cometh in print because he would be known is like the fool that cometh into the market because he would be seen."[31]

While Lyly's analogy evokes the commodification of discourse in what Alexandra Halasz has called "the marketplace of print," it is instructive also in construing print as a space one might "cometh into."[32] For whereas manuscripts tended to be passed among existing social networks, moving along (sometimes quite extended) paths of personal acquaintance, printed books were typically available to any willing buyer.[33] Print, like "the market," thus functioned for Lyly as a metonym for the public: the virtual space glimpsed in the circuit of communication that linked writers to readers. This public was a *social imaginary*—a community constituted, in Michael McKeon's definition, by the "explicitating act of self-reference" that brought together writers and readers who might never have met in person.[34] The relative anonymity of this relation provoked elaborate attempts to personalize it: the period's elaborate prefaces, which hailed "Gentlemen Readers," "the well disposed Reader," or "all courteous readers," are perhaps best read as attempts to manufacture tangible communities through the act of address.[35] Meanwhile, the stock figure of Nemo or Nobody (a fixture on stage, in ballads and pamphlets, and even as the sign of the stationer John Trundle's shop) captured the mystery of publicness, which gathered nobodies into that collective somebody known as "the reader."[36] In a certain sense, as circulating fictions of personality and presence, Elizabethan personae answered the challenges of public discourse.

But they also embodied publicity's peculiar social logic: like Nobody, they were virtual denizens of a virtual space.

The virtues of virtuality were made clear by the brief but explosive career of Martin Marprelate, the impish face behind which an anonymous group of reformists waged a guerrilla campaign of anti-episcopal polemic in 1588 and 1589. Martin's persona was in the first place a mode of evasion, a way of concealing the identities (and the number) of those who wrote and printed the pamphlets issued in his name, and in the second place, a tactic of argument: lacking an actual identity, he repelled personal invective of the kind that he gleefully hurled. Above all, however, Martin was a fiction of popular dialogue—one drawn in the image of Piers Plowman, who, as Jones points out, was invoked by the Marprelate pamphleteers as Martin's "Gransier."[37] Eric Vivier has recently shown how Martin's irreverent, sardonic voice mirrored the style of his nemesis, John Bridges; in "answering Bridges according to his folly," Martin punctured his air of authority.[38] At the same, the pamphlets' performative energy made them antihierarchical not just in argument but in form. They are boisterously dialogic, their margins filled with notes that, in Jesse Lander's analysis, alternately amplify and contest Martin's arguments in the main text, thus conjuring the public to which they appeal.[39] Moreover, Martin himself seemed a form of plural identity. Both "person and stance," as Joseph Black puts it, "Martin and *a* Martin," his style encouraged imitators and successors—successors like Martin Junior, whose appearance in 1589 mocked the impotence of the bishops' attempts at suppression.[40] Even the state-hired cadre of anti-Martinists added to the impression of Martin's ubiquity, aping his distinctive style in their counterblasts and thus becoming, despite themselves, versions of their opponent.[41]

The Marprelate pamphlets thus suggest the aptness of personation for print. Yet it is important to avoid the impression that personae were in any simple sense products of the rise of print. For one thing, as we have seen, the traditions that lie behind them significantly predate the invention of the printing press. More importantly, the "rise of print" is itself a narrative in need of qualification. As Wendy Wall, Arthur Marotti, Harold Love, H. R. Woudhuysen, Margaret Ezell, and others have shown, the book trade did little to displace the production of manuscripts.[42] Manuscript circulation, in fact, offered certain advantages over print: at least notionally, manuscripts could be kept closer than books sold publicly, and they were therefore especially fit for politically sensitive writing. Such sensitivity may partially explain Sidney's request to his sister to keep the manuscript of *The Covntesse of Pembrokes*

Arcadia "to your selfe, or to such friendes, who will weigh errors in the ballaunce of good will."[43] The felt difference between the two mediums—between print and "disclosure," in Wendy Wall's subtle account, and the comparative closure of manuscript circulation—itself concentrated the class and gender tensions that in Wall's argument underwrote changes in the styles of authorial self-presentation in early modern England.[44]

But it can be equally misleading to frame the relation between manuscript and print in oppositional terms, for the mediums in many ways complemented each other. Presentation copies of printed volumes often came adorned with authorial additions or marginalia in script.[45] Readers, of course, annotated copiously, scribbling in the margins of their books, adding indexes and finding aids, or copying poems and sententiae into commonplace books of their own.[46] Printed books themselves solicited such uses, encouraging commonplacing, for instance, by marking sentences with inverted commas or manicules.[47] Nashe's *Haue with You to Saffron-Walden* (1596) went further, including on one page a framed, empty box in which readers were urged to render their own judgments of Nashe's enemy, and the object of the pamphlet's satire, Gabriel Harvey. In a superb analysis of this pamphlet, Jane Griffiths shows the defamiliarizing force of the blank, which works against the printed page's finality "in order to convey what is incomplete and impromptu."[48] The space points up the hybrid status of the book, gesturing both to the medium in which readers encounter the pamphlet and to the medium in which they are invited to complete it. Such gestures were typical of the media consciousness that the coexistence of manuscript and print cultivated. Observing that the earliest recorded use of the word *manuscript* dates to the 1590s, Peter Stallybrass suggests that the concept is itself "parasitic upon printing": "Before printing, there was writing, no end of writing, but no manuscripts."[49] Once the choice was no longer automatic, the fact of medium (and of mediation) could emerge from the background.

The complex interactions of manuscript and print thus focused attention on the dynamics of textual mediation, and personae (as beings that lived in and through their ongoing circulation) were a signal instance of this attention. This much is clear simply from the frequency with which they generated reflexive fictions of textual transmission—in many cases fictions that meditate directly on the passage between manuscript and print forms. Greene's ghost, in his eerie visits from the grave, is perpetually in search of someone to deliver his latest manuscript to the press. We meet Pierce Penilesse, too, as a writer with a manuscript to sell; and when he returns in *Haue with You*, the text unfolds as a conversation among Nashe's friends, who inspect a manuscript draft of the soon-to-be printed pamphlet. (That the conversation itself forms the pamphlet's foundation is a characteristically defamiliarizing paradox). Colin Clout, for his part, stands at the center of Spenser's elaborate experiment in paratextual intervention, *The Shepheardes Calender* (1579). In these cases, personae concentrate a fascination with the processes by which writing finds its way to readers, their stories emplotting the mechanisms, and incorporating the multiple agents, of manuscript transmission and print publication. We might say, in fact, that they encode a form of identity that inheres in its mediation, that obtains precisely in its passage through the circuits of textual communication. Hence Nashe's description of Pierce as a *paper* monster: Elizabethan personae, that label suggests, are the prodigious embodiments of their media.

Such conflations of text and person were ubiquitous. In *A Hundreth Sundrie Flowres* (1573), George Gascoigne inserted his surname into the titles of poems like "Gascoigne's Woodmanship" and "Gascoigne's Anatomy." These possessive nouns do double duty—framing Gascoigne as at once the authorial subject behind his poems and as their narrative object—and in doing so they encourage readers to grasp identity as a textual phenomenon, arising from the relations among the poems scattered across the volume.[50] A still more striking example is the remarkable popularity in the 1580s and 1590s of Euphues, the young prodigal first introduced in John Lyly's 1578 romance *Euphues. The Anatomy of Wyt*. Spurred by the book's success—the first edition was followed by two further editions in 1579, with more to follow—Lyly published a sequel, *Euphues and His England*, in 1580. But Euphues also began to migrate into the work of other writers. The earliest appropriation, Anthony Munday's *Zelauto* (1580), framed itself, in its extended title, as "a freendly entertainment to Euphues, at his late ariuall into England."[51] Robert Greene used the name in *Euphues His Censure to Philautus* (1587) and *Menaphon Camillas Alarum to Slumbering Euphues* (1589). Thomas Lodge cited him in *Rosalynde. Euphues Golden Legacie* (1590) and *Euphues Shadow* (1592), and two years later John Dickenson put him in the title of *Arisbas, Euphues Amidst His slumbers* (1594).[52] Seemingly ubiquitous, Euphues was, in the description Douglas Bruster, "the first textual citizen of early modern London, an artificial person whom one could expect to meet with some frequency in this rapidly expanding metropolis."[53]

Euphues's emergence as an autonomous, untethered character at large owed much to the way Lyly represented him. In a prefatory epistle to the women readers of *Euphues and His England*, Lyly assumed the secondary role of intercessor, addressing them "in the behalf of Euphues." The epistle treats Euphues as a strange conflation of person and object: in one passage, Lyly recommends the book as after-dinner reading, noting that it is better "to hold Euphues in your hands, though you let him fall" than to prick yourself while drowsily sewing.[54] The personal pronoun is the grammatical signature of the epistle's broader prosopopoetic strategy—of the implication that book and character might have thoughts and desires of their own. This way of talking about Euphues is partly a function of the romance plot. Having forsworn his prodigality at the end of *Euphues. The Anatomy of Wyt*, Euphues returns in the sequel as an oddly retiring protagonist. He accompanies his old friend (and erstwhile rival) Philautus from Athens to Italy and then England, but avoids the romantic intrigues that entangle Philautus. Leaving his friend to woo in London, Euphues returns to Athens, where he begins to write: the final pages of Lyly's sequel are dominated by Euphues's treatise on England and Elizabeth and by a letter of advice on marriage that he sends to the newlywed Philautus. Euphues seems at last to have outgrown Lyly's plot. No longer a character within the narrative, he reconstitutes himself as a voice of sententious moral authority speaking from beyond its borders.

On the other hand, Euphues's retreat to the margins is a reminder that his own narrative trajectory remains unfinished. Unlike Philautus, whose marriage marks his turn away from romance wandering and into the quiet of domestic stability, Euphues remains unmarried, alone, and (for all of his scholarly resolve) restless—determined, we are told, "to sojourn in some uncouth place until time might turn white salt into fine sugar; for surely he was both tormented in body and grieved in mind."[55] It is a sojourn that seems more midpoint than end; but the story, Lyly implies, will not be his to resume: "And so I leave him, neither in Athens nor elsewhere that I know. But this order he left with his friends, that if any news came, or letters, that they should direct them to the Mount of Silixsedra, where I leave him either to his musing or his muses."[56] Lyly's valediction is striking for the independence it grants his protagonist, who is given not just a farewell but a forwarding address. *Euphues and His England* has gradually reduced Euphues to the textual forms that carry his wisdom back to Philautus (and to us) from afar; now the prospect of his future mediation carries him beyond the boundaries of the romance altogether. Waiting to receive (and perhaps to send) further news and letters, he is released into an afterlife whose final chapters will be left to Euphues to write for himself—or, rather, left to his readers.

Euphues thus seems to move beyond Lyly's romance at precisely the moment when he is most fully seen as a mediated presence. Or, to reverse the logic, it is when we recognize Euphues as an independent, extratextual being that his textual medium is brought forward to our attention, realized as a virtual space that he (and others like him) might inhabit. Martin Marprelate would enter the same space a decade later, and their crossed paths point up their similarities. Both are possessed of prodigious verbal styles that simultaneously distinguish them and compel imitation. Both are fictions that move beyond their sources: Euphues in the works of Lyly's imitators, Martin in the counterblasts that he inspired. And both are sustained by a constitutive hybridity: they are caught between the poles of author and character, narrator and narrative agent, real person and imaginary being. The same is true of the personae examined in the chapters that follow. Each one occupies a different place on the line between fiction and reality, but all of them court the confusion of the one with the other. It was this ambiguity that encouraged writers and readers to imagine them as autonomous beings.

In their autonomy and mobility, Elizabethan personae bear a striking resemblance to the "detachable" characters of eighteenth-century fiction whose reception David Brewer has traced. Brewer's account of "character migration"—the process by which readers imagined the further adventures of Lemuel Gulliver or Pamela Andrews—aligns the phenomenon with Franco Moretti's concept of the "social canon": the collective preservation of a set of shared texts that forges "a sense of ongoing kinship with one's fellow readers."[57] Brewer's characters may belong to a later moment of literary (and media) history, but the social canonicity they disclose is hardly restricted to the novel. Gavin Alexander and Mike Rodman Jones have shown how imitations of Sidney and reappropriations of the plowman figure, respectively, sustained communities of early modern readers (and writers) across time and space.[58] Most recently, Natasha Simonova's study of rewritings of and sequels to fictions from the *Arcadia* to *Clarissa* discovers the continuation as a genre of its own—a genre defined by a project of collaborative writing and reading.[59] The sense of "ongoing kinship" that these studies explore mattered a great deal to the readers whose efforts propelled the afterlives of Elizabethan personae, for one of their central effects was to give shape to the communities of readers who recognized them and welcomed their returns. "The fact that all writers of continuations must begin as readers of the source text," Simonova writes, "means that each continuation is also a record of reading and reception."[60] The same is true of personae: in a way that few other literary artifacts are, they are manifestly the products of collective and collaborative imagination, with each rewriting an explicit and concrete instance of reader response.

Personae had much in common, then, with other forms of appropriative reception. Like continuation and rewriting more broadly, they concentrated the diverse forms of agency at work in early modern literary culture: they were the products of the writers who brought them to life, the stationers who sold them, the editors who curated their afterlives, the readers who (touched or outraged by them) picked up their pens in response. In important respects, however, personae were different. For one thing, as fictions of literary production and reception, they were naturally reflexive, and so they cultivated a particularly self-conscious brand of social canonicity. As we shall see, to read or rewrite Greene's ghost or Colin Clout was necessarily to be drawn into a reflection on the very terms of literary community.

More importantly—and more strangely—personae seemed not only to focus the agency of others but also to exert an agency of their own: they accosted readers, wooed them, pleaded with them, and in the process demanded the writing of their afterlives. Personae are in this sense examples of the nonhuman agency that lies at the heart of Bruno Latour's revisionist sociology. For Latour, action is "borrowed, distributed, suggested, influenced," effected by subjects and by objects alike.[61] Such agency may be in some sense an illusion—a displacement of our own action—but perhaps it is better to say that it is the job of culture to make things that wield a power of their own. In leaving Euphues on Mount Silixsedra, Lyly honors his protagonist's ability to act on us: to hail the audiences who remember him, to inspire imitations, to elicit concern or curiosity or nostalgia, to bring together those who participate in the telling of his ongoing story. Personae demonstrate the power of literary forms to do things to readers, even as they underscore our tendency, when confronted with such agency, to personify it.[62] They are artifacts that act like persons.

Literary Public, Literary Field

In telling the story of such personae, *Paper Monsters* joins a growing body of work on what we can call, for lack of a general term, early modern personation. One branch of this work closely tracks the social dynamics of literary (and especially print) culture. Andrew Hadfield, for example, identifies "self-publicity" and personal insult as key tactics in the hothouse climate of polemical dispute in the 1590s.[63] Richard McCabe's recent study of early modern patronage, on the other hand, positions the persona as a central trope in the "art of dedication" by which writers cultivated patrons and, implicitly, readers.[64] Personality emerges in these studies as a way of navigating the demands of writing at a moment when literary production straddled economies (patronage and market) and media (manuscript and print). The contextual focus of such criticism is usefully complemented by a rich vein of formal and theoretical work on problems of character and personification. Most recently, Andrew Escobedo has argued that personifications in early modern texts disclose an understanding of the will as something separate from and in excess of the individual agent's judgment and control: they are, he writes, "trajectories of volitional energy that have taken on a life of their own."[65] The theory of agency that Escobedo recovers has much to say to the personae I study here: personae share what he calls the "wayward independence" of premodern personifications. Indeed, in describing their "transactional" force—their function as relays between agent and world—Escobedo points the way back to the questions that concern Hadfield and McCabe.[66] Personae continually find their way into the more prosaic transactions of polemical confrontation and patronal support precisely because they move between inside and outside, person and object.

Douglas Bruster arrives at this insight from the other direction. In "The Structural Transformation of Print in Late Elizabethan England," a chapter in his *Shakespeare and the Question of Culture*, Bruster traces the emergence, at the end of the sixteenth century, of "a new fluidity between person and thing," a fluidity that reframed "the relationship between authors and books, between characters and persons, and between readers and books."[67] For Bruster, this "embodied writing" betrays the workings of a "nascent public sphere," albeit one characterized by the very opposite of impersonal debate—by "a personalism that licensed readers' attention to paper bodies."[68] My own argument differs in key respects from this one. I take Elizabethan personae to be less the products of "the personalization of print," for instance, than of the reflexive consciousness of a hybrid media culture.[69] Perhaps more significantly, I eschew the implicit teleology behind Bruster's invocation of the Habermasian public sphere. Nevertheless, this book is crucially indebted to Bruster's work. For not only were the personae I study here central examples of the embodied writing of the 1590s, they were also at the heart of the period's reckoning with the conditions of literary publicity.

The publics traversed by Pierce, Euphues, and Colin Clout were in no necessary way linked to the rise of the rational-critical sphere that Jürgen Habermas influentially traced to the end of the seventeenth century. They were, instead, something more malleable and plural—"forms of association," in the language favored by the recent Making Publics project at McGill University, that arose outside of preexisting communities and were sustained by the circulation of discourse.[70] "A public," writes Michael Warner, "is a relation among strangers," a relation grounded in the premise of mutual anonymity; hence, it is "a space of discourse organized by nothing other than discourse itself." Publics are in this sense fundamentally rhetorical things, existing, as Warner argues, only "by virtue of being addressed."[71] For Elizabethan writers, the abstractness of this relation could seem strange, albeit increasingly unavoidable, as the emergence of consumer readerships left them to wrestle with the challenges (to borrow Nashe's phrase) of "mak[ing] ourselues publique."[72] Publicity came with exposure, but it also brought distance—the distance that separated writers from diffuse and unpredictable audiences that could be reached only via the mediating efforts of printers and booksellers. And this distance meant that acts of public address rested on a tacit act of imagining: on what Warner calls "the poetic function of public discourse."[73]

The serial, semifictional personae of the 1580s and 1590s arose in part as responses to the publicness of late Elizabethan literary discourse: they were the virtual persons called forth by emerging forms of virtual community. At the same time, they were central to the production of publicity: their charismatic fictions of address, their projections of personality onto the page, were a way of conjuring public sociality into being. In their periodic returns, moreover, they conferred on their reading publics a sense of durability: the sense that Pierce and Greene and Philisides were returning again and again to "us." Personae made publics, then; but they also made them objects of attention. Their stories were stories of circulation and social formation, stories that foregrounded the readerships who awaited their appearances. In this sense, as I will argue in Chapter 1, personae enabled a reflexive discourse (albeit a fictional one) on the terms of Elizabethan publicity—and on the questions of identity and value that arose in an increasingly public literary culture.

This discourse reflected the formation of what Richard Helgerson influentially called the early modern "literary system," that "system of authorial roles" made necessary by the "sudden increase in the production of poetry" in late sixteenth-century England.[74] As it became more visible, literary production demanded a conceptual framework to support it, and Sidney,

Nashe, Puttenham, Webbe, and others obliged. Over the course of the 1580s and 1590s, literature began, in Georgia Brown's words, "to be conceived as a valuable activity in its own right, with its own personnel, rules, history, and conventions."[75] The personae that I study here were one of the ways that literary culture reflected on and systematized itself—not least by framing the writing, circulation, and reception of texts as processes that were themselves worthy of narrative reconstruction. Yet they also reveal the essential unruliness of late Elizabethan literary culture, an unruliness belied by the concept of a literary "system," with its divisions (Helgerson's key insight) into the dialectically opposed categories of amateur, professional, and laureate. It is a scheme that illustrates brilliantly the self-fashioning strategies of Helgerson's laureates—those poets who refuse both the amateurs' haughty retirement and the professionals' popularity—and yet its categories are suspiciously slippery. Sidney, for instance, takes his place as an amateur, a poet who professed not to have elected his vocation, but what are we to make of his installation, some years after his death, as something very much like a laureate?[76] For that matter, what distinguishes amateurs from professionals, many of whom evince a characteristically amateur distaste for print? Are these issues of self-fashioning alone, or should circulation and reception—processes that are surely constitutive of any literary culture—matter as well? Helgerson's model breaks down, Brown suggests, when it treats as firmly established categories that were still in formation. For her, the period's "emerging discourses of literary professionalization" were distinctly paradoxical, rooted less in the production of authority (laureate or otherwise) than in the languages of shame and marginality.[77] Pierce in his pennilessness and Colin Clout in his abjection suggest the force of Brown's argument, which asks us to approach the literary system from its fluid margins—from the boundaries where questions of literary legitimacy and aesthetic value were contested.

To attend to these contests, or "struggles," is to frame a system that looks more like what we might call a literary field. While my approach draws on theories of publics and publicity, then, it is informed equally by Pierre Bourdieu's sociology of cultural fields: those spheres of cultural production in which the symbolic capital of artistic legitimacy competes with the economic capital that predominates in the broader "field of power."[78] The two approaches are, in fact, closely linked: for Bourdieu, cultural fields emerge against the backdrop of a consuming public, but they are also effects of, and engines for, the differentiation of distinct publics. Bourdieu's case study is nineteenth-century Parisian intellectual culture, where an energetic avant-garde positioned itself against mass culture (on the one hand) and the middlebrow prestige of bourgeois institutions (on the other). In the avant-garde's rejection of a mass consumer public, Bourdieu detects the logic of a subfield of "restricted production," in which writers value symbolic capital among peers over the material benefits of popularity.[79] It is through this sphere of restricted production that a literary field attains *relative autonomy*, a term that, for Bourdieu, indicates less an escape from the field of power than a reversal of its incentives: the elevation of internal criteria of value over economic ones—of prestige over profit.

As an account of how a work "might index . . . the social world around it," Bourdieuian sociology has in recent years found increasing sway in literary studies.[80] Yet its value to early modern studies is far from clear. Early modern London lacked nineteenth-century Paris's avant-garde, with its commitment to "art for art's sake"; more significantly, it lacked the pronounced opposition between restricted and mass cultural production that would ground such assertions of aesthetic autonomy. The most productive applications of Bourdieu to early modern studies have therefore worked to excavate the specific logic of a very different literary culture. Lori Humphrey Newcomb, for example, has traced the emergence of the distinction between popular and elite literature between the sixteenth and the eighteenth centuries; Edward Gieskes, meanwhile, has examined the tensions between an existing patronage economy and a nascent "self-legitimating field of cultural production" on the Elizabethan stage.[81] My account of the early modern literary field is careful to observe these differences too; the skirmishes for prestige and legitimacy that I trace appear here as fitful and ambivalent movements toward the relative autonomy that would characterize modern cultural fields. It was a process that routed itself through the self-reflexive fictions of Elizabethan personae: if their ubiquity in the 1580s and 1590s depended on their embodiment of the virtual logic of public, textual community, it also hinged on their ability to make visible the symbolic stakes of literary competition.

At the same time, I suggest a new path for sociological work on early modern texts—one that construes aesthetic artifacts not merely as products or reflections but as active mediators (to use a term of Latour's) of distinction and affiliation.[82] Because they were social artifacts, personae encoded the networks in which they circulated, and in turn they gave those networks structure: they constellated groups of writers and editors and printers and readers, marking off insiders from outsiders, poets from hacks. More fundamentally, in giving the texture and continuity of narrative to the processes of literary production, they allowed late Elizabethan literary culture to conceive of itself as a unified sphere—that is, as a field.

Persona and Author

The fact that these processes of field formation were realized through personae, rather than authors, is striking. For Bourdieu, struggles for legitimacy in the literary field are closely tied to the author function. "It is clear," he writes in *The Rules of Art*, "that the interest in the personage of the writer or the artist grows in parallel with the autonomization of the field of production and with the correlative elevation of the status of producers."[83] Indeed, it is not hard to see authors as the heroes of Bourdieu's account: their determination to "make their mark," he suggests, is what spurs the dialectical wheels of cultural change.[84] Authorial names are where the symbolic capital at stake in the field accrues.

In this sense, Bourdieu's literary history is entirely typical, continuous with the broad current of scholarship that sees authors as functions of capital, symbolic or otherwise. In Joseph Loewenstein's influential account, the literary author function emerged in tandem with the gradual rethinking of copyright in the seventeenth and eighteenth centuries.[85] Largely determined by the competition among stationers, authorial rights were born "as back-formations within the development of industrial copyright," and not until the passage of the Statute of Anne in 1710 was intellectual property decisively shifted from publishers (who had long controlled it through the guild regulations of the Stationers' Company) to authors.[86] There is, then, a risk of anachronism in the centrality of the author to literary histories of early modern England. To be sure, scholars have long recognized the difficulties involved in the concept; much of the finest historical criticism of the last two decades, in fact, has sought to reevaluate the category of authorship. Marcy North's work on anonymity, for instance, has contested narratives that too readily attribute to the Renaissance the rise of authorial individuality; instead, she suggests, the withheld name can point to overlooked forms of social authorship.[87] Kevin Pask, on the other hand, has historicized those narratives themselves, locating them in the emergence, over the course of the seventeenth century, of the genre of the poet's life-narrative.[88] Historians of drama, for their part, have demonstrated the collaborative nature of Elizabethan and Jacobean playwriting, emphasizing the distance between modern expectations of artistic autonomy and the demands of the early modern theater.[89] And Stephen Dobranski and Natasha Simonova have explored the relation between writers and the readers who continue, rewrite, and adapt their works—testing their own agency by measuring and working with or against the author's.[90] I have learned a great deal from each of these studies, and in the rest of this book I rely on them often. But I want to suggest that our rethinking of the author as literary category has not yet been thorough enough. For even the most skeptical approaches tend to preserve the author, however reconceived, as their object of analysis, as do (if only implicitly) the monographs that continue to divide their chapters on the principle of authorial identity.

A literary history read through its personae looks very different. The motive agents of such a history are fictions that are, in their own way, real—fictions whose peripatetic afterlives bring into view the full range of literary producers and disclose the self-reflexive discourse of the culture in which they move. The personae I follow here cross genre and medium and authorial corpus; they link different writers to each other, and, as documents of constant rewriting, argue the inseparability of literary production and reception. Exploring their archives offers a view of Elizabethan literary culture that is both stranger and truer than the one that we have come to know.

One of my aims is to write a literary history without authors. But one reason to do so is to better understand the fictional imaginary that lies behind our relation to them. For the characters I study here are a special kind of person: they are fully textual creatures, beings who are treated as real despite existing only on the page and in the minds of readers. They exhibit, in short, the sort of abstracted and delimited identity that we now associate with authors, those odd persons who exist only as functions of the circulation of discourse. In Foucauldian accounts, the author function is a means of delimiting the field of reader response. Elizabethan personae, by contrast, animate and expand it. They allow us to see authors, too, as collectively imagined fictions—as abstracted, virtual selves called into being by the publics that receive and reimagine their texts. Like personae, authors are material forms; they are characters come to life.

* * *

In each of the chapters that follow, I trace the path of a particular persona, developing a diachronic account of its individual path—however idiosyncratic—through various texts, and through time. Those paths frequently intersect:

1592, in fact, is the year in which Robert Greene died and the year in which Thomas Nashe published *Pierce Penilesse*—the respective subjects of Chapters 1 and 4. The narrow timespan recognizes the historical specificity of late Elizabethan literary culture, a culture in which semifictional personae pervaded the pamphlets and poetry sold in print and in which Spenser and Sidney could find their personae crossing paths with those of the popular pamphleteers Greene and Nashe. While the book's argument is in important respects progressive—beginning with the foundational problems of circulation, publicity, and textual community in the first half before taking up issues of literary distinction and value in the second—its central force is therefore cumulative: it is in the intersecting microhistories of Robert Greene's ghosts, of Colin Clout, of Philisides and Astrophil, and of Pierce Penilesse that their complex negotiations of publicity and circulation, of poetic distinction and aesthetic value, at the turn of the century come into view.

The first chapter explores the picaresque afterlife of Robert Greene. Greene's final writings had come to center on the story of his fitful journey from prodigality to repentance, a story that culminated in a trio of startling pamphlets—all published immediately after his death in 1592—in which he set aside romance fiction in order to address his readers (and declare his penitence) directly. In the ensuing months and years, Greene would be repeatedly resurrected as a ghost, returning each time with a new text intended for his old readers. His hauntings positioned Greene as a fictional character rather than biographical person, and in doing so they gave the lie to his late writings' performance of penitent sincerity. At the same time, they pointed up the essential virtuality of the publics for whom Greene wrote—publics that could now be seen, like the writers who addressed them, as evanescent, purgatorial fictions.

A key dimension of Greene's appeal was the fantasy of presence that his charismatic voice fueled. Presence was an especially vexed question for lyric poetry, a mode oriented by an idea of oral "voice" but one that circulates, inevitably, as text. My second chapter examines the paradoxes of lyric dissemination—at a moment when the migration of manuscript verse into print foregrounded them—by following Spenser's pastoral alter ego, Colin Clout, through his serial appropriations. For those who invoked him, Colin grounded a fiction of community oriented by a myth of spontaneous pastoral song that, as citable, iterable textual commodity, he simultaneously discredited. This tension, I suggest, manifests in Colin (both in Spenser's poetry and beyond) in the form of an oddly proleptic nostalgia: a sense that he is somehow already lost and gone, even as he roams the literary circles of the 1590s.

Colin's fiction of community was compelling because it was open to whoever invoked him and yet evoked the privileged remove of a world apart. In Chapter 3, I explore the busy afterlives of Philip Sidney's twin personae, Philisides and Astrophil, taking them, too, as examples of the power of personae to affiliate and to exclude. Introduced in the old *Arcadia* and *Astrophil and Stella*, respectively, Philisides and Astrophil were characters whose esoteric personal allegories marked them as written for an audience of familiars—and thus as devices designed to hold at bay more distant readers. This dynamic shaped the manuscript circulation of Sidney's texts, but it also sustained an important countercurrent in his posthumous print reception: a current that reimagined him as an exclusive coterie figure even as his works gained wide popularity. Placed in opposition to the public at large, the coterie that Astrophil and Philisides grounded emerged as an image of restricted production set apart from (and in opposition to) the broader literary field.

Distinctions like these—between coterie and public, popular and elite writing, good poets and bad—occupied a central place in turn-of-the-century literary discourse, provoked in part by a book trade that brought elite texts like Sidney's into the same arena as cheap pamphlets. The book's fourth chapter pursues the discourse of distinction in the strange life of Pierce Penilesse, and in the notorious pamphlet quarrel between Thomas Nashe and Gabriel Harvey, in which Pierce played a starring role. Never quite sure what to make of Pierce, critics have been particularly torn over the question of his sincerity: does Nashe deploy the persona in earnest solidarity with London's "penniless" print writers, or to insist on ironic distance from them? This debate, I suggest, reproduces the terms of the Nashe-Harvey quarrel itself, which unfolded as a battle over whether Nashe ought to be identified with or distinguished from his fictional double. The resulting confusion concentrated the quarrel's central concerns: the viability of distinctions of literary value and the nature of the authority that might enforce them.

While the first two chapters tackle the problem of virtual personhood, the latter two thus unpack the embeddedness of such persons in systems of status, authority, and value. Together, they discover in the persona the idea of a specifically literary identity. I therefore conclude with a coda that follows the persona into the seventeenth century, and into a collision with the author whose path it had helped to pave. Two brief case studies—the lyric anthology *Englands Helicon* (1600) and Robert Burton's *The Anatomy of Melancholy*

(1621)—illustrate, first, the persona's place in the conceptualization of the abstract, literary identity that we now associate with authorship and, second, the persona's conversion into a fundamentally authorial and characteristically ironized mode of self-reflexive metafiction.

This book, then, is a literary history—a history of a form. It may thus seem to belong to one side of the endless (and, one begins to suspect, largely ritual) debates between form and its opposite of the moment: between form and politics, form and history, form and the material.[91] But I find myself skeptical of these oppositions. The last two decades of scholarship in the history of the book have made it clear that literary "forms" are never quite *im*material: that a genre's history is inseparable from the history of its mediation, a poem's effect from its setting on the page. "Literature exists, in any useful sense," writes David Scott Kastan, "only and always in its materializations."[92] On the other hand, material culture (precisely insofar as it is a "culture") is never free from form; hence, as András Kiséry and Allison Deutermann suggest, "we also need to ask how literary forms shape the perception and use of the medium."[93] Asking such questions steers us away from the risks of naturalization. It urges us to see media not as the agents of history, bequeathing manuscript or print culture to us, but rather, to borrow Lisa Gitelman's definition, as "socially realized structures of communication."[94] Elizabethan England's personae dwell in and give life to the social realization of their structures of communication. They are paper monsters: born to and sustained by the forms of textual circulation that bring them back again and again—and to which they impart their own uncanny vitality.

CHAPTER 1

Robert Greene's Ghosts

In the opening pages of *Greenes Newes Both from Heauen and Hell* (1593), Barnabe Riche recounts an evening stroll along the outskirts of London. As he passed "between *Pancredge Church* & *Pye-corner*," Riche recalls, things took a sudden turn for the fantastic: he was confronted by what he would describe as a "most grislie ghost," which blocked his path and—when Riche hurried to the other side of the street—faced him there as well, "that passe I might not, vnlesse I should runne ouer him."[1] When, at last, a shaken Riche asked the ghost's name, the answer he received was a striking one. "I am the spirite of *Robert Greene*," it declared, "not vnknowne vnto thee (I am sure) by my name, when my wrytings lately priuiledged on euery post, hath giuen notice of my name vnto infinite numbers of people that neuer knewe me by the view of my person" (*GN*, sig. A_2^v). One of Elizabethan England's most prolific writers, Greene had died on September 3, 1592, only months before the publication of *Greenes Newes*, and in Riche's pamphlet he cuts a simultaneously strange and familiar figure, arriving as a household name turned ghastly spectacle.

For Riche, this story's interweaving of the prosaic facts of authorship and supernatural fiction was surely the point, a reflection of the paradoxes that came with being a public name. It was one of the peculiarities of publication, after all, that writers could be known—or, in Riche's more ambivalent phrase, "not vnknowne"—by a great many readers who had never met them face-to-face. In Riche's account, print is at once a vehicle of mass dissemination ("on euery post," "vnto infinite numbers") and a stubborn preserver of anonymity, occluding an author's face ("the view of my person") and hence rendering it an object of fascination.

Such fascination may have been a general condition of print publicity, but it gathered with particular intensity around Greene, who was both singularly popular—sixteen of his books, in new editions and reissues, were published in 1592 alone—and, thanks to his tireless self-fashioning as a repentant prodigal, a literary celebrity *avant la lettre*.[2] This self-fashioning began in the paratexts of the romance fictions he published in the late 1580s: in writing stories of erotic intrigue, he lamented, he had rendered himself as dissolute as his books' inconstant heroes. His continued writing and publication began to play out a drama of deferred penitence, with a fresh apology (and a promise to stop writing "wanton" romances) accompanying each new text. Greene's gradually unfolding autobiography continued in a series of cony-catching pamphlets, where he claimed the role of public servant, protecting innocent readers from the rogues whose frauds the pamphlets chronicled. And it culminated in a series of pamphlets, published in the weeks and months after his death, in which he sensationally described his descent into vice and his final, dying repentance.[3] By the end of 1592 Greene had established himself, as the subtitle of a recent collection of criticism has it, as "England's first notorious professional writer."[4] His notoriety helped ensure his popularity even after his death. Ten years later, in 1602, Samuel Rowlands told the story of a gentleman uninterested in the new books hawked by a bookseller's apprentice: "Can'st helpe mee," he asks instead, "to all *Greenes* Bookes in one Volume? But I will haue them euery one, not any wanting."[5]

Riche's street-corner encounter was just one of several ghostly returns for Greene in the 1590s. Within months of Greene's death Henry Chettle had revived him in *Kind-Harts Dreame*, a kind of print séance in which Greene and other spirits visit the title character in a dream; *Greenes Newes* was published around the same time.[6] Five years later John Dickenson produced *Greene in Conceipt* (1598),[7] a romance delivered during another visit from the underworld, and four years after that Rowlands summoned Greene once more, this time as a sponsor for his (largely plagiarized) rogue pamphlet *Greenes Ghost Haunting Conie-catchers* (1602).[8] Greene's precocious authorial celebrity has received increasing critical attention recent years, most notably in *Writing Robert Greene*, the aforementioned collection of criticism.[9] But the pamphlets that resurrected him have received less attention: only Lori Humphrey Newcomb, in a brief account of Greene's posthumous canonization; Arul Kumaran, who places them in the transition between patronage and market economies; and Steve Mentz, for whom the pamphlets frame the ambiguous cultural position of prose fiction, have given them sustained attention as a group.[10] This is surely in part a function of their eccentricity. The ghost pamphlets are very different texts—*Kind-Harts Dreame*, a dream vision;

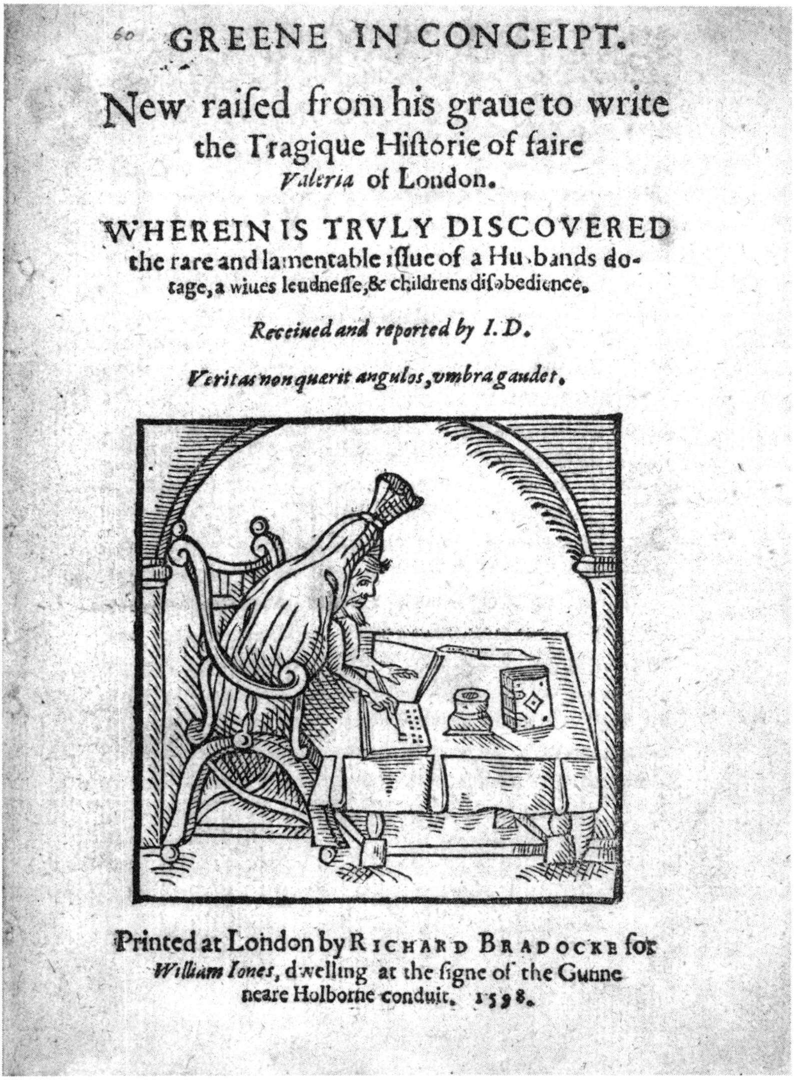

60

GREENE IN CONCEIPT.

New raiſed from his graue to write the Tragique Hiſtorie of faire *Valeria* of London.

WHEREIN IS TRVLY DISCOVERED the rare and lamentable iſſue of a Husbands dotage, a wiues leudneſſe, & childrens diſobedience.

Receiued and reported by I. D.

Veritas non quærit angulos, vmbra gaudet.

Printed at London by RICHARD BRADOCKE for *William Iones*, dwelling at the ſigne of the Gunne neare Holborne conduit. 1598.

Figure 1. John Dickenson, *Greene in conceipt New raised from his graue to write the tragique historie of faire Valeria of London* (London, 1598). RB 31354. By permission of the Huntington Library, San Marino, California.

Greenes Newes, a picaresque satire; *Greene in Conceipt*, a romance—but they share a fascination with the idea that Greene could be brought back to life, in print if not in fact.[11] His ghost arrives, in each case, as a surprisingly embodied presence—"of face amible," reports Kind-Hart, "of body well proportioned, his attire after the habite of a schollerlike Gentleman, onely his haire was somewhat long."[12] The title page of *Greene in Conceipt* made this "schollerlike Gentleman" visible for Dickenson's readers, featuring a woodcut that shows the spectral author at a table, quill in hand, writing in an open book, his head wrapped in a burial shroud (fig. 1).

But the ghost pamphlets were linked by more than a fantasy of face-to-face contact; they were also fictions of mediation. In each case Greene visits because he has a text in need of an audience. For Dickenson, it is the romance narrative that takes up most of *Greene in Conceipt* (a story, Greene says, that he overheard the heroine, Valeria, telling in Elysium); for Chettle, a complaint against his detractors; for Riche, an account of Greene's picaresque travels in heaven and hell. The visits are always brief; after quick conversations Greene hands over his messages and departs, tasking his hosts with seeing to their publication. "The matter that I would request thee to performe," he tells Riche in *Greenes Newes*, "is the committing of these papers to the Presse" (*GN*, sig. A_2^v); the spirits who visit Kind-Hart, for their part, encircle him at the end of their dream and, "thrusting into my hand all their papers, they at once charged mee to awake, and publish them to the world" (*KH*, sig. B_3^v). It is fitting that the title page of Dickenson's printed book depicts Greene at work penning a manuscript: the stories of his returns operate precisely in the passage between manuscript and print. In each case, the successful delivery of the script to the press—made concrete by the existence of the pamphlet itself—marks the culmination of the story of Greene's return, its circulation in print materially fulfilling his ghostly wishes and sustaining, albeit more modestly, his posthumous presence.

The ghost pamphlets thus frame the relation between Greene and his readers in two distinct ways. His in-person visits, on the one hand, allow a fantasy in which the relation between writer and reader is embodied, in which Greene could become thrillingly present. On the other hand, his hasty appearances and disappearances leave the texts that narrate them to dwell on the fact of his separation from his readers; they can encounter him, and he them, only by way of a complicated process of mediation. The fiction of haunting sustains both, allowing the fantasy of personal presence even as it figures the writer's distance from his audience. In the preface to *Greene in Conceipt*, Greene's spirit tells Dickenson how Valeria had told him her story—her cuckolding of her husband, her lover's inconstancy, her descent into poverty—and how he had decided it needed a wider audience. Greene had negotiated with Mercury, he explains, so that "this my bodies bloudlesse remnant might reuisite the earth, to finde some one who receiuing fro[m] mee the plot and groundworke of this rare subiect, might performe thereon in my behalf, that which by reason of deaths defects my selfe now ca[n]not."[13] If Greene's death thus figured the practical separation of writers from their readers, the need for and reliance on mediation, his ghostliness evoked the disembodiment and the sporadic rhythms of print, the medium that returned him to London serially but unpredictably and impermanently. Greene could visit at any time, but his presence was inevitably fleeting and fragile.

The pointed ephemerality of Greene's ghosts registered anxieties that went to the heart of literary production at the end of the sixteenth century, when an expanding book trade rewarded writers like Greene with growing, but also increasingly diffuse, readerships.[14] To write for these audiences, the ghost pamphlets suggest, was to encounter something worryingly unknowable. It is of course easy to overstate the differences between manuscript and print. The pamphlets, in their stories of transmission from one to the other, in fact point up their codependence; they draw on both the mystery of mass production and the fascination of secretive literary exchange. Yet the ghost pamphlets are also concerned with what distinguishes the two mediums. Or rather, as reflexive tales of textual transmission, they participate in the construction of those differences. To read Riche, Chettle, and Dickenson is to encounter the manuscript as an object of personal exchange, something carried by Greene himself and passed to each of them by hand; on the other hand, it is to see the printed text as something alien: dependent on the intervention of third parties and mysteriously carried, by the opaque workings of "the Presse," to "the world." In asserting these distinctions, the pamphlets appear as early instances in the conceptual formation of what we have come to call "print culture." They bear a striking similarity, indeed, to familiar narratives of the rise of print—narratives like Walter Ong's, who wrote that while "manuscript culture had preserved a feeling for a book as a kind of utterance, an occurrence in the course of conversation," the printed book "was less like an utterance, and more like a thing."[15] While book historians since Ong have learned to treat such narratives skeptically, the ghost pamphlets suggest that they require not wholesale rejection but genealogical excavation.[16] Greene's ghost, that is, points up the long and complicated history by which print came to be seen as bloodless and impersonal.

What seems to have occupied Riche, Chettle, and Dickenson most of all was their sense of the press's openness: anyone could walk into a bookstall and ask for Greene's books. In this respect, Greene's desired audience was a public: a community of notional strangers, brought into being only in and by the act of address. "A public," Michael Warner writes, "might be real and efficacious, but its reality lies just in this reflexivity by which an addressable object is conjured into being in order to enable the very discourse that gives it existence."[17] The curious fictionality of publicity helps to explain the galling absence of Greene's ghost, who disappears as soon as he dispatches his manuscripts. It helps to explain, too, the charismatic first person that grounds each of the pamphlets: the power of the ventriloquized voice ("I am the spirite of *Robert Greene*") lies in the fantasy of contact it encourages, the fantasy of a dead man reanimated and, almost as thrilling, of an author made present. Greene's ghost thus stands as an artifact of the reflexive act of imagination by which a public, as a virtual community, constitutes itself.

At root, indeed, Greene' s peripatetic afterlife encodes a story about the poetic logic of literary publicity—about what it meant, in Thomas Dekker's pregnant phrase, "to be a man in print."[18] Being in print and in public, Greene's hauntings suggest, was not simply a matter of material dissemination, of names privileged on posts; it was an existence both determined and imperiled by its constitutive fictionality.[19] This chapter begins, therefore, by examining the evolving modes of Greene's fiction, tracing the emergence of his enigmatic persona from a growing tension in his later works between fictional artifice and personal disclosure. It then turns to the mutual implication of fiction (as a formal category) and literary publicity (as a social one). In reclaiming Greene's persona—in imagining a spectral Greene caught between truth and fiction, life and death—Chettle, Riche, and Dickenson turned him into a mobile allegory for the experience of circulation. For the writers who resurrected him, the ambiguous fictionality of Greene's ghost became a way of recognizing—and reckoning with—the virtual reality of the publics that all of them sought to reach.

Personal Fictions

Robert Greene made his name as a writer of what we now call romances, the increasingly popular prose narratives that in the sixteenth century constituted "a genre without a name."[20] A young and precarious form, fictional prose was trailed by the suspicions of moralizing critics who worried about the corrupting influence of amorous narratives and, more fundamentally, about the possibility that fiction was simply a form of deception. "Throughout the sixteenth century," Robert Maslen has argued, "prose fiction seems to have been regarded, by its authors as well as its readers, as the most slippery of literary mediums."[21] During the 1580s Greene and others moved to forestall the charge of deception by clearly marking their texts as fictions, consolidating a set of conventions largely derived from their most influential sources: Italian novellas that circulated in popular translations from the late 1560s and John Lyly's romance *Euphues*, published in 1578.[22] From the novellas Greene and his counterparts borrowed the veneer of exotic distance afforded by foreign settings and by names like Philautus, Narbonus, Zelauto, and Mamillia; from Lyly they borrowed the rhetorically elaborate style eventually called euphuism.[23] Most significantly, they gravitated toward omniscient third-person narrators whose remove defused suspicions of scandalous topicality. Impersonal narration encouraged what David Margolies terms the "objectification" of Elizabethan fiction: the disappearance of explicit contact with and guidance from the author, which left readers "to find the meaning in the story alone."[24]

Greene was a master of this kind of storytelling. Consider the opening lines of one of his final works, the posthumously published *Greenes Groats-worth of Witte*: "In an Iland bounded with the Ocean there was somtime a Cittie situated, made riche by Marchandize, and populous by long peace, the name is not mentioned in the Antiquarie, or els worne out by times Antiquitie, what it was it greatly skilles not, but therein thus it happened."[25] In a single sentence Greene conjures up a distant time and a place too remote, apparently, even to be named; soon, to add to the effect, he introduces characters named Gorinius, Lucanio, Roberto, and Lamilia. He does all of this with such a carefully impersonal syntax—*there was a city, the name is not mentioned*—that the narrator seems to vanish from the story he is telling almost entirely. The book may be called *Greenes Groats-worth*, but here, at least, there is no Greene.

Yet by 1592, when the book was published, Greene had begun to chafe against the conventions that he could nonetheless still produce on cue. Indeed, tensions were quietly present much earlier, in works like *Arbasto, The Anatomie of Fortune*, a romance published in 1584. *Arbasto* is typical not only of Greene's books in the 1580s but also of the genre more broadly, its narrative trafficking in familiar characters and themes: erotic temptation, betrayal, belated penitence. The protagonist and title character is the young king of Denmark, but his story begins in France, where he is busy waging war and, soon enough, falling in love with the daughter of his enemy. Arbasto's love for Doralicia, the French princess, is a problem for all the obvious reasons, but also for a more unusual one: her sister, Myrania, has fallen in love with him. When Arbasto is captured and imprisoned, it is Myrania who engineers his escape—but only on the promise of marriage. He feigns affection, even after they return to Denmark, but he continues to woo Doralicia from afar, sending letters both to her and to her father, to whom he proposes a trade of one daughter for the other. Eventually, and inevitably, Myrania discovers the letters; she dies of grief after bitterly reproaching Arbasto, who is suddenly stricken with guilt. Deposed by the Danish nobles, he retires to a quiet hermitage, where he whiles away his days contemplating the vagaries of fortune.

Because it is in most respects unremarkable, the romance is a useful example of the narrative conventions of late-Elizabethan prose fiction—its grandiloquent rhetoric, boldly impassioned characters, and mazy plots. Take this passage, in which Myrania laments her misfortune in loving Arbasto:

> But alas, poore Myrania could not feele one minute of suche ease, for she vncessantly turned the stone with *Sysiphus*, rolled on the wheele with *Ixion*, and filled the bottomlesse tubs with *Belydes*, in so much, that when she coulde find no meanes to mitigate hir mallady, she fell into these bitter complaints.
>
> Ah *Myrania*, ah wretched we[n]ch *Myrania*, how art thou without reason, which sufferest reason to yeelde vnto appetite, wisedome, vnto sensuall will, and a free mind vnto seruile loue: but I perceyue, when the vine riseth, it wreatheth about the Elme: when the hop groweth high, it hath neede of a poale, and when virgins wax in yeares, they followe [that] which belongeth to their youth. Loue, loue, yea but they loue expecting some good hap, and I alas both loue, and liue without all hope, for *Arbasto* is my foe, and yet if he were my friend, he liketh not me, he looketh only vpon *Doralicia*.[26]

Most of the distinctive habits of the genre are gathered here. There are the typical features of euphuism: the accumulating isocolons, balanced oppositions, gentle alliteration, and rhetorical questions. There are, too, the seamless blend of narration and equally eloquent self-address, the unhesitating shifts into soliloquy—*Arbasto*'s narrator, like those of many of its counterparts, seems able to read the minds of the book's characters, and he transcribes their private thoughts as if they were public speeches. No apology or explanation is offered for this omniscience; the narrator's impersonality, his perch above and removed from the events and people he is describing, seems to be taken for granted.

The problem is that the narrator is Arbasto himself—a character within the story rather than an impersonal voice outside of it. In narrating omnisciently, Arbasto creates difficulties. Privy, as the story's narrator, not only to his own thoughts but also to Myrania's and Doralicia's, he must as a character forget what he has heard, so that he can be genuinely surprised when the events anticipated in their soliloquies come to pass. (By the time Myrania reveals her love to Arbasto, he has already reported several soliloquies in which she meditates on it.) The illogic is a strain on the story, and at least once Greene acknowledges as much: at the end of the soliloquy quoted above, Arbasto qualifies his report with the phrase "as I supposed," retroactively framing the speech as a hypothetical reconstruction.[27]

These inconsistencies register Greene's dissatisfaction with the emergent conventions of prose romance. The calculated exoticism and impersonal narration intended to protect works of fiction from the charge of deception also threatened to denature them: affirming nothing, to borrow Philip Sidney's phrase, risked communicative isolation. These strategies of fictional signposting thus reproduced at the level of form the separation of author and audience that texts encountered in the process of circulation. *Arbasto* is an artifact of this tension. It was not the only text in which Greene confronted the challenges of the genre he had chosen—his predilection for frame tales, with their detailed scenes of storytelling among familiars, discloses an interest in imagining the narrative utterance as an intimate rather than anonymous act.[28] But in *Arbasto* the conventions of fictional narration were turned on their head. The flaws in the book's narration reveal something more than artlessness. They reveal a desire to transform an objective fiction into a subjective story, to render the story and its telling a personal interaction.

The relation between these two modes, the objective and the subjective, is under constant scrutiny in *Arbasto*. Greene's protagonist is a person and a storyteller, but also an "anatomy," an icon. We first encounter him, in the framing report of an unnamed traveler, as a kind of emblem—"in his left hand," we learn, he held "the counterfeit of fortune, with one foote troade on a polype fish, and with the other on a Camelion, as assured badges of hir certaine mutabilitie"—and the drama of the frame narrative is generated, in large part, by the traveler's belief that there is a story behind the picture and his desire to hear it.[29] That story has to be coaxed out of an Arbasto who seems happier to signify silently than to be drawn into dialogue, and when he decides to tell it, the question of what kind of story it is remains.[30]

For Arbasto, it is a story of exemplary, objective demonstration: "Sit downe, and thou shalt heare what trust there is to be giuen to inconstant fortune." His questioner, by contrast, hopes for a story that will reveal Arbasto himself: "I hope youre highnesse will pardon my vnwitting wilfulnesse, and take (had I wist) for an excuse of so suddaine an offence, whiche graunted, the desire I haue to heare of your strange hap, doo make me passe manners in beeing importunate with youre Maiestie, to heare the tragicall chance of this your strange change."[31] Katharine Wilson has suggested that the two modes—the iconic and the personal, image and story—are, in the end, mismatched. "The picture," she writes, "does not tell the story—even if Arbasto is determined to believe otherwise," for Arbasto's counterfeit of fortune obscures his own agency in his tragic fall.[32] His story implicates him, in other words, in a way that the emblem did not; and in telling it to the traveler, he is drawn into an act of confession. By the end of his story, Arbasto seems to understand what has happened. His final words abandon the language of typological, third-person exemplarity with which he began in favor of a straightforward first person: "Thus thou hast heard why in meane estate I passe my daies content: rest therefore satisfied, that thus I haue liued, and thus I meane to die."[33]

If the turn of events that brings Arbasto to tell his own story is what gives him depth as a character, it also holds the prospect of reorienting the reader's relation to Greene's text. Readers, after all, respond differently to character narration than to impersonal narration. As Tzvetan Todorov observes, we treat the latter as poetic, and therefore exempt from the "test of truth," but we treat the former as real within the story, and hence subject to it. Making Arbasto the storyteller means opening his story to questioning; it asks readers to consider what we feel about him, whether we believe him.[34] The effect is stronger, perhaps, because of his interlocutor, the unnamed traveler with whom we meet Arbasto and whose thirst for his tale sparks our own. We are drawn in almost to the point of being included with him in the charged personal exchange that the story becomes. Yet we are, finally, left on the outside. While the frame narrative serves to negotiate Arbasto's shift from object to subject, it also has the effect of walling off Arbasto's discourse from us, of containing it within the bounds of fiction. We are never in any real doubt about the significance of his story; we never believe that Arbasto is confessing anything real to us, however real it may be to his nameless interlocutor *within* the fiction. This is why, although his interlocutor has forgotten Arbasto's original emblematic status by the end of the story, the work can still be offered to Greene's readers, on its title page, as an "*anatomy* of fortune." Greene's attempt to turn objective into subjective narrative, to turn prose fiction into a personally motivated discourse, is brought up short by the inescapable fact of its fictionality.

What *Arbasto* makes clear is that the problems of literary publicity and of fictional narration are, at least in one crucial respect, analogous. They are problems of *address*: who is speaking to whom and why?[35] If the felt anonymity of author and audience forcefully raised this question, the conventions of Elizabethan prose fiction compounded it. *Arbasto*'s lesson was that fiction itself was the issue: that to tell a made-up story was to sacrifice personal directness, to relinquish the communicative claims an utterance might make on its addressee. In the years that followed, Greene began to test the boundary between fiction and reality, weaving strange claims of historical veracity into outlandish romances and then, more aggressively, turning himself into a peripheral character in the cony-catching pamphlets that he wrote between 1590 and 1592. Steve Mentz and Linda Woodbridge have shown how cony-catching texts used documentary realism as an alibi for what were, in effect, storehouses of romance and jestbook tropes, and Greene enthusiastically capitalized on the ambiguity, fashioning himself as a fearless truth teller.[36] Most interesting, however, is *Greenes Never Too Late*, a romance published in 1590. Although the story it tells bears the conventional signposts of fictionality—it is set in Bergamo, its characters have Italian names, it is told with a typical mixture of eloquent letters and melodramatic soliloquies and interspersed lyrics—Greene hints that it is something more.[37] Described on its title page as "a true English historie," the story-within-the-story that commands most of the pamphlet's pages is indeed set in England, and it is told with assurances that the reported events actually happened.

As in *Arbasto*, the challenges of fiction arise in *Never Too Late* as the text works through the problems of narrative discourse: whose story is being told, and who is telling it? It begins, like the earlier romance, with a frame narrative in which a first-person speaker meets a stranger whose story he then solicits. Like Arbasto, *Never Too Late*'s Palmer is a kind of cipher, a figure whose appearance is in equal parts significant and opaque: "eyther some penitent pilgrime that was very religious," judges the narrator, "or some despayring louer that had bin too too affectionate."[38] Like *Arbasto*, he is an emblem in need of a story—penitent for what, and traveling where?—and when his interlocutor asks him to tell it, the stage is set for the kind of story Greene was increasingly interested in telling: a narrative of self-disclosure, in which the impersonality of "objective" fiction gives way to the intimacy of confessional revelation. The Palmer's tale, however, turns out to be not about him at all but about a man named Francesco, and the text moves in a wholly different direction. Francesco's is a familiar story of prodigality: he marries a beautiful woman and overcomes her father's objections, only to ruin his good fortune, falling under the sway of a courtesan and wasting his fortune in the city. He eventually falls so far as to become a playwright, making enough money to squander all over again. Only at the last moment, when word reaches him of his wife's heroic constancy back home, does he repent.

The Palmer's substitution of this story for his own comes on multiple levels as a frustration. It is, in the first place, a refusal of narrative closure, with the revelation of his own history deferred just when his audience is most interested in learning it. It is also a refusal of the kind of narrative immediacy that the romance seemed to promise: in telling Francesco's story, the Palmer can retreat to the safely impersonal redoubt of the third person. Most simply, as the Palmer acknowledges, his withholding is a breach of courtesy, a failure to reciprocate his interlocutor's hospitality: "Hospitalitie is so precious, as no price may value. Then, if I should not graunt anie lawful demaund, I might seeme as little pliant to humanitie, as you lyable to courtesie: and therefore if the Gentlewoman your wife and you will sit vp to heare the discourses of a traueller, I will first rehearse you an English Historie acted and euented in my Countrey of *England*: but for that the Gentleman is yet liuing I will shadowe his name, although I will manifest his follies; and when I haue made relation I will shew why I directed the course of my Pilgrimage onely to *Venice*."[39] The Palmer's solicitous reply is an attempt to repair his affront. Francesco's story may not be his, but he hints that it bears some meaningful relation to him—a relation that depends, it seems, on its being true. In his insistence that Francesco is real, and his story "acted and euented," the Palmer preserves the possibility that telling it will lead to a revelation; in stressing the gap between Francesco's pseudonym and his real identity, he tantalizingly points to a moment when the latter would be unveiled. If this hint sparks the reader's interest in Francesco, it also points back to the storyteller, for it places a burden on the Palmer's credibility. What kind of belief, his audience is led to ask, does his story merit? How does he know what he knows, and what is his relation to "Francesco"? These questions revive the seemingly foreclosed prospect of self-disclosure: in seeking Francesco's concealed identity, we find ourselves once again wondering about the Palmer's.

The most tempting possibility, advanced by Meredith Skura, is that Francesco *is* the Palmer and hence that the Palmer's story is an autobiography, after all. The Palmer seems to invite this reading with his declarations that Francesco is yet living, from the same country, though under a false name. The sequence that he proposes—"when I haue made relation I will shew why I directed the course of my Pilgrimage onely to *Venice*"—hints at a continuity between the two parts, as if his pilgrimage were in fact the latest chapter of Francesco's history. The identity of Francesco and the Palmer is further suggested in the frame narrative, where on a few occasions we listen in on the Palmer's private meditations and it becomes clear that his pilgrimage is a penance for his own youthful prodigality. "The Palmer," Skura writes, "could easily be taken for an older, wiser Francesco, looking back if not on his own adventures then on something very like them."[40]

And what of Greene himself? His presence in the text has long been taken for granted by critics eager to read *Never Too Late* as a "thinly veiled autobiography" or "quasi-autobiographical romance."[41] What gives the game away is Francesco's turn to playwriting—an allusion to Greene's own recent theatrical forays, and more than that a plunge into the contemporary, local space of late Elizabethan London. Nandini Das has argued that Greene's fictions gradually moved from "old romance" toward a kind of realism, with *Never Too Late*'s "Troynouaunt" serving as "essentially Greene's contemporary London, where the socially displaced and morally errant hero becomes involved with prostitutes and the world of theatre and hack writing."[42] Perhaps the most telling instance of this convergence comes in the Palmer's proem to the story of Francesco: "In those dayes when Palmerin reigned King of great *Britaine*, famoused for his deedes of Chiualrie . . ."[43] It is, on first read, a conventional gesture—a displacement into another time—but it unravels as soon as it is uttered: Palmerin had descended not from traditional legend but from the series of sixteenth-century Portuguese romances that, thanks to Anthony Munday's translations, had recently attained wide popularity in England. "In those dayes wherein Palmerin reigned" thus meant the bookstalls of London, circa 1590. The line begins with a promise to guide its readers away from the real world but ends by thrusting them back into it.[44]

Such double motions seem to constitute the text as a whole. Its successive frames produce a series of duplications: Greene, who offers his text as a "Powder of Experience," is displaced by the Palmer, himself forged as a moral educator by hard experience; then the Palmer is displaced, too, his prodigal past transferred to Francesco. Each duplication estranges Greene's readers, denying closure to one story while opening another. The deferrals heighten anticipation for the moment when the various figures the text produces will turn out to be one, when Francesco will be revealed to be the Palmer and the Palmer to be Greene. This tug of war troubles Das's account of romance's merging with realism; *Never Too Late* instead puts fiction and truth in irreducible conflict and leaves its readers waiting for the moment when the latter will break through the former.[45]

But no such moment comes. As Skura observes, when the Palmer inscribes some parting verses for his host, the first words—"In greener yeares"—pun on the name of the book's author.[46] This, however, is as close as the text comes to confirming the identities it has led its readers to presume. When the Palmer finishes Francesco's story, in *Francescos Fortunes: Or, The Second Part of Greenes Never Too Late* (1590), he speaks about his own past and his reasons for traveling to Venice, but only briefly and obliquely. He inscribes his poems, and then he departs: "After they had broken their fast, and the goodman of the house courteouslie had giuen him thankes for his fauor, the Palmer set forward towards *Venice*: what there he did, or howe hee liued, when I am aduertised (good Gentlemen) I will send you tidings. Meane while let euerie one learne (by *Francescoes* fall) to beware, least at last (too late) they be enforced to bewaile."[47] In these last lines the characters who seemed ready to merge with each other are once again separated out. The Palmer is sent on his way to Venice, a narrator whose services are no longer needed; Francesco is left a didactic object, an emblematic warning of the pitfalls of love; and Greene turns outward to address his readers. Only a final equivocation stands in the way of their divergence: in referring to the Palmer's subsequent travels, Greene invests the Palmer with a life beyond the page. It is a fitting conclusion to a text built of such ambivalences. *Never Too Late* and *Francescos Fortunes* construct fictions in order to entertain their dismantling, only to leave them in place, eroded but intact, pointing to a disclosure that is never made.

Such a breakthrough came only in *Greenes Groats-worth of Witte* (hereafter referred to as the *Groatsworth*). The authorship of the *Groatsworth* is an unsettled question. From the beginning, there have been suspicions that its real author was Henry Chettle, who denied the charge—though he admitted editorial involvement—in the preface to *Kind-Harts Dreame*. Recent stylistic analyses have split on the question: though some attribute the text to Chettle, the most recent analysis, by Brian Vickers, restores it to Greene.[48] My reading proposes the *Groatsworth* as a culmination of Greene's shifting relation to his fictions, and so I advisedly refer to Greene as its author. Yet it is perhaps no less exciting to suppose that the *Groatsworth* was the first appropriation of Greene's persona—and hence that those who seized on Greene's name also recognized and fulfilled his rebellion against the constraints of fiction.

Whether by Greene or Chettle—or by someone else—the *Groatsworth* is in obvious ways a close rewriting of *Never Too Late*; its protagonist, Roberto, like Francesco, abandons his wife, squanders his wealth, and eventually finds himself writing for the stage.[49] But the parallels run much deeper: the *Groatsworth* is a formal sequel to *Never Too Late*'s own ambivalent fictionality. Like *Never Too Late*, the *Groatsworth* announces itself as a fiction even as it hints at a submerged stratum of referential truth. Even the text's opening lines, which seem designed to signal the *Groatsworth*'s fictionality, turn out to do the opposite: the "Iland bounded with the Ocean" is transparently Britain, and the city "situated" in it London—a city that was in fact "made riche by Marchandize" and that is indeed rarely mentioned in the "Antiquarie." From the beginning, the *Groatsworth* invokes the conventional rhetoric of fiction to subvert it, to herald a moment when the charade might end and Greene might tell his own story, in his own voice. But whereas *Never Too Late* maintains the fictional cover of Francesco until the bitter end, the *Groatsworth* finally does work its way around to the climactic revelation it foreshadows.

The *Groatsworth* begins with the death of the miserly usurer Gorinius, who leaves his money to his wasteful younger son, Lucanio; to Roberto, the elder son and—to all appearances—a virtuous scholar, he leaves a single groat, telling him to buy with it the titular groatsworth of wit. Consumed with envy, Roberto conspires to steal his brother's new wealth. He enters into a plot with the courtesan Lamilia, who promptly seduces and swindles Lucanio, but rather than pay Roberto, she exposes his scheming to his brother, who rejects him and leaves him penniless. Roberto then falls in with a group of players; he begins writing plays and living loosely, his unnamed and long-suffering wife nearly forgotten. At last he is reduced to his final groat, and, recalling his father's bequest, he is brought to penitence, lamenting his failure to buy wisdom when he had the chance. It is at this point that the fiction breaks: "Heere (Gentlemen) breake I off *Robertoes* speach; whose life in most parts agreeing with mine, found one selfe punishment as I haue doone. Heereafter suppose me the said *Roberto*, and I will goe on with that hee promised: *Greene* will send you now his groats-worth of wit, that neuer shewed a mites-worth in his life: and though no man now bee by, to doo mee good: yet ere I die, I will by my repentaunce indeuour to doo all men good."[50] The facade simply drops away in these lines: the past tense gives way to the present, third-person pronouns to first-person, Roberto to Greene himself, and emphatic deictics (*heere* and *heereafter*) point to the here and now of writing and reading as "character, narrator, and author," in W. W. Barker's words, "collapse into a single subject."[51] Fiction is left behind along with Greene's prodigality; now, in the moment of his reformation, he addresses his readers directly—apologizing, promising atonement, soliciting belief.

The *Groatsworth* was the most striking of a series of pamphlets—all published shortly after Greene's death in 1592—that offered narratives of personal repentance. *Greenes Vision: Written at the Instance of His Death*, a dream vision featuring Chaucer and John Gower, and *The Repentance of Robert Greene Maister of Arts* both insisted on the truth of the story they told, a story in which Greene at last made good after a life of dissolution. For his nineteenth-century biographer, Nicholas Storojenko, the pamphlets displayed their author's "boundless sincerity," a self-lacerating moral honesty that he called Greene's "most attractive feature."[52] And none of them performed their sincerity more dramatically than the *Groatsworth*.

Yet it is worth wondering how final the pamphlet's banishment of fiction really is. Greene is at pains to portray it as absolute: the text's climax is his own emergence as a sincere, and sincerely repentant, voice. Plot's distractions give way to Greene's direct, unmediated address to his readers; narration gives way to presence and self-disclosure. But there are reasons for skepticism. The narrative legibility of Greene's repentance, after all, depends on his implicit continuity with the fictional character he displaces: we can understand what happens at the end only by understanding his story to be Roberto's, and Roberto's his. Greene's voice compels, that is, because of the story that frames it; we are persuaded of his sincerity to the extent that the foregoing fiction prepares us to accept it. The ambiguity is written into the text's climactic reversal: in asking readers to "suppose me the said *Roberto*," Greene reinstates the logic of fictional supposition just where and when it ought to vanish. The climax of the *Groatsworth* is not only Roberto's transformation into a real person; it is also Greene's transformation into an imaginary one.

At His Dying Request

The *Groatsworth*'s turn to the first person, and to a disposition of penitent sincerity, effectively rewrote the rhetorical relation between Greene and his readers. His address to them became personal in the sense that he was now asking them to think and feel something particular about him; his final works demanded not just attention but faith, trust, sympathy. If this meant that he was increasingly a textual projection, it also meant, conversely, that his works were increasingly imbricated in his persona. It was a shift with complex effects. The possessive titles with which Greene's works had begun to be published were at first, presumably, the work of their publishers. "In the Stationers' Register," Newcomb observes, "Greene's name [was] itself a valuable property," a paratextual "shroud" that marketed the popular writer and, at the same time, a commodity ready to be appropriated.[53] But if the titles of *Greenes Orpharion* and *Alcida Greenes Metamorphosis* were assertions of copyright, or advertisements, the possessives came to mean something more in the repentance pamphlets. The legitimacy of the *Groatsworth*, the *Repentance*, and *Greenes Vision* depended on Greene's having written them: anyone could tell Alcida's fictional story, but his repentance was a story only he could properly tell. They were "Greene's" in a way that the *Orpharion* and the *Metamorphosis* were not.

Even as the repentance pamphlets carved out for Greene a subtle claim to authorial possession, however, they also pointed up the intermediary roles of their publishers. The circumstances of his death were the subject of energetic rumor—it was unclear if he had indeed repented before dying or if, as some alleged, he had gone out in a final burst of debauched excess—and the gossip no doubt stoked demand for the pamphlets that purported to record his coming good.[54] His passing, Henry Chettle wrote in *Kind-Harts Dreame*, left "many papers in sundry Booke sellers hands," and the weeks and months that followed saw a scramble toward publication (*KH*, sig. A_3^v). William Wright entered the *Groatsworth* in the Stationers' Register on September 20, 1592, less than three weeks after Greene's death; John Danter followed suit barely two weeks later, on October 6, by registering the *Repentance*. (Thomas Newman never registered the rights to *Greenes Vision*, but his prefatory epistle suggests that it, too, was published shortly after Greene died.) The pamphlets were naturally competitors, and their very multiplicity cast doubt on all of them, rendering their assurances of authenticity mutually discrediting: "collectively," as Alexandra Halasz observes, "the pamphlets place each other under suspicion."[55] Newman advertised *Greenes Vision* by avowing that "manie haue published repentaunces vnder his name, but none more vnfeigned than this," acknowledging in the process (perhaps inadvertently) that none was above suspicion.[56] The *Groatsworth* drew the most scrutiny, much of it centered on Chettle. Each of the pamphlets, however, was ready to defend its own veracity:

a preface attributed to Greene in the *Repentance* calls its account "true and vnfained," and the title page of the *Groatsworth* insists that it was "written before [Greene's] death and published at his dyeing request."[57]

The various interests at stake in the publishing frenzy are hard to distinguish. Arul Kumaran has argued that the wave of texts that followed Green's death constituted a "pamphlet moment," in which writers sought to capitalize on an emergent consumer market's demand for satire.[58] No doubt there was an element of opportunism driving publishers too. Their competition may well have been partly collusion: Danter was involved in printing the *Groatsworth* for Wright, even as he held the rights to the *Repentance* (though he apparently recruited Cuthbert Burby to provide the capital for the latter text's publication—Burby's name rather than Danter's appears on its title page.) Chettle, too, was multiply implicated. The *Groatsworth* was registered to Wright "vppon the perill of Henrye Chettle," an unusual phrase that suggests Chettle had played some role in its acquisition, and John Jowett has argued that Chettle had also procured the *Repentance* for Danter.[59] There would have been a certain logic to playing up the rivalry and the suggestions of fabrication, for doubt about the truth of Greene's repentance must have stoked interest in the pamphlets that reported it. But there also seems to have been genuine discord among the involved parties. On March 5, 1593, two disputes involving Danter were heard in the court of the Stationers' Company: one with Chettle and the other with Burby.[60] The existence of more than one manuscript telling the story of Greene's repentance may have been the cause, with Burby frustrated that the *Repentance*, which he published after Danter brought it to him, was not the only pamphlet on the subject, and Danter angry with Chettle, a longtime partner, for procuring the *Groatsworth* for Wright rather than for Danter himself.[61] Before long, Wright would publish *Kind-Harts Dreame* and Danter the sonnet collection *Greenes Funeralls*, their apparent competition for the rights to Greene's final words spilling into a commercial rivalry over his posthumous legacy.

The competition among the publishers of the three repentance pamphlets amounted to a dispute over textual property, but an unusual kind of textual property. Since the pamphlets were sufficiently different from each other, the rights to copy were not at stake; at issue, rather, was the authenticity of the texts involved. The episode thus reflected Joseph Loewenstein's account of authorial possession as a back formation of contestation among early modern stationers: the relative value of the *Groatsworth*, the *Repentance*, and *Greenes Vision* came to depend on the attribution of authorship.[62] The question, in other words, was not what belonged to Wright or Danter—it was what truly belonged to Greene.

This was why each pamphlet was so eager to insist that it was genuinely Greene's work. The *Groatsworth* and the *Repentance* went even further. The *Groatsworth* presents a letter from Greene to his estranged wife, described as "founde with this booke after his death."[63] A similar letter comes at the end the *Repentance*, which also includes a list of "Certaine Cauiats sent by *Robert Greene* to a frend of his (as a farewell:) written with his owne hand" and a prayer that he had uttered "in the time of his sicknesse."[64] It would surely have been hard to prove that these extraneous materials were not themselves faked, but they are presented as corroborating evidence. Left behind and discovered by chance, they offer ostensibly private authentication for the narrative of repentance told in the texts intended for publication.[65] They even suggested that the texts could themselves be read as found documents, not just narratives but artifacts of their author's reformation. A paratext in the *Repentance*, indeed, frames the writing of the manuscript as a critical moment in the conversion: "After that he had pend the former discourse (then lying sore sicke of a surfet which hee had taken with drinking) hee continued most patient and penitent; yea, he did with teares forsake the world, renounced swearing, and desired forgiuenes of God and the worlde for all his offences."[66] Greene's text is subsumed here into an overarching narrative, a story in which the act of writing serves as prelude to the real climax, his penitential prayers and death.

It was a story that only a publisher or editor could tell. And while Wright and Newman were less aggressive than Burby in adding their own words to Greene's, they likewise took on modest narrative roles, rehearsing Greene's penitent death in prefatory epistles, on title pages and, in the case of the *Groatsworth*, in the fragmentary documents that complemented the main text. The result was a further confusion of the roles of author and publisher: while the repentance pamphlets afforded Greene a new possessive claim, they also made Wright, Burby, and Newman into storytellers—participants in the collective fashioning of Greene's persona. The pamphlets themselves were, therefore, distinctly multivocal. Greene's first-person narration, in each case, arrives only after the publisher's prefatory materials prepare us for it, and it is bracketed on the other end by the presence of the miscellaneous documents. The texts rotate between voices and perspectives, shuttling Greene between the roles of narrative object and subject; they guide him into the role of telling the story, already under way, of his prodigality and reform.[67] By the time Greene emerges as the first-person narrator of his story, he has already come into view as a character, his narrative particularity grounding his direct address to his readers. The repentance pamphlets thus turned Greene's persona into a jointly owned property and a collaboratively narrated character. In doing so, they pointed the way for those readers who would wish to rewrite his story, to make him their own. What is striking is that this happened when Greene emerged most fully into his own voice: he became most appropriable at the very moment his presence to his readers became most persuasively personal.

Ghost Stories

For Chettle, Riche, and Dickenson, reanimating Greene's persona called for a delicate balance. Their Greene would be, could only be, a fiction of their own making, but it was important that he still come off as a person with an independent existence. The ghost pamphlets, therefore, imitated the division of agency that they found in the repentance pamphlets. Riche's title page articulates the division clearly: "GREENES | Newes both from *Heauen and Hell.* | Prohibited the first for writing of | Bookes, and banished out of the last for | displaying of *Conny-* | *catchers. Commended to the Presse* By B.R" (*GN*, sig. A_1^r). The familiar possessive name, heading the page in capital letters, labels the text as Greene's, with Riche consigned to smaller type and mere initials and credited only with a minor role in the text's acquisition by the press. *Greene in Conceipt* similarly presents its real author as little more than a stationer's agent. Its title page also advertises Greene's name in capitals and adds Dickenson's initials at the end: "Receiued and reported by I.D."[68] Riche and Dickenson framed themselves, like the publishers of the repentance pamphlets, as intermediaries, responsible for editing and arranging for the publication of what they pretended were still Greene's manuscripts. The imitation continued inside, with a prefatory epistle in each pamphlet telling the story of Greene's haunting visit and the text he brought with him. Once this story of provenance was done, Greene would take over, his report from heaven and hell (in *Greenes Newes*) and the romance of Valeria (in *Greene in Conceipt*) accounting for the pamphlets' remaining pages.

The pamphlets were careful to establish a link between their ghosts and the biographical Greene who preceded them. They are littered with references to his books: *Never Too Late*, the *Groatsworth*, *A Quip for an Upstart Courtier* (1592), and the cony-catching pamphlets all find their way into *Greenes Newes*. That list creates what Newcomb describes as "an early canon of Greene's topical and autobiographical works" at the expense of his romances (though *Never Too Late* is arguably both).[69] In *Greene in Conceipt*, Greene's ghost maintains the distinction, inscribing his romance and cony-catching works onto his life's moral arc: "I am hee whose pen was first emploied in the aduancement of vanitie, and afterward in the discouering of villanie."[70] In *Kind-Harts Dreame*, he takes aim at his detractors: "Hauing with humble penitence besought pardon for my infinite sinnes, and paid the due to death, euen in my graue was I scarse layde, when Enuie . . . spit out her poyson, to disturbe my rest" (*KH*, sig. E_1^r). This strategy of citation was itself drawn from Greene's late works, which had used the rubric of prodigality and repentance to recall the romances of his earlier career as evidence of his sinful dissolution. Greene's returns asked his readers to remember his earlier incarnations, to see him as a character not so much invented as brought back.

When they were called on to recognize him, his readers were themselves made suddenly visible: it was their sustained attention, as much as anything, that ensured Greene's afterlife. In the opening lines of the main text of *Greenes Newes*, he directly solicits a readership that he presumes is an old and friendly one:

> Be not dismaied (my good freends) that a deade man shoulde acquaint you with newes, for it is I, *I per se I, Robert Greene, in Artibus Magister*, he that was wont to solicite your mindes with many pleasant conciets, & to fit your fancies at [the] least euery quarter of the yere, with strange & quaint deuises, best beseeming the season, and most answerable to your pleasures. Hauing therefore so many times taken the true measure of your appetites, & finding the very height of your dispositions inclined to nouelties, that you might the rather see howe willing I am to satisfie your humors, I haue sent you heere the whole discourse of my aduentures, what hath betyde me since I left the terrestriall worlde, with a very true report of my infernall trauailes. (*GN*, sig. A_4^r)

As Riche's Greene tells it, he and his readers share a history of intimacy. His literary career and the processes of publication and reception that shaped it are imagined here as a courtship: he solicits their conceits, fits their fancies, and answers their pleasures. The passage discloses the rhythms of publicity: the periodic, "punctual" temporality of circulation—"euery quarter of the yere," Greene tells his readers, I come back to you—that, for Michael Warner, convinces us that publics live across time, that they have "activity and duration."[71] Greene's public survives because he keeps addressing it. Each return affirms the public's ongoing existence and, more than that, encourages the sense that it is a collection of familiars, and this latest text just one more gathering of friends.

To imagine a diffuse public readership in this way was to endow it with a presence and an agency that were normally elusive. The ghost pamphlets were explicit and public acts of reception, the work of Greene's most attentive readers and thus enactments of the kind of dialogic exchange that their writers were so keen to imagine. His persona and his readership consequently sustained each other—whenever one of Greene's readers decided to write another sequel to his story, his reading public was made real and tangible again along with his ghost. In the process, his persona was turning into the kind of open imaginative space that David Brewer has called a "textual commons." For Brewer, the afterlives of fictional characters in the eighteenth century created spaces for "readers who imagine themselves as part of a public, a virtual community interested in the same things as they are"; a given character would serve, in its rewritings, as "the commons around which the virtual community organizes itself."[72] Greene's persona similarly enabled the convening of the virtual community of his readers, anchored (and made visible to each other) by their participation in the telling and retelling of the persona's ongoing, open-ended story.

It made sense, then, that the ghost pamphlets would gravitate toward dialogue, that Greene's returns would be motivated, seemingly, by a simple need for someone to talk to. The dynamic is most pronounced in *Kind-Harts Dreame*. Chettle's pamphlet gathers a cacophonous collection of personae—a balladeer, a medic, a juggler, and Richard Tarlton—each of whom arrives with a particular complaint, directed toward a particular audience: Tarlton, for example, confronts opponents of the theater, while the medic, Dr. Burcot, calls out "the impudent discreditors of Phisickes Art," and Greene, for his part, condemns the detractors whose abuse he can no longer ward off after death (*KH*, sig. C_4^v). The eclectic cast creates a scene of converging publics, all addressed at different points but summoned to the same textual place. Chettle's persona Kind-Hart floats in and around them, promising to ensure the transmission of each letter into print and intermittently offering his own commentary; the pamphlet's final section presents "his Censure on the Apparitions seuerally" (*KH*, sig. G_4^r). His is a discourse constructed out of a reflexive, or perhaps a parasitic, engagement with those that he transcribes. Kind-Hart's authority, in Alexandra Halasz's perceptive analysis, flows from his movement between different roles in the marketplace of print—writer, editor, compositor, publisher—and between the text's different personae.[73] Gathering them, and addressing their audiences, allows Chettle to present his persona as entering into a preexisting public (or publics) rather than having to invent one out of whole cloth.

Perhaps more powerful than speaking to or alongside Greene, however, was the fiction of speaking *as* Greene. Indeed, each pamphlet builds toward the uncanny moment when Greene would again speak directly to his readers. Each gives considerable space to what are presented as his own words: the letter on his detractors in *Kind-Harts Dreame*, the report from the afterlife in *Greenes Newes*, the romance that he brings from Elysium in *Greene in Conceipt*. These moments of textual immediacy recall the personal presence that had energized the repentance pamphlets and the *Groatsworth* in particular, a presence that Greene suddenly seemed to recover: here he was, incredibly, addressing himself to his readers once more, his voice reproduced by the surrogates who spoke as and for him—which is to remember, of course, that Greene's voice was really Chettle's, Riche's, or Dickenson's in disguise. Greene's hauntings were fits of ventriloquism, his person and voice emerging for fleeting moments by occupying those of others and, in the process, allowing his surrogates to come into the public eye in the guise of someone familiar. It was this availability to others that made him a "textual commons," for to speak as Greene was to inhabit a personality and a style of address that writer and reader alike could believe already to exist.

But if the force of these stories of haunting rested on their ability to reproduce the charismatic first-person rhetoric of the repentance pamphlets, Chettle, Riche, and Dickenson at the same time began to unpack Greene's performance of sincerity. The repentance pamphlets had abounded with assertions of their authenticity—"I trust heerein thou shalt perceiue my true and vnfained repentance," Greene had written in the *Repentance*—and those truth claims returned along with his persona in the ghost pamphlets.[74] But they came back as parodies. Chettle's Kind-Hart is stunned when he awakes and the papers left him by the ghosts fall from his hand, "which," he declares, "confirmed my dreame to bee no fantisie" (*KH*, sig. B_4^r). Riche's Greene promises "a very true report of my infernall trauailes" (*GN*, sig. A_4^r), while Dickenson's insists that he had known Valeria, the protagonist of the book's romance fiction, when they lived in London. These claims were transparently false, given away by the fantastical narratives they affirmed, by their tone of ironic play, and occasionally by direct hints.[75] They consequently advertised the fictionality of the texts that made them—and the fictionality, by extension, of Greene's persona. Greene's performance of penitent sincerity, they suggested, was really his most cunning poetic invention. At once emphasizing their continuity with the Greene presented in the repentance pamphlets and pointedly displacing him into the realm of poetic invention, the ghost pamphlets toyed with the idea that he had always been, at some level, a creature of the imagination.

Greene's afterlife thus brought a buried fiction to the surface. His persona's manner was, in its rewritings, no less sincere than it had been in the repentance pamphlets, but that sincerity could now be recognized as a rhetorical production. So too, more broadly, could the act of public address itself. Pointing out that Greene's persona was an imaginative invention stripped away the idea—which his posture of sincerity had left tantalizingly open—that there could be any direct, unmediated relation between writer and public. Instead, the ghost pamphlets suggested that this relation was a virtual one, and in doing so they focused attention on the poetic, "world making" aspect of public address.[76] This effect is brought home when Riche has Greene insist that he really is Greene, "*I per se I*," a ubiquitous phrase whose roots in grammar school hornbooks betray the rhetoricity of Greene's performance of presence.[77] For Greene, the address that constituted the virtual community of his readers needed to feel real—it needed the immediacy of a personal encounter—and that feeling depended on what Riche suggested was a tacit leap of the imagination.

Greene's ghostly afterlife became a story about that leap, and the pamphlets that told it an unusually sustained meditation on the conditions of literary publicity, which consisted at once of uncanny presence and debilitating absence. When Greene returned, delivering a text for his frightened interlocutor to publish, his appearances renewed the fantasy of immediate presence, but they also compromised it, rendering his returns transient, his person somehow deficient. In *Kind-Harts Dreame*, Greene's ghost and the letter he brings—an oblique retort to his detractors—leave Chettle's alter ego bewildered: "With *Robin Greene* it passes *Kindharts* capacity to deale; for as I knowe not the reason of his vnrest: so will I not intermeddle in the cause" (*KH*, sig. G_4^v). A few years later Dickenson's title page announced his return as a kind of miracle, advertising over its woodcut portrait a Greene "new raised from his graue." Yet the startling intensity of Greene's visible presence is slowly drained over the course of Dickenson's preface, until he is no more than a "bloudlesse remnant" of his former self.[78] By the time his ghost leaves, Dickenson's point seems to be that Greene can exist for his readers *only* "in conceipt," brought before them at the end of a process of transcription and publication from which he has long since vanished.

The most searching of the ghost narratives came in *Greenes Newes*. Unlike Chettle, who included other ghosts along with Greene, or Dickenson, who used him to frame a romance fiction with a different protagonist, Riche built his entire pamphlet around Greene, offering it as a first-person report of his experiences in the afterlife. The story takes the form of a surreal quest, with Greene wandering first to heaven, where he is turned away by Saint Peter over the "partialitie" of his writings (*GN*, sig. C_1^v), then in search of purgatory, which is revealed to be a mirage—a figment, he is told by a miller he encounters on the way, of the imaginations of "madde men and fooles" (*GN*, sig. G_3^r). Finally he reaches hell, where the rogues he exposed in his cony-catching pamphlets recognize him, and Lucifer, "willing to appease their passions with any punishment, commaunded mee presently to bee thrust foorth of hell gates and charging me so to remaine a restlesse spirite, wandering through the world, and neuer after to make any returne agayne to that place" (*GN*, sig. H_2^v). The double banishment cleverly plays on the ambiguity of Greene's repentance: having ended his life on uncertain terms, he is neither redeemed nor condemned after death. Instead, he remains in a moral and narrative limbo.

Riche's pamphlet is peculiarly concerned with this middle space: the space Greene journeys through as he seeks each successive destination, and the space he is cast back into when each fails. It is not purgatory, at least not properly speaking; Riche's extended debunking of the doctrine (and the accompanying flurry of anti-Catholic satire) makes that much clear. Rather, it is a world of literary bits and pieces—a fabliau told by a bricklayer and another by the miller, a cony-catching tale offered by a mercer in heaven. Greene's companions in his quest are Cloth and Velvet Breeches, the adversaries from his satiric dream-vision *A Quip for an Upstart Courtier*, and their conversations are filled with references to his writings ("I am now to put you in mind of an other of my Bookes, called *Greenes neuer too late*: O that you had but read ouer that Booke in time, but nowe it is too late for me to spend such wishes, and more later for you to redresse your former follyes" [*GN*, sig. B_2^v]). Having dispelled the Catholic purgatory, Riche produces in its place a purgatorial anthology of print entertainment: a representation, Mentz suggests, of "the uncomfortable position of early modern prose fiction, which can rest in neither a humanist's heaven nor an outlaw's hell."[79] After his expulsion, Greene is himself consigned to this untidy gallery of fictions. "I remayne now (as I haue tolde you)," he tells Riche's readers, "a walking spyrite, restlesse and remedilesse to wander through the world" (*GN*, sig. H_2^v–H_3^r).

For Riche, it seems, what has replaced purgatory is the nowhere of fictional reference. In the pamphlet's debunking of the doctrine, indeed, this is more or less what Riche reveals it to be:

> The foundation wheron it was layd, was lyes and foolish fantasies, the rest of the vpper buildings, was dreames and doting deuises. All the whole edifice, was of such lyght and rotten stuffe, that after they had beene two or three hundred yeeres patching & peecing it together, a poore silly Swaine naked and thred bare, called *Trueth*, blowing against the building but with a little blast of breath, the gale was of such force against it, that the whole matter & substance, together with the Founders, Patrons, Proctors, Protectors & Defenders, were al blown immediatly into Hell. (*GN*, sig. G_3^r)

Stephen Greenblatt argues that purgatory was always a poetic idea, always caught up in an impulse to imagine and represent an afterlife; here Riche, following William Tyndale and the Protestant reformers who had cast it out, unmasks purgatory as a fiction, his language invoking the vocabulary of the Elizabethan case against poetry—*lyes*, *foolish fantasies*, *dreames*. The ghosts of Greenblatt's purgatory lived on in the theater, and Riche's purgatory, too, is secularized and moved into the realm of the aesthetic.[80] But while purgatory, in Greenblatt's argument, gave the stage a template for the awesome conjuring power of performance, Greene's hauntings—for Riche but also for Chettle and Dickenson—seem to mean something different: they offer a window onto the liminality of fictive discourse, the strangeness of its proximity to but difference from the real world. When Greene averred that his report from heaven and hell was "very true" in *Greenes Newes*, or when he affirmed the veracity of Valeria's story in *Greene in Conceipt*, he reversed the logic that his contemporaries typically assigned to fictional tales: he allowed readers to imagine fiction not as a lie in the real world but as a true utterance from a different one. Fiction in Greene's hauntings short-circuits reference: it is a report from a place that does not exist, a message that evaporates in its delivery.

Just how different this world really was is one of the tantalizing questions posed by the pamphlets, which mix the trappings of the supernatural with the real world of contemporary London. It is a signal eccentricity of the ghost stories, indeed, that Greene continually returns from the dead for so mundane a reason as to deliver books to the press. Yet Riche, Chettle, and Dickenson had come to see the publics that Greene revisited as potent fictions in their own right, as virtual communities formed by means of a fragile act of collective imagination. In a study of *Tarltons Newes Out of Purgatorie* (1590), Richard Preiss describes purgatory as an allegory of mediatization: it is, he suggests, a space that marks "the hybrid territory . . . between theatre and print."[81] Greene's purgatory of fictions likewise encodes the pressure of medium and mediation. For the writers of his afterlife, purgatory was finally the purgatory of print publicity, and the attenuated existence of Greene's ghost a version of what might await writers who ventured into the public eye.

Near the end of *Greenes Newes*, Greene turns outward to address his readers once again. "Sometimes," he warns them,

> I will bee *Robin Goodfellowe*, and will meete with a wanton wench in a darke corner, and let her blesse and crosse her selfe as well as she can, I will put her in such a bodily feare, that for fortie weekes after, shee shall thinke that young bugges are crawling in her belly. Sometimes I will shew such dreames & vysions to women whilst they be sleeping, that they shall make theyr Husbands Cuckolds when they are waking.
>
> Sometimes I will trans-forme my selfe into diuers shapes, and will walke through all trades, all Sciences, and all occupations, and some I will infect with the spirite of *Auarice*, some with miserie, some with deceipt and all manner of subtiltie, that they shall leaue no practise vnsought for, whereby to rake and gather pelfe, to leaue to theyr heyres, that the olde Prouerbe might bee verified: *Happy are those children, whose Fathers goe to the deuill.* (*GN*, sig. H_3^r)

The future that Riche's Greene imagines for himself here is constrained by the terms of his permanent half-life. He can visit readers, but only occasionally and only fleetingly, in the temporality of pamphlet publication; he is resigned to mischief around the margins of a world he can haunt but never again belong to. What Greene is left with is the hollowed-out existence of an enduring, but also enduringly homeless, fiction. It is only in his restless and remediless wanderings that he can return to London: to Riche on a darkened street, to Chettle and Dickenson in dreams, to the readers for whom he always brings some new text from abroad. Still, even this is a kind of life; fleeting or not, what Greene promises is that his relationship with his readers is not dead. His tone is strangely altered—something close to aggression replaces the solicitous courtesy of the pamphlet's opening lines—but his first-person voice has perhaps never been so forceful in its appeal to his readers. He now exists, more apparently than ever, only when he can address them.

* * *

For all of their ironic playfulness, the ghost pamphlets were thus reckonings with the challenges of literary publicity—the opacity, the distance, the ephemerality that it seemed to enforce. To live in this transitory, ethereal space—to be a man in print—was, in a sense, not to be a person at all. Rather, Riche and his peers suggest, it was to be a ghost. But understanding the practice of literature in these terms had benefits too. The foremost, and the one I want to close this chapter by pointing to, was that thinking of Greene as a virtual being—as a persona—was a way of abstracting a particularly literary identity, of separating literary persons from persons in the fuller sense. In making this kind of abstraction available, the stories of Greene's haunting gave their readers a way of coming to terms with, and of talking about, an emergent literary system. His name could serve, as it did for Gabriel Harvey, as a hammer with which to bludgeon literary adversaries: "But *Greene* (although pitifully blasted, & how woefully faded?) still flourisheth in the memory of some greene wits, wedded to the wantonnesse of their owne fancy, and inamored vppon euery new-fangled toy."[82] For Harvey, writing soon after his death, Greene's afterlife recapitulated his prodigal youth, his wanton romances still seducing fresh readers. For others, the name evoked a modern, vernacular literary pantheon: in Thomas Dekker's imagining of a celestial garden of English poets, playwrights and pamphleteers, Greene's spirit sits near Spenser and Chaucer, laughing with Christopher Marlowe and George Peele as they welcome Nashe into their company.[83]

But the point is best illustrated by returning to *Kind-Harts Dreame*. Chettle's resurrection of Greene is, at least in one respect, an outlier: whereas Riche's and Dickenson's versions of Greene desperately seek access to the public that he could no longer reach himself, Chettle's Greene speaks guardedly. He affirms his repentance and denies the scurrilous rumors about his death, but it is hard to say what he wants. Much of his letter is spent urging his interlocutor to hit back at their common enemies—"Awake . . . reuenge thy wrongs, remember mine"—only for him to retract the request: "All this had I intended to write, but now I wil not giue way to wrath, but returne it vnto the earth from whence I tooke it: for with happie soules it hath no harbour" (*KH*, sig. E_2^r). Kind-Hart's reactions tell a conflicting story. Later, he will say that passing judgment on Greene's letter is beyond him. In the moment of its reading, however, the letter is mysteriously compelling: "Had not my name beene *Kind-Hart*, I would have sworne this had beene sent to my selfe; for in my life I was not more pennilesse than at that instant" (*KH*, sig. E_2^r).

But the addressee of Greene's letter is not Kind-Hart, nor is it a general readership; instead, it is Thomas Nashe's persona Pierce Penilesse. In making Pierce the object of Greene's ghostly address, Chettle responded to the second edition of Nashe's pamphlet *Pierce Penilesse His Supplication to the Diuell*, which was published after Greene's death and apparently before the writing of *Kind-Harts Dreame*. In a preface, Nashe had complained that the unauthorized printing of the first edition had prevented him from giving Pierce additional documents to send to hell with the devil's messenger, among them a letter "to the Ghost of *Robert Greene*, telling him, what a coyle there is with pamphleting on him after his death."[84] Perhaps more than any other scene in Greene's hauntings, this exchange evokes the peculiar world to which Greene's persona pointed: a social imaginary in which the virtual embodiments of English letters might live together. In this imaginary, personae anchored relations among themselves, relations that transposed and reconceived the social dynamics that obtained in the actual world of publication and reception. As we will see in the next chapter, no persona did this so powerfully, or so ambivalently, as Colin Clout.

CHAPTER 2

Rehearsing Colin Clout

A year after a ghostly Robert Greene accosted Barnabe Riche, the poet Barnabe Barnes told of another marvelous encounter. This time, the roles were reversed. Barnes himself (or rather his alter ego Parthenophil) was the unexpected visitor, and the person he met, in the midst of a tour through Arcadia, was Colin Clout: "Here *Colin* sittes," Barnes wrote, "beneath that oken tree / Eliza singing in his layes."[1] The differences between the two encounters reflect the generic distance between Colin and Greene's ghost. Of course Greene, a loquacious amalgam of satire and amorous romance, would come looking for company; and of course Colin Clout, an anxious and retiring avatar of pastoral melancholy, would flee it—would need to be found out. But these differences point up what the two moments, and the personae at their centers, have in common. Like Riche's ethereal Greene, Colin seems to live beyond the text that discovers him, indeed beyond any particular text at all. Like Greene, Colin is a collective and public fiction, a combination of imaginary character and historical author who came to exist, in the responses of readers and writers like Barnes, as a person at large in the literary public. In Barnes's poem, as in Riche's pamphlet, the moment of encounter sends a thrill down the spine—the thrill of meeting Colin in the flesh, sitting "here," right in front of us.

By the time he made his way into Barnes's *Parthenophil and Parthenophe* (1593), Colin Clout had already undergone a long and complicated history. When Edmund Spenser introduced him in *The Shepheardes Calender* (1579)—as the mask "under which," in the commentator E. K.'s gloss, "this Poete secretely shadoweth himself"—he was himself borrowing a name that belonged to others.[2] Clément Marot had made "Colin" the authoritative voice in the

Eglogue sur le trepas de ma dame Louise de Savoye (1531), the poem that Spenser would imitate in the elegy for Dido that appears in the *Calender*'s November eclogue.[3] The same year, or shortly before, John Skelton's *Here after foloweth a lytell boke called Collyn Clout* was published in London. An astringently satirical attack on Cardinal Thomas Wolsey, the poem would soon become Skelton's most popular work, going through several editions in the middle decades of the sixteenth century and inspiring at least one pre-Spenserian imitator.[4]

In Spenser's hands, Colin became the pastoral double for the "new Poete," and ever since, he has been taken as a cipher for Spenser's laureate ambitions. His characteristic melancholy has long seemed to disclose an uncertainty about the possibility of a poetic vocation; so Kreg Segall, building on a line of thinking developed by Richard Helgerson and David L. Miller, can write that Colin thematizes Spenser's "anxiety over the meaning of 'poet.'"[5] Patrick Cheney, in his study of Spenser's career, is more sanguine: for him, Colin is a success, if a preliminary one, an "inaugural stage within the 'perfect paterne of a poete.'"[6] Colin in either case belongs to the choreography of Spenserian self-fashioning, the reflexivity of his fictions pointing us to the author behind him. But Colin was always something more—and something more complicated—than a poetic signature. More than a self-image, Skelton's Colin was an evasion: a displacement of authority onto a stock character in the tradition of Piers Plowman—an anonymous "clout" or "clod" out of which the voice of popular complaint might emerge.[7] Colin Clout was a doubled figure from the beginning, a persona that pointed at once toward and away from the poet who claimed him. So it was perhaps to be expected that—on the other side of Spenser's appropriation—Colin would emerge again as a portable, circulable fiction, a figure to be reimagined by writers like Barnes.

For Barnes, Colin's appeal lay in the world that the name conjured: a world of shepherds and nymphs in which song is natural and contagious. It is by finding a place alongside Colin—and Astrophil and Stella as well—that Barnes can establish himself as Parthenophil, a Petrarchan lover cast into the space of Sidneian and Spenserian pastoral. Nor was Barnes alone: the ability to evoke a world in miniature was quickly becoming Colin's calling card. Like the other personae examined in this book, Colin encouraged narrative reimagining. But unlike Greene's ghosts, Colin sparked little in the way of sustained rewriting, unless one counts Spenser's own returns to his alter ego in *Colin Clouts Come Home Againe* (1595) and Book 6 of *The Faerie Queene* (1596). Instead, Colin was evoked in passing: dutifully saluted in prefaces, written into eclogues and epigrams and satires, even summoned onto the stage. To cite Colin was to use him as a kind of shorthand, a name capable on its own of summoning two worlds in one—on the one hand the Elizabethan literary field, in which "Colin Clout" was interchangeable with "Edmund Spenser," and on the other the pastoral environs of the *Calender*, in which poets could imagine themselves to be, like Colin, singing shepherds. Elizabethan personae combined the form of citational reference with a capacity for fictional world-making, and Colin took that combination to its highest (or at least its most compressed) form.

If Greene's ghost belonged to satire and prose romance, Colin moved in the world of lyric poetry. He did so at a moment of transition for English verse: one marked by the gradual entrance of verse forms into print, both in poetic miscellanies and, increasingly as the century wore on, in single-author works.[8] The eclogue was one such form; the sonnet sequence—which became an intensely fashionable sector of the book trade in the 1590s—was another. Despite his roots, Colin moved freely between kinds, appearing in sonnets as easily and as frequently as in pastorals. Indeed, he fostered generic cross-pollination, mingling pastoral and Petrarchan modes in what could be imagined, in his light, as a seamless lyric world. Barnes's Arcadia—a space shared by Astrophil and Colin, personae with very different generic lineages—makes this point well. So does Richard Barnfield, who hailed "great *Colin* chiefe of sheepheardes all" in his own sonnet sequence, *Cynthia* (1595), thus bringing a field of English poets into view as a pastoral community convened under Colin's presiding authority.[9] If the printing of poetry in the second half of sixteenth century encouraged what Matthew Zarnowiecki describes as a "metacritical awareness of [the] new medium," Colin seemed to embody that reflexive media consciousness.[10] His appearances located lyric, a mode centrally concerned with the projection of voice, in scenes of organic presence—as when Parthenophil finds Colin sitting, and singing, right *here*—even as they reckoned with the inevitable fact of circulation. From this perspective, Colin has more in common with Greene's ghost than we might suspect: both concentrated a fascination with the forms of personality and community that textual circulation could support.

This chapter is about Colin's emergence as a portable symbol of what we might call lyric presence. But it is also about the curiously paradoxical symbol he became. Consider this passage from Thomas Edwards's *Narcissus*:

Collyn was a mightie swaine,
In his power all do flourish,
We are shepheards but in vaine,
There is but one tooke the charge,
By his toile we do nourish,
And by him are inlarg'd.[11]

In these lines, a pastoral scene frames contemporary poets as shepherds gathered around one "mighty swaine." Edwards's mention of Colin has a familiar memorializing reverence, a sense of homage to a departed literary forebear. It is an impression strengthened by the lines' verb tenses, which divide the moment between past and present, between "*Collyn* was" and "We are." Yet the elegiac grammar is misleading: when Edwards published *Narcissus* in 1595, Spenser was still alive and actively writing. The year 1595, in fact, marked his public return to his pastoral persona, in the long eclogue *Colin Clouts Come Home Againe*. The nostalgia that colors Edwards's lines is thus strangely premature: it is as if Colin and the pastoral scene that he evokes belong to a world dislocated from the present, available only in a mode of poetic recollection.

This sense of temporal dislocation became the defining condition of Colin's circulation. Edwards was hardly alone in invoking him nostalgically. On the contrary, a proleptic sense of absence pervaded Colin's later appearances, both in the works of other poets and, arrestingly, in Spenser's own treatment of his alter ego. We might recognize in nostalgia the characteristic affect of citation and rewriting, the forms that animate personae like Colin: to cite, to allude, to invoke is always to point backward, toward a moment that can be remembered because it has passed. More particularly, however, this belatedness reflects the urgency of the pastoral myth of organic community and oral song—a myth set against, and perhaps foreclosed by, the textual forms in which the poets who invoked Colin wrote and the marketplace in which they published. The resulting ambivalence centered on Colin, who at once embodied this fantasy and, because he could deliver it only by becoming himself a portable commodity, dispersed and disenchanted it.

The pages that follow, then, develop a pair of interrelated arguments. First, they offer an account of Colin as something more than Spenser's reflexive double—as instead, or in addition, a detachable persona, written into the culture at large in a way that a focus on Spenser's writings alone must miss.

His circulation made him a corporate character; at the same time, it established him as a legitimating figure in a nascent literary field. Second, the chapter traces the paradoxes of lyric as Colin came to represent it: a form premised on a fantasy of oral presence that Colin, as a circulating, textual symbol, seemed to unravel. In the event, these lines of argument are thoroughly intertwined. For the community that Colin anchored—the field assembled around him—depended at once on the sense of presence that he symbolized and the forms of mediation that threatened to dissolve it. It was this contradiction that lay behind the curiously proleptic nostalgia with which he was so often invoked, as well as the strange distance of Spenser's own returns to the persona that had once been his.

Colin's Domain

The Colin whom Spenser claimed from Skelton and Marot was a blend of genres and styles. From Marot, he brought the associations of pastoral elegy; from Skelton, those of complaint and satire. Spenser tapped the latter vein frequently, confronting episcopal authority in "Maye," "Julye," and "September"; as Jane Griffiths suggests, Spenser's Colin can be read as mediating a tradition of Skeltonian social critique given new urgency at a moment of fresh religious tension.[12] Even as it draws on this vein of critique, however, the *Calender* insulates Colin from it—or rather, the book disperses it into the diffuse melancholy that characterizes Colin as forlorn Virgilian lover. The anonymizing plurality of Skelton's Colin accordingly becomes in the *Calender* something close to the opposite: an insinuation of secreted identity, with Colin, as the poet's pseudonym, grounding a network of personae representing "the persons of divers other his familiar freendes and best acquayntance" (p. 64). Offering an "imagined community," in Michelle O'Callaghan's description, that transposes "an actual community of friends and patrons said to exist just outside its pages," the *Calender* frames social relations in the terms of utopian simplicity: "No doubt," wrote George Puttenham a decade later, "the shepheards life was the first example of honest felowship."[13] In this imagined community, poetry is the heartbeat of social life, and Colin (as Hobbinol insists in "June") is its mascot: "*Colin*, to heare thy rymes and roundelayes, / Which thou were wont on wastfull hylls to singe, / I more delight, then larke in Sommer dayes" (lines 49–51).

It was this naturalization of poetry that lay at the heart of Paul Alpers's argument, in a seminal essay, that the *Calender*'s aim was to fashion an independent "domain of lyric." Alpers's essay arrived at the height of the New Historicism, and it sought to answer that movement's critique of (in its view) an earlier criticism's naïve commitment to aesthetic autonomy. It was a critique that gathered with particular energy around pastoral, a mode whose green worlds seemed especially liable to aestheticist misreading, as free spaces set apart from history.[14] For Alpers, the opposition between history and the aesthetic was a false one. Rather, he insisted, "the claim to relative autonomy, by means of something like aesthetic 'space,' was Spenser's historical . . . aim in *The Shepheardes Calender*."[15] Such a claim was necessary precisely because of poetry's thorough sociopolitical implication—because poets in Tudor England were so often compelled to justify and motivate their writings as a form of courtly service. In the fiction of the *Calender*, by contrast, poetry needs no motivation: Spenser's shepherds sing because that is what shepherds do. The governing primacy of poetry in the eclogues frames pastoral as politically or institutionally alternative—a *domain* of lyric whose relative autonomy suggests a comparison to Pierre Bourdieu's concept of the literary field. The term, Alpers explains, answers the challenge of aesthetic space by construing it "in terms of rule and authority."[16]

But why *lyric*? Though easier to pass over, this is perhaps the more difficult term: why not a domain of pastoral, or simply a domain of poetry—concepts that would stand on arguably firmer generic ground? Never the most stable of terms, early modern lyric is an especially fraught category at present, for recent scholarship has emphasized the degree to which modern understandings of lyric are distorted by a perhaps distinctively post-Romantic association with first-person subjectivity—with the presence of a poetic voice speaking to itself, not heard but overheard. In the strongest version of the argument, lyric is a nineteenth- and twentieth-century invention, a category that has overtaken and effaced a much wider range of discrete verse forms; it is a mode of reading that forcibly construes its diverse historical objects *as* lyrics.[17] Premodern lyric is, in this sense, an anachronism, a category produced by the imposition of modern reading practices onto older texts. On the other hand, as Heather Dubrow observes, the term *lyric* was used regularly in sixteenth- and seventeenth-century texts, where it referred to a wide range of kinds, including musical texts but also poems evidently not intended to be sung.[18] Moreover, as Stephanie Burt argues, any number of earlier poems evince the privacy or inwardness that we are tempted to reduce to a modern idea of lyric subjectivity.[19] Nor is the lyricization argument, as it has come to be called, altogether novel. It draws much of its inspiration from earlier accounts of the readerly force that underlies lyric—most notably Paul de Man's declaration that "the lyric depends entirely for its existence on the denial of phenomenality as the surest means to recover what it denies."[20] But de Man's point is ideological rather than narrowly historical. Lyric, his account suggests, might be found wherever phenomenal presence is attributed to or sought from poetry.[21]

I take *lyric* to be a meaningful term in its flagging of this ideological force—in the way it foregrounds the figuration of voice and presence, which linger as motivating fictions even, or perhaps especially, for primarily textual forms. The phenomenality of lyric mattered a great deal in the second half of the sixteenth century, a period marked by the increasing popularity of what Zarnowiecki identifies as "a new work of art, the printed book of lyric poetry."[22] Of course, as Arthur Marotti and others have shown, this new work of art in no way displaced its predecessors: manuscript circulation thrived as a medium alongside print—a reading of Joshua Eckhardt's study of manuscript miscellanies alongside Zarnowiecki's account of printed ones makes this much clear—and poems and poets moved back and forth between them.[23] It was precisely their coexistence, however, that left the choice of medium contingent, and that made a reflexive awareness of mediation inescapable. "Lyric poetry lives in the present," Zarnowiecki writes, summarizing this reflexive consciousness, "but poems on paper (and in other media) extend through time, and proliferate in number, and are changed in the process."[24] Writing and reading lyric in the late sixteenth century meant entering into the teeth of this contradiction—the contradiction of a form at once essentially immediate and necessarily mediated.

When I use the term *lyric* in what follows, then, I do so in order not just to refer to the broad array of verse forms that gathered around Colin—forms that go well beyond the pastoral eclogue or elegy—but also to register the fragile "attribution of aesthetic presence" that lies behind all of them, an attribution whose very urgency points up the unavoidability of mediation.[25] As it turns out, Alpers seems to have had something similar in mind. At the end of his essay, he takes up Colin's final poems, arguing that their power lies in their ability to "endow the expression of loss with what has the feeling of lyric presence."[26] Lyric on these terms is less a formal category than a phenomenal one: it names the mode of distinctively poetic *experience* to which we must appeal in order to establish the uncertain autonomy of Colin's domain.

Colin is in certain respects a doubtful source for such presence. He is, after all, absent more than he is present in the *Calender*. In "Januarye," he breaks his pipe and abandons his flock, returning in "June" only to disappear again until "November." The broken pipe marks Colin's estrangement from his fellow shepherds, an estrangement that will endure, in various forms, over the entirety of the *Calender*. Outside of "June" and "November," which are themselves reflections on his exceptional place among his peers, Colin avoids the dialogic exchanges that characterize the life of the *Calender*'s pastoral. In "Januarye" and "December" he speaks alone; in "Aprill" and "August" his poems are recited by others in his absence. In his alienation, Roland Greene suggests, Colin encodes a tension between individual poetic voice and the dialogic lyric practiced by his fellow shepherds—a tension resolved only, and imperfectly, in the final eclogue.[27] Where his peers address verses to each other, Colin begins instead with apostrophes. He does so most dramatically in "August," where his sestina (recited by Cuddie) opens with a series of apostrophic turns—"Ye wastefull woodes . . . / Ye carelesse byrds . . . / Thou pleasaunt spring" (lines 151–55)—that forcefully redirect the poem's address. The sestina is itself a particularly isolating form, eluding conversation by internalizing its own responsive echoes, and for Colin it seems to enact a mode of poetry that refuses any interlocutor at all. "Heere," Colin insists, with a deictic that seems to refer to the woods and the sestina alike, "will I dwell apart / In gastfull grove" (lines 169–70).

Yet it is Colin's stubborn determination to "dwell apart" that provokes the *Calender*'s most powerful articulations of pastoral community. When Hobbinol praises Colin's "rymes and roundelays" in "June," the description is offered as a memory, a reminder of the songs that Colin once sang and might sing again. In "Aprill," too, Colin's absence introduces what Segall calls an "aesthetic gap" in what would otherwise be a pastoral world at peace: "Hys pleasaunt Pipe," Hobbinol tells Thenot, "whych made us meriment, / He wylfully hath broke, and doth forbeare / His wonted songs, wherein he all forewent" (lines 14–16).[28] The moment calls to mind Susan Snyder's distinction between two versions of pastoral: one spatial, the other temporal. In the latter, the *locus amoenus* is encountered as already lost, surviving "only as a frustrating memory, a marker of present alienation."[29] Colin's exile enforces just such a pastoral of process, framing an opposition between idyllic past and inadequate present that weighs on Hobbinol's mournful past tense. From this perspective, what is lost with Colin's departure is the unified present that lyric reaches after. In its place, we are left with the secondary time of recollection.

Recollection, at least, is how Colin's poems survive his refusal to sing. The centerpiece of "Aprill"—and arguably of the *Calender* as a whole—is his lay for Eliza, a royal encomium that doubles as a display of virtuosity:

> Ye dayntye Nymphs, that in this blessed Brooke
> doe bathe your brest,
> For sake your watry bowres, and hether looke,
> at my request:
> And eke you Virgins, that on *Parnasse* dwell,
> Whence floweth *Helicon* the learned well,
> Help me to blaze
> Her worthy Praise,
> Which in her sexe doth all excell. (lines 37–45)

Colin's lay begins by situating itself in a carefully elaborated here-and-now—addressing "ye" nymphs, pointing to "this" brook, asking its audience to "hether looke"—that in turn reflects the *Calender*'s central fiction: the community of shepherds united by the spontaneous performance of poetic song. But in "Aprill" Colin is absent, and he does not sing his own lay: instead, Hobbinol "records" it (to use the poem's own term), offering it to Thenot as proof of Colin's brilliance. We are thus some distance from the lay's here-and-now, and in this later moment Hobbinol can only wistfully recall the time of its original utterance, when Colin had sung the lyric "as by a spring he laye, / And tuned it unto the Waters fall" (lines 35–36). The lay is thus an oddity. In a collection of eclogues governed by the fiction of spontaneous song, it is a poem that has become, as Louis Montrose puts it, "a public trust, a document of cultural history."[30] By separating the poem from the moment of its performance, Hobbinol introduces the idea that poems might be reproduced as texts: that they might exist apart from, and hence outlive, the moment of their utterance.

Recitation, and by extension poetic transmission, had been long been central concerns of pastoral: in Virgil's *Eclogue* 9, Moeris rehearses verses once sung by an absent Menalcas; and in *Eclogue* 5, Mopsus recites a song of his own that he had recently carved on a beech tree. Such moments suggest the constitutive doubleness of pastoral, its setting of a fiction of simplicity within a richly traditional genre. Pastoral happens in the moment, but it also encodes its own history. In "Aprill," Hobbinol's recitation points toward textualization; it is a case study in what it means for a poem to become public. "Perhaps paradoxically," Zarnowiecki observes, it is "Colin's withdrawal from the community of poets" that submits him to the processes of cultural reconstruction.[31]

It is only when he must be invoked, and his songs rehearsed in absence, that a distinction between poet and performer becomes necessary, or even pertinent; it is here, in other words, that Colin comes into view as an *author*. The effect is even clearer in the parallel episode in "August," where Cuddie recites Colin's sestina. After the recitation, Perigot offers his judgment: "O *Colin, Colin*, the shepheards joye, / How I admire ech turning of thy verse: / And *Cuddie*, fresh *Cuddie* the liefest boye, / How dolefully his doole thou didst reherse" (lines 190–93). For Perigot, rehearsal serves as a nearly sufficient compensation for Colin's absence. Invoked as a poetic author, as a *turner* rather than a *rehearser* of verse, Colin can be addressed as if he were really present. If Colin can thus be summoned back to presence, the sestina and the lay can be projected into a future in which they will be rehearsed again and again—in which they will be cited and repeated as documents. As indeed they were: unsurprisingly, these two poems were excised and reproduced more than once in the years after the *Calender*'s publication. William Webbe, for instance, included "the rufull song of *Colin* sung by *Cuddie* in the *Sheepheards Calender*" as an example of a sestina in his catalogue, published in 1586, of English verse forms.[32] And when the lyric miscellany *Englands Helicon* appeared fourteen years later, it included the lay for Eliza, carefully extracted from its setting in "Aprill" and offered as a self-standing lyric.[33] Alienation in the *Calender* is, in Catherine Nicholson's words, poetry's "paradoxically enabling condition."[34]

In Colin's absence, the practices of re-creation—of recollection, recording, repetition—are what might restore and maintain the threatened pastoral idyll. For Zarnowiecki, the work of recording registers a kind of cultural optimism, drawing Colin, despite his recalcitrant solipsism, back into sociability and, at the same time, enabling the survival of his poetry. He is, as Wendy Wall writes, "often invisible but persistently audible."[35] And yet rehearsal is a matter of some ambivalence in the eclogues: if it promises to redress Colin's absence, it also redoubles the sense of loss—the irretrievability of a moment that can only be "dolefully" retold and reenacted. This was an effect that the temporality of reproduction, both plumbing the past and preserving for the future, only heightened. To recite Colin's songs is to recall the lost moment of their performance, but it is also to anticipate the transmission of the eclogues themselves—and of the pastoral *locus amoenus* as a whole—as texts. The pressures of this double time become, over the course of the *Calender*, increasingly difficult to escape. Even Colin's late return in "November," which seems to herald a restoration of pastoral harmony, is framed from the beginning by the prospect of poetic circulation: "Now somewhat sing," Thenot urges him, "whose endles sovenaunce, / Emong the shepeheards swains may aye remaine" (lines 5–6). What Thenot wants is a song that is already an artifact of endless memory, a song that can be experienced, even in the present, as separate from it. And for once, Colin provides what is asked of him: his poem, an elegy for the shepherdess Dido, seems designed to detach itself from its moment. Like his earlier, rehearsed set pieces, it begins with an apostrophic address—"Up then *Melpomene* thou mournefulst Muse of nyne" (line 53)—that turns away from Thenot and carries him, and us, toward an abstracted timelessness.

Elegy is, of course, itself a form quintessentially concerned with "sovenaunce," with the memorialization of both subject and poet, and Spenser hints that the death in question is not Dido's alone.[36] The refrain, repeated with variations at the end of each stanza, rhymes "O heavie herse" (that is, Dido's casket or corpse) with "O carefull verse." The "care" of Colin's poem is its sorrow but also its attentive crafting—the care evident, to recall Perigot's praise from "August," in the "turning of thy verse." Like Dido's tomb, the elegy itself is an object built to last: *herse* and *verse*, the rhyme hints, are versions of each other. And we might also hear in Colin's refrain an echo of the related rhyme in "August," *verse-rehearse*. The prospect of literary transmission, of the production and reproduction of texts, is by this point the unavoidable context for Colin's poetry, so that even in the moment of its utterance the elegy is cast as an object of nostalgia, a performance already calcified into a literary object. Only here is the dark pun at the heart of Cuddie's "rehearsing" in "August" given full rein. To have one's verses re*hearse*d—to have them reproduced, cited, made into artifacts—is, Spenser suggests, its own form of death. Colin thus embodies an equivocation that lies at the heart of pastoral: the evocation of a golden age that can only be glimpsed as memory.

Hovering around the edges of this reading is *The Shepheardes Calender*'s own status as an irreducibly textual artifact—an artifact dependent on the forms of transmission that Spenser so anxiously broaches in "Aprill" and "August." As Richard Halpern has argued, "the pastoral myth of an organically unified world" sits uneasily alongside E. K.'s commentary, which continually reminds us that the *Calender*'s eclogues were *written* by "the Poete."[37] Framed by an apparatus that anticipates a scene of literary reception, the world of the eclogues seems to dissolve. In Andrew Mattison's striking reading, the *Calender* both invests in and relinquishes the idea that pastoral might meaningfully represent poetic activity. "Pastoral's simplification of agrarian life," he writes, "stands in for the simplicity of poetic production that Spenser acknowledges as desirable but unworkable."[38] This simplicity fails for Mattison because poetic inspiration requires a complexity of experience that escapes pastoral convention; Spenser's sense of himself as a poet with the experience necessary to write thus requires the diminishment of his pastoral double. But perhaps it fails less at the moment of poetic inspiration than at the moment of textual mediation—the moment when the charmed scene of pastoral dialogue runs up against the realities of material circulation.

In "To His Booke," an *envoi* that appears, unusually, at the beginning of the volume, Spenser's other alter ego, Immeritô, tells his "little booke" how to answer the question of its provenance: "A shepheards swaine saye did thee sing, / All as his straying flocke he fedde." Here the fantasy of pastoral orality is projected outwards, as a myth to govern the actual circulation of this material book. But Immeritô's instructions reveal the tactic's contradictions. A swain safely ensconced within the pastoral fiction might "sing," but singing and speaking are precisely what the *book* cannot do. To glimpse this fantasy of oral expression is to watch it harden into the fixed, durable form of the written text—whereupon it is promptly encoded as a nostalgic object, an innocence lost in the real world of public circulation. Colin, as both swain and public name, is caught in this contradiction, left to refer to a myth that expires in its invocation.

Portable Autonomy

Certainly Colin's myth was a potent one. On its publication in 1579, *The Shepheardes Calender* was an immediate and a lasting sensation; new editions appeared in 1581, 1586, 1591, and 1597. Colin indeed seemed more ubiquitous and influential as the years passed. In the early decades of the seventeenth century, as O'Callaghan has shown, the so-called Spenserian poets emerged as a "print community" of imitators: their willful outmodedness, as a form of Elizabethan nostalgia, carried with it an implicit critique of Jacobean politics.[39] But in the 1590s—before he acquired this oppositional register—Colin was if anything even more popular, his name circulating in poetic circles as a kind of currency. It is customary to draw a distinction between "the Colin of the 1570s" and "the Colin of the 1590s": the first, as Rachel Hile suggests, a pastoral persona only loosely linked with the *Calender*'s author; the second, an aggressive conflation in which "Colin Clout" transparently signified "Edmund

Spenser."[40] The irony of this shift was its coincidence with another: Colin's emergence as a character for others to cite, reclaim, reimagine. He was most surely Spenser, that is, when he was no longer Spenser's; or, put another way, the more he recognizable he was as an author-effect, the more mobile he became as a character.

Colin's influence no doubt had much to do with the surge of verse publication in the years after the *Calender*. In the sonnets, elegies, and epigrams that saluted him, he served as a versatile sign of affiliation, evoking a fellowship that transcended categories. "If so you come where learned *Colin* feedes, / His louely flocke," wrote Thomas Lodge in the induction to his sonnet sequence *Phillis* (1593), "pack thence and quickly hast you; / You are but mistes before so bright a sunne, / Who hath the Palme for deepe inuention wunne."[41] Lodge's gesture hints at the expansion of pastoral, which could now merge with the Petrarchan wave that followed the publication of *Astrophil and Stella* in 1591. At the same time, it registers the contradictions that had begun to gather around Spenser's persona, who is imagined as both humble shepherd and brilliant sun—someone whom an aspiring poet might approach but must then "quickly haste" from.

What may be most evocative in Lodge's induction is his portrait of Colin as a person at large: feeding his flock in a pastoral space of his own, beyond the confines of any particular text, waiting for readers to happen upon him by chance. In charting this space, Colin suggested that others might enroll themselves in it—that they might become literary shepherds like him. He was a moveable source of self-invention, a fiction around whom other poets could constellate themselves. Michael Drayton, for instance, made apologies for his epyllion *Endimion and Phoebe* (1595) by striking a pose of modesty: "Deeare *Collin*, let my Muse excused be, / Which rudely thus presumes to sing by thee, / Although her straines be harsh vntun'd & ill, / Nor can attayne to thy diuinest skill."[42] Drayton's pivot is telling: it is by first paying his respects that he can claim a position alongside Colin, as a fellow poet addressing a shared public audience. William Smith opened his sonnet sequence *Chloris, or The Complaint of the Passionate Despised Shepheard* in a similar vein, with a dedicatory poem (fig. 2), addressed to "Collin, my deere and most entire beloued," that promised sonnets in dressed "weedes . . . plaine, such as poore shepheardes weare" yet brave enough to "vvande[r] . . . deuoid of feare."[43] Colin's name hovers over the page, his role as presiding sponsor rendered typographically in the page's commanding capitals and italics. Joseph Hall, in a 1597 book of satires, likewise declined to enter into a contest with the master: "At *Colins* feet I throw my yeelding

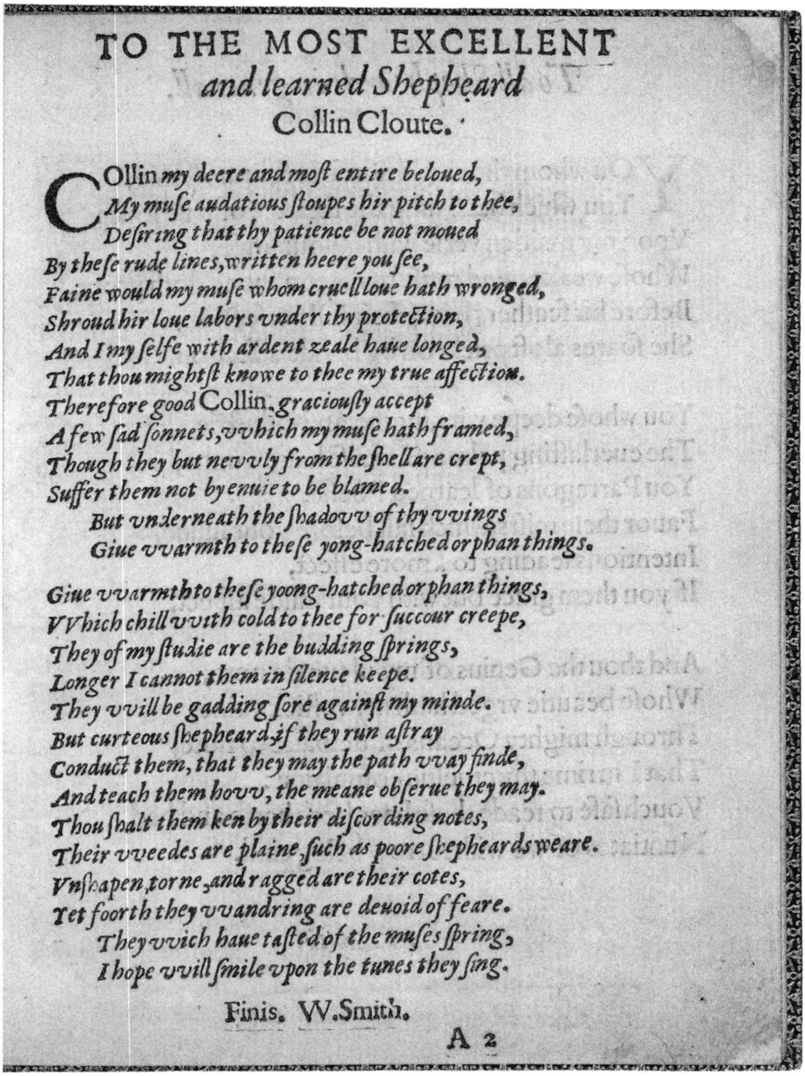

TO THE MOST EXCELLENT
and learned Shepheard
Collin Cloute.

C*Ollin my deere and moſt entire beloued,*
My muſe audatious ſtoupes hir pitch to thee,
Deſiring that thy patience be not moued
By theſe rude lines, written heere you ſee,
Faine would my muſe whom cruell loue hath wronged,
Shroud hir loue labors vnder thy protection,
And I my ſelfe with ardent zeale haue longed,
That thou mightſt knowe to thee my true affection.
Therefore good Collin, *graciouſly accept*
A few ſad ſonnets, vvhich my muſe hath framed,
Though they but nevvly from the ſhell are crept,
Suffer them not by enuie to be blamed.
But vnderneath the ſhadovv of thy vvings
Giue vvarmth to theſe yong-hatched orphan things.

Giue vvarmth to theſe yoong-hatched orphan things,
VVhich chill vvith cold to thee for ſuccour creepe,
They of my ſtudie are the budding ſprings,
Longer I cannot them in ſilence keepe.
They vvill be gadding ſore againſt my minde.
But curteous ſhepheard, if they run aſtray
Conduct them, that they may the path vvay finde,
And teach them hovv, the meane obſerue they may.
Thou ſhalt them ken by their diſcording notes,
Their vveedes are plaine, ſuch as poore ſhepheards weare.
Vnſhapen, torne, and ragged are their cotes,
Yet foorth they vvandring are deuoid of feare.
They vvich haue taſted of the muſes ſpring,
I hope vvill ſmile vpon the tunes they ſing.

Finis. VV.Smith.

A 2

Figure 2. William Smith, *Chloris, or The complaint of the passionate despised shepheard* (London, 1596), sig. A_2^r.
By permission of the Folger Shakespeare Library.

reed: / But let the rest win homage by their deed."[44] Such gestures were soon ripe for mockery. By 1598, John Marston could single out Colin as an object of particularly ludicrous poetic veneration: "Here's one must invocate some lose-legg'd dame, / Some brothell drab, to helpe him stanzas frame . . . Another yet dares tremblingly come out, / But first he must invoke good *Colyn Clout*."[45]

Marston's quip makes clear how much Colin's citations had to do with the problem of "com[ing] out," of entering into the public eye. Drayton's and Lodge's gestures of deference were also gestures of likeness and proximity: to be in Colin's shadow was at least to be near him. Each such gesture, in reaffirming the force of Colin's prestige, also strengthened the sense that his pastoral domain demarcated a network of professional affiliation in the real world. Drayton was one of several poets to adopt shepherd-personae as colleagues of Colin's. In *Idea the Shepheards Garland* (1593), he offers his own alter ego Rowland as a replacement for Colin—who has, we are told, lain "his pipes to gage, / And is to fayrie gone a Pilgrimage"—as the center of pastoral sociability.[46] Colin was soon surrounded by personae "invocated" alongside him. It was in such invocations that Colin's domain was gradually realized, formed by the network of poets gathered under distinctively literary identities. In *The Affectionate Shepheard* (1594), for instance, Richard Barnfield listed a series of shepherd-poets who suffered at the hands of love, starting with Colin and ending with Drayton's Rowland: "By thee great *Collin* lost his libertie, / By thee sweet *Astrophel* forwent his ioy. / By thee *Amyntas* wept incessantly, / By thee good *Rowland* liu'd in great annoy."[47] Pastoral translation identified one as a poet; more importantly, it placed one into meaningful relations with other poets. And the force of this translation was necessarily changed by its emergence as a corporate project. For Alpers, the domain of lyric had been bounded by the covers of *The Shepheardes Calender*. Colin's circulation, however, made this domain public and real: it was now an enduring, and a genuinely collective, social body.

But what was it a body of? Unlike the Jacobean Spenserians, who cohered around a shared style and politics, the shepherds who orbited Colin in the 1590s were a generically and socially eclectic group. What Colin grounded, that is, was less a particular "school" than the literary field broadly conceived. In a neutral sense, that term is surely uncontroversial. But I want to press on its more specific meaning, drawn from Bourdieu's sociology of art, as a cultural arena that sets itself apart from the encompassing field of power by determining its own boundaries and criteria of legitimacy. A literary field, Bourdieu suggests, is always bound by the economic logic of the world that surrounds it, yet it depends on the ability to project a sense of independence, to conceive of itself as a "world apart," endowed with a "specific logic" of its own.[48] The terms of that logic are symbolic (as are the rewards, in the form of prestige, that might accrue in it), and in this sense participation hinges on a kind of translation—on one's willingness to enter into the rules of the game, to believe in its founding *illusio*. Colin's pastoral myth enacted just this sort of translation: to enter it was to become a new person—indeed a new *kind* of person—and to be ushered into a world irreducibly different from and yet tethered, by the allusive logic of the pseudonym, to the real world. In its overtness, indeed, the fantasy of the poet as shepherd crystallizes the fictive investment that underpins Bourdieu's relatively autonomous fields.

As casual and as fleeting as they might seem, then, Colin's returns consolidated a system of literary affiliation. Those who cited him recognized his domain as having specific criteria for membership: one had to be a poet, and ideally a good one. They developed, too, a repertoire of affiliative practices: one adopted pastoral weeds, performed modesty, addressed others in their shepherd-personae. And they cultivated in the process a sense of tradition—a tradition linked by the accumulating references to Colin, which also, implicitly or explicitly, became references to references to Colin—that codified his field and hence made it durable. These acts constituted the pastoral domain as something more than a fiction; they gave it the force of a material reality, the purchase of an actual social formation: in a word, an institution.

The institutionalizing effect of Colin's appearances, and their articulation of a particularly literary legitimacy, is especially clear in William Smith's dedication to Colin in *Chloris*. Richard McCabe observes that the poem deliberately echoes the *envoi* of *The Shepheardes Calender*, in which Immeritô seeks Sidney's patronage, by appealing to Spenser's alter ego:[49]

> *Collin*, my deere and most entire beloued,
> My muse audatious stoupes hir pitch to thee,
> Desiring that thy patience be not moued
> By these rude lines, written heere you see,
> Faine would my muse whom cruell loue hath wronged,
> Shroud hir loue-labors vnder thy protection,
> And I my selfe with ardent zeale haue longed
> That thou mightst knowe to thee my true affection.
> Therefore good *Collin*, graciously accept

A few sad sonnets, vvhich my muse hath framed,
Though they but nevvly from the shell are crept,
Suffer them not by enuie to be blamed.
But vnderneath the shadovv of thy vvings,
Giue vvarmth to these yong-hatched orphan things.[50]

Smith, like Immeritô, wants the "protection" of an elite guardian who, he hopes, will pardon his audacity. But his appeal proposes a relation not between patron and client—nor even the more complex relation of Spenser to Sidney, both a patron and a fellow poet—but between poets. As McCabe puts it, the dedication imagines "the possibility of an alternative to social patronage, an empowerment of poetical 'gifts' by the poetically 'gifted.'"[51] The less tangible protection that Smith sought certainly had advantages: a patron might refuse a hopeful client, but Colin Clout authorizes *Chloris* simply by virtue of his invocation. Thus, by the end of the volume, Smith can thank him for a job well done: "It pleased thy graue shepherdhood / The Patron of my maiden verse to bee, / When I in doubt of raging Enuie stood, / And now I waigh not who shall *Chloris* see."[52]

But Smith's dedication also reveals the ambiguities of Colin's position. To frame Colin as a poetic sponsor was not only to substitute a form of symbolic capital for the economic capital of patronage, but also to assign him a special distinction. Even as Colin offered an imitable image of the poet, then, his symbolic force depended on a sense of his difference from his fellow shepherds. And the more he became a substitute for patronal protection, the less at home he was in the undifferentiated society of pastoral. When Thomas Edwards describes him as a "mighty swaine," or Richard Barnfield calls him "great *Colin* chiefe of sheepheardes all," the attribution of grand authority contradicts the shepherd's humble simplicity, and the idea of kinship—that Colin's invokers are shepherds like him—is undercut by distance. For Smith, Colin's "graue shepherdhood" likewise stands in contrast to his own "orphan things." As if to drive home the opposition, *Chloris* includes a second prefatory poem, this one addressed "To all shepheards in general," a group of fellow professionals from whom Colin seems to stand apart, not a colleague but an authoritative, legitimating outsider.[53] Citing Colin in this case both conjured a pastoral community and suggested his estrangement from it.

Often this estrangement was felt as a form of nostalgic belatedness. After Spenser's death in 1599, retrospection was of course inevitable. "Ah," wrote Francis Davison in 1602, "where is Collin and his passing skill?"[54] John Weever had already supplied the answer three years earlier: "*Colin*'s gone home, the glorie of his clime, / The Muses Mirrour and the Shepheards Saint."[55] In the ensuing decades, the Spenserian poets made a habit of invoking him. Phineas Fletcher, for instance, wrote that he might be called any name at all—"But never mounting *Colin*; *Colin*'s high stile will shame me."[56] If the shared work of mourning served to convene a community in Colin's image, the weight of grief also threatened to dissolve it. In a poem mourning Elizabeth's death in 1603, Richard Niccols lamented that neither Spenser nor Drayton was able to lead the work of poetic commemoration: "Wher's Collin Clout, or Rowland now become, / That wont to leade our Shepheards in a ring? / (Ah me) the first, pale death hath strooken dombe, / The latter, none encourageth to sing."[57] Niccols's lines evoke a self-contained literary field—a "ring" of poets gathered under the presiding pastoral authority of Colin and Rowland—but also a notably fragile one, riven by the problems of the world beyond it: Spenser's death and Drayton's struggle for patronage.[58] The *ubi sunt* topos paints the shepherds' ring in a ruefully nostalgic light, casting it, like Colin's recited lyrics in *The Shepheardes Calender*, as an image from a halcyon past lost to a troubled present.

But Colin had made a habit of vanishing long before Spenser himself died. Even in the 1580s and 1590s, invoking him seemed to depend on a sense that he was already gone—if not dead then exiled from the society of whoever addressed him. Drayton had complained in 1593 of Colin's departure "to fayrie," and in doing so he echoed Gabriel Harvey's commendatory verses in Spenser's *The Faerie Queene*. There Harvey had reprised the role of Hobbinol in order to limn a pastoral world mourning Colin's absence:

> Thy louely Rosalinde seems now forlorne,
>   and all thy gentle flockes forgotten quight,
> Thy changed hart now holdes thy pypes in scorne,
>   those prety pypes that did thy mates delight.
> Those trusty mates, that loued thee so well,
> Whom thou gau'st mirth: as they gaue thee the bell.[59]

Colin is gone, of course, because Spenser has traded pastoral for epic, but it is a change coded in social as well as generic terms. Harvey's Hobbinol recalls that Colin once "didst stirre to glee our laddes in homely bowers"; now, however, he seeks to "delight the daintie eares of higher powers."[60] The simplicity of homosocial pastoral fellowship suddenly seems a quaint memory against the grander and more complicated setting of the court.

Harvey's verses drew on a vein of nostalgia endemic to pastoral, and one particularly linked in the *Calender* to the persona of Hobbinol, who laments Colin's exile and rehearses his lay in the April eclogue. In the *Calender*, as we have seen, this sense of belatedness was rooted in the practices of recollection and reconstruction by which Colin and his poems were preserved in absence. Remembering Colin now, ten years later, Harvey was also remembering the act of remembering Colin, and in this sense the very act of citing Spenser's persona seemed to confirm his absence, his relegation to the past. From one angle, the sense that Colin was always already gone strangely reinforced the autonomy of the field that his appearances marshaled. His very pastness separated his domain as a "world apart" in temporal as well as spatial terms; it was a world available only via retrospective recovery. And yet that pastness also threatened the sense of presence on which Colin's domain depended—the presence claimed when Drayton appeals to him to "let my Muse excused be," or when Lodge imagines his fellow poets happening on Colin, feeding his sheep alone. If Colin could not be summoned *now*, if the act of reimagining him only distanced him further, then what was the point? The paradoxical effect of Colin's circulation, in short, was that the fiction of autonomy that he carried was most potent precisely when it seemed at risk of vanishing altogether.

Several years before the arrival of *The Faerie Queene*—before, that is, the idea of Colin's absence could be attributed to Spenser's turn to epic—Colin's death had punctuated the subplot of George Peele's *The Araygnement of Paris*, a play that offered the first significant reimagining of Spenser's persona.[61] The play dramatizes the contest of beauty between Venus, Juno, and Pallas, in which Paris is arraigned as judge. Having named Venus the most beautiful, he is bewitched by the slighted goddesses with love for Helen of Troy; he abandons the shepherdess Aenone for this new love and so finds his way to the brink of the Trojan War. In the third act, this pre-epic plot pauses for the entrance of a group of shepherds—among them Hobbinol, Diggon, and Thenot—and, in Colin, a new lover, pining with unrequited love for the beautiful Thestylis.

Although he is the center of this subplot—again concentrating the vicarious interest of those around him—Colin makes only one appearance, entering at the beginning of Act 3 in order to announce his imminent death:

O gentle loue, vngentle for thy deede,
  Thou makest my harte
  A bloodie marke
With pearcyng shot to bleede.

Shoote soft sweete loue, for feare thou shoote amysse,
For feare too keene
Thy arrowes beene,
And hit the harte, where my beloued is.
To faire that fortune were, nor neuer I
Shalbe so blest
Among the rest,
That loue shall ceaze on her by simpathye.
Then since with loue my prayers beare no boot,
This doth remayne
To cease my payne,
I take the wounde, and dye at Venus foot.[62]

Colin, in his fatal steadfastness, appears as a counterpoint to the unfaithful Paris; he stands, too, as a monument to pastoral as it is superseded, dying into permanence as a shepherd-lover even as Paris moves into the world of Homeric epic.[63] This is inescapably the Colin of the *Calender*: sad and alienated and unlucky in love; given to self-regarding lyric virtuosity; his solipsism reflected in the turning-away of the opening apostrophe. Naturally, then, this poem too seems to turn, in the moment of its utterance, into a removable and reproducible text—a text like the lay for Eliza, with which it would appear, as an excerpted lyric, in *Englands Helicon*. When Colin returns to the stage, he does so as a dead body, with Venus herself presiding over his burial. "Let *Colins* corps be brought in place, and burned in the plaine," she decrees, "And let this be the verse. *The loue whom Thestylis hath slaine*."[64] The playbook's italics separate the memorial verse, marking it as the material residue of Colin's life. His death is thus a translation into a textual artifact, with the form of the epitaph standing—like the rhyming couplet *herse* and *verse* in "November"—as a sign of the convergence of corpse and inscription.[65]

The form of the epitaph, in fact, seems to linger behind Colin; its poignancy and summary brevity are typical of his appearances in the 1580s and 1590s. Like Colin, the epitaph appears at the intersection of life and death, presence and absence: it marks a permanent and fixed place for the memory of someone gone. Epitaphs, proposes Scott L. Newstok, are inherently rehearsals: "Even on the tomb proper they invoke some other absent voice, 'in quotation marks,' as it were."[66] In Colin's appearances, as in epitaphs, writing supplies a lesser presence in compensation for what is felt as a more absolute absence. And perhaps, too, the act of citing Colin carries something of the epitaph's quasi-official force, translating his person into the institution of the literary domain. Like graves, institutions rest in the past, in a sense of tradition that authorizes and directs those who belong to them. For this reason, as the sociologist Bernard Lahire argues, they are always mediated, dependent on the capacity of writing "to mark our presence even when our body is absent." They are "like sanctuaries haunted by the absent or dead: texts constrain the action of the living, while those who produced them have long since departed."[67] Lahire's description of institutional haunting helps to explain the force of Colin's citational afterlife: to cite Colin was to foreground the processes of mediation through which his domain would be built. As the origin around whom an authorizing past was to be codified, Colin's role entailed his absence—or, rather, his spectral, mediated presence. The proleptic nostalgia that trailed him was precisely the sign of his institutionalizing force.

And yet this nostalgia disclosed at the same time a contradiction in the idea of the lyric domain: the phenomenal presence at its heart is precisely what cannot be preserved and put to work in absence. Encountering Colin, the portable source-text of this domain, brought the contradiction home: as a reproduction—a textual artifact—he carried this sense of presence with him only to dissolve it in the moment of his invocation, displacing it into an imagined past prior to his mediation.

Perhaps for this reason, those who appropriated Colin often gave particular attention to the moments in the *Calender* that anticipated a shift from oral song to textual artifact. The "Aprill" lay, in particular, intrigued Spenser's fellow poets, its retrospective mode providing a model for those who would go on to borrow Colin for their own texts. For the anonymous author ("E. C.") of the sonnet sequence *Emaricdulfe* (1595), the "Aprill" lay was Colin's signature achievement. In one sonnet, he promises his beloved the praise of a poet more eloquent than himself: "Thy vertues *Collin* shall immortalize, / *Collin* chast vertues organ sweetst esteem'd, / When for *Elizas* name he did comprise / Such matter as inuentions wonder seem'd."[68] There is something touching in the self-awareness with which the poet delegates the task of immortalization to someone more capable of it. Who better than Colin, whose lay for Eliza had already proved its, and his, longevity?

While *Emaricdulfe* looks forward to Colin's future immortalizing work, however, "Aprill" more often tempted its readers to go backward in time—to the scene of originary performance that the eclogue withholds. And the most striking reimagining came from Barnabe Barnes who, in *Parthenophil and*

Parthenophe, conjured as vividly as anyone the pastoral domain as myth of Elizabethan letters:

> Here *Colin* sittes beneath that oken tree
> *Eliza* singing in his layes.
>
> Blest is *Arcadiaes* Queene, kneele swains, and say
> That she (which here cheefe Nymph doth rayne)
> May blessed liue, to see the'extreamest yeare.
> For sacrifice (then) Lambes and kiddlinges kill:
> And be by them *Eliza* glorified,
> The flower of loues, and pure virginitie:
> This *Delian* Nymphe doth amaise.[69]

These lines recapitulate much of the "Aprill" lay—they offer an audience of shepherds, the nymphs that had occupied a central place in Colin's poem, and the celebration of the virgin queen. The difference, of course, is that Colin is here as well, singing his own song rather than relying on Hobbinol's recitation. Barnes allows us to glimpse a perfected "Aprill," one that redresses the alienation of the pastoral community in Spenser's eclogue by reintegrating Colin as its central member. Where "Aprill" had consigned Colin's poetry to the past, accessible only in the memories of his friends, Barnes imagines him as present both in space and time: "Here *Colin* sittes."

But perhaps it is not quite right to read this moment as a reintegrated present. What *Parthenophil* offers may be less a revision of "Aprill" than a prehistory, a reconstruction of the lost originary scene in which Colin sang the lay himself. Or perhaps it is more complicated still: on closer inspection, is it Colin who blesses the Arcadian queen, who tells the swains to kneel—or is it Parthenophil? Barnes's poem leaves the speaker of these lines ambiguous, allowing the lay to be at once Colin's and not Colin's, poem and paraphrase, the original of the "Aprill" lay and yet one more belated rehearsing of it. The result is a Colin oddly dislocated in time: brought forward into Parthenophil's present tense even as he is memorialized; excavated from *Aprill*'s buried past even as that eclogue's fiction of literary transmission is carried one step further. If he thus seems to be trapped in the amber of Parthenophil's memory, the world that he inhabits seems frozen as well: evoked as a nostalgic vision of a literary community that has already passed away.

Coming Home

The April eclogue had a lasting hold on Spenser too. Two years after the appearance of *Parthenophil and Parthenophe*, he published the long eclogue *Colin Clouts Come Home Againe* (1595); the six-book *Faerie Queene* followed a year later. Each offered a return to Colin and, in a different way, to the lay for Eliza—by now seemingly the founding myth for Colin's literary domain. In *Colin Clouts Come Home Againe*, the lay reappears in an imagined future in which his poems in praise of the queen are still sung:

> And long while after I am dead and rotten:
> Amongst the shepheards daughters dancing rownd,
> My layes made of her shall not be forgotten,
> But sung by them with flowry gyrlonds crownd.[70]

In Book 6 of *The Faerie Queene*, the lay returns in another image of pastoral figures "dancing rownd"—the circle of nymphs and muses atop Mount Acidale—that conjures the lost, ecstatic moment of Colin's song. The latter has long been an object of critical fascination, its rapturous glimpse of aesthetic bliss seemingly a key of some kind to Spenser's poetry. For Harry Berger Jr., the scene's power lies in its recuperative vision, in which—in a play on the word's double meaning—"the earliest recreation becomes the latest recreation."[71] Rebecca Helfer carries the idea further. In a study of Spenser and the arts of memory, she reads Acidale as not a return but a prehistory: a depiction of the lost originary singing of the lay that in "Aprill" Hobbinol had reenacted.[72] This return—or rather, on this reading, Colin's *first* appearance—brings out the question of priority that lurks behind the multiple Colins of the 1590s. If "Aprill" and Acidale are each other's originals, they are also mutually derivative, legible insofar as they are retellings of each other.

Spenser's returns to Colin are in this sense a critical convenience. They furnish a ready-made frame for narratives of a poetic career—narratives that find Spenser taking the measure of his achievements, or reckoning with a transformed sense of what laureateship might mean.[73] Colin in these readings belongs to Spenser, and only more so as time passes, so that in *Colin Clout*, as William Oram suggests, he emerges unmistakably as "the poet's avatar."[74] No doubt this is all true: the Colin who appears in the later eclogue surely bears a closer resemblance to the biographical Spenser. But to follow Colin from the *Calender* to *Colin Clout* to Book 6 of *The Faerie Queene* is to forget that Colin had lived in the meantime—that he had been carried away from Spenser's control and made a kind of public property. Spenser's returns were in this sense reclamations—reassertions of Spenser's rights over his own alter ego—and, by extension, acknowledgments of the degree to which Colin had, in the intervening years, been estranged from him. This is the effect, at least, of Colin's appearances. Calidore is wandering aimlessly through the fields of *The Faerie Queene*'s pastoral when he happens upon him, seemingly by chance; the encounter is startling, almost miraculous. Had Calidore taken a different path, the poem allows us to believe, Colin might simply have been left to his own devices, undiscovered by the poem. Approaching carefully, Calidore treats Colin as less a person to be addressed than a curiosity to be described. Eventually, after far too long, the narrator identifies him—"That jolly shepheard, which there piped, was / Poore *Colin Clout* (who knowes not *Colin Clout*?)"—but even then he is kept at a distance, eyed from beyond the circle as *that* shepherd *there*.[75] His public career has rendered him a person with a life of his own, someone whom even Spenser can only hope to meet by chance on the commons of pastoral.

Spenser was, in this sense, merely the latest in a line of writers to discover and reimagine Colin, and his returns to "his" persona were accordingly encounters with an uncannily distanced double. To the extent that Colin came to stand as Spenser's laureate self-image, then, he did so by framing it as something unexpectedly alienated from Spenser himself—as a position made and maintained by the collective efforts of those who invoked Colin's name. Laureation on these terms is less a matter of self-fashioning than of citation; it is the process by which one becomes a public image. Perhaps this is why the forms of citation themselves filter into Spenser's meetings with Colin—in the parenthesis, for instance, that marks his persona's appearance in *The Faerie Queene*. Andrew Hadfield has warned against reading the question within the parenthesis as a straightforward allusion to Colin's fame, pointing out that Spenser would use the same formula in the *Mutabilitie Cantos* with a deliberate, self-marginalizing irony: "Who knowes not *Arlo-Hill*?" (VII.vi.36.6). It may be that this moment, too, works to isolate a special group, to distinguish "those who knew Spenser's earlier career and adoption of this particular persona from those who had not read his work."[76] Then again, one did not need to have read Spenser to know Colin; his was a name that a reader in the 1590s could hardly have avoided. If there is something coy in Spenser's question, then, it seems to be less a function of what it withholds than of what it discloses: the

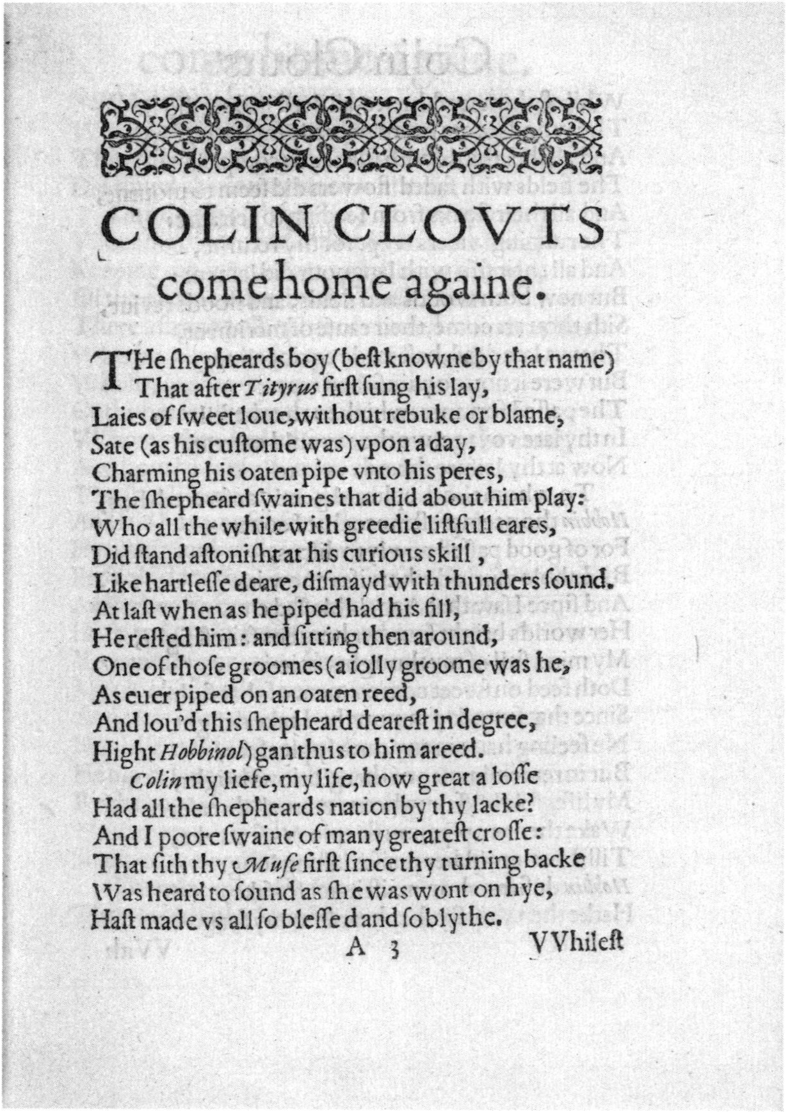

COLIN CLOVTS
come home againe.

THe ſhepheards boy (beſt knowne by that name)
That after *Tityrus* firſt ſung his lay,
Laies of ſweet loue, without rebuke or blame,
Sate (as his cuſtome was) vpon a day,
Charming his oaten pipe vnto his peres,
The ſhepheard ſwaines that did about him play:
Who all the while with greedie liſtfull eares,
Did ſtand aſtoniſht at his curious skill,
Like hartleſſe deare, diſmayd with thunders ſound.
At laſt when as he piped had his fill,
He reſted him: and ſitting then around,
One of thoſe groomes (a iolly groome was he,
As euer piped on an oaten reed,
And lou'd this ſhepheard deareſt in degree,
Hight *Hobbinol*) gan thus to him areed.
Colin my liefe, my life, how great a loſſe
Had all the ſhepheards nation by thy lacke?
And I poore ſwaine of many greateſt croſſe:
That ſith thy *Muſe* firſt ſince thy turning backe
Was heard to ſound as ſhe was wont on hye,
Haſt made vs all ſo bleſſed and ſo blythe.

A 3 VVhileſt

Figure 3. Edmund Spenser, *Colin Clouts come home againe* (London, 1595), sig. A_3^r. By permission of the Folger Shakespeare Library.

recognition that Spenser can no longer claim Colin as in any simple sense his own. The parenthesis is, in this sense, an act of reference: to Spenser's own Colin but also to Drayton's, Peele's, Lodge's, Barnes's, Hall's, and Smith's Colins—and to the public literary domain that they fashioned through him.

Colin Clout, too, finds its way back to Colin by way of parenthesis. In the first edition, the title of the eclogue—printed on the title page and again after the dedicatory epistle (fig. 3)—looms above the first line, which introduces "the shepheards boy (best knowne by that name)." The reference to "that name" points us back to the edges of the poem, where Colin stands above and beyond it, as a sort of alienated monument. Caught between text and paratext, he is imperfectly absorbed into Spenser's eclogue, which regards him with a respectful distance—the verb *know*, which greets him in *The Faerie Queene* as well, evokes the perspective of public recognition rather than close familiarity—even as it begins to tell his story.[77] The parenthetical asides also casually reveal a difference between the eclogues of *The Shepheardes Calender* and Spenser's later poems: the former are for the most part dialogues, but the latter are narrated and hence give us access to Colin only through the narrators who recount his story. If Colin in his later Spenserian iterations is an object of citation and reference, he is thus also mediated in another sense: he is subjected to the agency of those who retell, reconstruct, and rehearse him.

"Recollection," writes Helfer, is what "builds Colin's house of fame," and in *Colin Clout* the arts of memory are everywhere.[78] The poem's governing mood of nostalgic return is clear from its title and driven home by the allusion, in its first line, to the opening of the *Calender*'s January eclogue: "A shepeheards boye (no better doe him call)" (line 1).[79] But its nostalgia is a complicated matter. *Colin Clout*'s homecoming is both topical—its occasion is Spenser's return to Kilcolman from London and the court—and, in its return to the eclogue form, generic.[80] Colin's revival of the pastoral mode seems early in the poem to answer the despair of the April and June eclogues. "Whilest thou wast hence," Hobbinol tells him, "all dead in dole did lie . . . But now both woods and fields, and floods revive, / Sith thou art come, their cause of merriment, / That us late dead, hast made againe alive" (lines 22, 29–31). If Colin's companions are cheered by his return, they are also intensely curious about his journey, just as Colin himself remains entranced by it. *Colin Clout* unfolds, accordingly, as a reconstruction of his time abroad, and in this sense it is a poem about the mixed pains and pleasures of retelling. When Hobbinol asks Colin to tell his story, he responds: "*Hobbin* thou temptest me to that I covet: / For of good passed newly to discus, / By dubble usurie doth twise renew it" (lines 37–39). These lines are thick with temporal movement: the opposition of a good "passed" only to be "newly" discussed; the re*new*al of experience through memory; the metaphor of interest accruing on capital.[81] The economizing metaphor bears a thread of optimism: an implication that memory is a viable currency, a bond that pays off. Its value is, Elizabeth Heale suggests, poetic: the endowing of "the authorial voice with the authority of experience."[82] But the metaphor also reminds us that Colin's retelling is ineluctably derivative, no more than interest gathered from the store of the past.

Colin certainly does his best to tell a profitable story. When Cuddie urges him to recite the poem he had exchanged with the Shepheard of the Ocean—"Of fellowship . . . Record us that lovely lay againe" (lines 96–97)—Colin answers with a winning performance. When Thestylis asks him to describe the Shepheard of the Ocean's poem, he offers his best paraphrase. In each case, he fulfills the social obligations that he had gallingly failed to meet in the *Calender*. Colin's willingness to be his own rehearser makes sense in a fictionalization of Spenser's visit to court. It remains unclear whether Spenser in fact recited from *The Faerie Queene* for Elizabeth; there is, as Hadfield concludes in his biography, no firm evidence that he did.[83] But Colin reports that Cynthia "to mine oaten pipe enclin'd her eare," turning his story into a story of literary reproduction. In the process, Cynthia's court emerges, like the pastoral idyll of Hobbinol and Colin, as both object and occasion of recollection: Colin is rehearsing a journey of poetic rehearsal.

At times this redoubling of recollection and mediation seems to unsettle the poem's grasp of its own origins. Critics have often observed the ambiguity of Colin's "home," which can seem to be the colonial hinterland of "my house of *Kilcolman*" or the metropolitan center of London, with its coterie of court poets. Each is a home and an exilic periphery; as Julia Reinhard Lupton suggests, exile is the concept through which Spenser arrives at an idea of "home."[84] Both homes concentrate the poem's nostalgic yearning, and both emerge at different moments as the sites of a deficient, belated present. Thus Colin's account of the glories of Cynthia's court leaves the *locus amoenus* of his pastoral home in the shade: "Why didst thou ever leave that happie place," asks Thestylis, and return "to this barrein soyle, / Where cold and care and penury do dwell" (lines 654–57). In a curious reversal, the pastoral world itself is disenchanted, outshone by the new *locus amoenus* of the court. Just as abruptly, however, the pendulum swings the other way, and Colin shifts from sublimation to satire, lacerating court as "no sort of life, / For shepheard fit" (line 688). His interlocutors can barely keep up: having been lectured on the virtues of Cynthia's court, the sudden disparagement comes as an affront. By the end of the poem, Colin finds himself rebuking them for their failure to appreciate Rosalind's singular grace—"For she is not like as the other crew / Of shepheards daughters which emongst you bee" (lines 931–32)—and, in doing so, falling back into the solipsistic isolation of *The Shepheardes Calender*. The poem's transposition of the complex into the simple, to borrow Empson's aphorism, leaves court and pastoral idyll as degraded versions of each other. Enfolded into a ramifying process of recollection and retelling, neither can sustain a claim to priority, and Colin, having been torn between two homes, ends up with none.

Spenser's return to Colin is in this sense a reckoning with the forms that had come to define the persona: recording, retelling, rehearsing, reproducing. It was Colin's emergence as a textual creature—as a citable shorthand for literary fellowship—that had enabled the circulation of the *Calender*'s pastoral myth. But in *Colin Clout*, where the community of shepherds buckles under the pressures of mediation, this institutionalizing turn is precisely the problem: the more pastoral comes to resemble the world from which it distinguishes itself, the less it can insist on its particular autonomy. Colin may have attained the permanence of an artifact, his name etched atop the volume's title page, but he did so at the cost of a pastoral world that, by the poem's end, no longer seems a serviceable home for his lyric domain. Arguably *Colin Clout* had never even attempted to offer such a home; at least, it never searches after the spontaneous presence that had been the *Calender*'s generative fantasy. Instead, we are from the beginning stranded in narrative, granted access to the words of the eclogue's shepherds only by way of the speech tags that mark the poem's own method of after-the-fact rehearsal.

Lyric Nostalgia

The Faerie Queene, though of course also a narrative poem, is more concerned to recover the lyric presence that Colin had come to symbolize. Calidore's pastoral sojourn has long struck readers as a deviation from the terms of epic romance: as a suspect refusal of the obligations that it imposes, or else (in Patricia Parker's reading) as a digression that casts the impetus of the quest as itself an uncertain good, a threat to the fragile, recreative calm of the poem's final book.[85] The discovery of Mount Acidale takes us still further afield, toward the private territory of lyric: the appearance there of Colin and his lass, as David Quint dryly notes, finds Spenser "taking a break from the poem . . . in order to write his sonnet sequence," the *Amoretti*.[86] I use the word *territory* deliberately: what is striking about Mount Acidale is that it *places* lyric, that it sets aside a space for it—a world apart, to recall Bourdieu's term, for Colin's poetic domain. That is not to say that it is the redoubt of the purely aesthetic: as a long sequence of historicizing readings have shown, Acidale's circle encodes the restricted space of the court, a nascent bourgeois domesticity, and the tension between rural property ownership and public commons.[87] But it is to suggest that the scene reflects Colin's central role in a pastoral myth that, by 1596, had come to authorize an emergent literary field's sense of itself as a discrete cultural space.

This world, like the court or the growing bourgeoisie, was exclusive, and in Book 6 we are made to feel our exclusion. Calidore focalizes the canto's narrative, and as he ascends Mount Acidale our perspective merges with his: like him, we are outsiders, unsure of what we have found. We hear "the merry sound / Of a shrill pipe" and, moving gradually closer, we see "a troupe of Ladies dauncing . . . Full merrily, and making gladfull glee" and, at their center, "a Shepheard piping" (VI.x.10.2–3, 7–9). Then, abruptly, Calidore stops:

> He durst not enter into th'open greene,
> For dread of them vnwares to be descryde,
> For breaking of their daunce, if he were seene;
> But in the couert of the wood did byde,
> Beholding all, yet of them vnespyde. (VI.x.11.1–5)

Fear keeps him out: the fear of being "descryde," but more powerfully the fear of breaking the spell and losing the marvelous vision spread before him. Somehow Calidore knows that entering the circle means destroying it, and so we wait with him in the woods, surveying the scene from afar. The narrator unfolds the vision meticulously, identifying three women near the center as "the Graces, daughters of delight, / Handmaides of *Venus*"; the beautiful damsel in the middle as "that iolly Shepheards lasse"; and finally the jolly shepherd himself as "poore Colin Cloute" (VI.x.15.1–2; VI.x.16.1, 4). This is the rhetoric of interpretation, brought forward from E. K.'s commentary on *The Shepheardes Calender* and assimilated into the narrative. If there is a textual apparatus, however, there is no text. Indeed, Spenser's reliance on a vocabulary of sight and vision points up the fact that Calidore has no access at all to Colin's song.

The scene is shattered when Calidore moves into the clearing: Colin puts down his pipe and the dancers, including the shepherd's lass, instantly vanish. Only Colin remains, lingering long enough to explain to Calidore what he has witnessed, in a speech, running to nine stanzas, that culminates in an apology to Gloriana herself for putting Rosalind at the center of his song:

> Sunne of the world, great glory of the sky,
> That all the earth doest lighten with thy rayes,
> Great *Gloriana*, greatest Maiesty,
> Pardon thy shepheard, mongst so many layes,
> As he hath sung thee in all his dayes,
> To make one minime of thy poore handmaid,
> And vnderneath thy feete to place her prayse,
> That when thy glory shall be farre displayd
> To future age of her this mention may be made. (VI.x.28.1–9)

Colin's retrospective account occupies a special place in criticism of *The Faerie Queene*, where it seems to offer a verbal realization of the fleeting transcendence of inspiration. Thus Berger, in a seminal reading: "Here two voices merge into one, Colin as he speaks, Spenser as he writes, the man momentarily transformed into the pure poetic voice, the recreative voice re-created, the past leaping to new life in the present. It is the moment of second sight in which the poet returns to his early fragment of insight, inspiration, or mere sportive pleasure and revises them, *sees* them for the first time. The past and present are juxtaposed as promise and fulfillment in a single poetic form."[88] Berger's account grasps the temporal scheme that underlies Colin's appearance, and indeed his entire public career: the recursive time of recollection, re-creation, recording, rehearsal. Poetry's power of recovery seems limitless, endowed with a synesthetic magic that recovers pure voice from second sight. This is Acidale as absolute presence, as *lyric*: a moment in which writing is experienced seamlessly as voice, with nothing lost in translation.

For Colin, however, the substitution is far from perfect. When Calidore greets him and asks who the vanished "dainty Damzels" were—"Right happy thou," he excitedly adds, "that mayst them freely see" (VI.x.19.6, 8)—Colin's reply is despairing:

Not I so happy, answerd then that swaine,
As thou vnhappy, which them thence didst chace,
Whom by no meanes thou canst recall againe,
For being gone, none can them bring in place,
But whom they of them selues list so to grace. (VI.x.20.1–5)

The moment of the ecstatic vision, Colin tells Calidore, was fortuitous, contingent on the whims of powers beyond his control, and hence irretrievable; there is no suggestion that remembering the experience might compensate for its loss. Spenser's use of the verb *recall* hesitates between its literal and metaphorical registers, as if to remind us that remembering a moment does not bring it back. Far from a reintegrated present, Acidale evokes the widening distance of a past that refuses renewal: the pure voice of lyric is precisely what eludes second sight, or what it can grasp only in its evanescence.

Colin thus emerges, in Spenser's final return to him, as a study in poetry's allergy to mediation. Book 6 of *The Faerie Queene* marks Spenser's wrestling with a persona that was no longer in any simple way his—a persona that he could reclaim only in spite and in the thick of his public circulation. It also marks his return to the questions of lyric textuality that had preoccupied *The Shepheardes Calender*. In the interim, Colin had become a public name; at the same time, the profile of poetry had changed, as the genres that we tend to call "lyric" emerged as consistently profitable sectors of the book trade. Spenser had published his own *Amoretti* three years earlier, amid a fashion that began with Sidney's Astrophil entering the public eye "in pomp," and by the turn of the century a series of anthologies—themselves designed to re-mediate the flood of published verse—could herald the riches of the national muse in titles like *Englands Parnassus* and *Englands Helicon*. Poems were, more unavoidably than ever, mediated forms, carried to readers (like Colin's lays to his fellow shepherds) as indefinitely reproducible reproductions; and while they might insist, like the title page of the *Amoretti and Epithalamion*, on having been "written not long since," to encounter them in the form of the book was to register one's arrival after the fact.[89]

What happens to lyric when it circulates? It is tempting to say that the idea of presence is lost, dispersed by the textual mechanisms that carry poems forward to new readers. But Colin's circulation reveals its enduring power—the power of an idea that is all the more captivating for being impossible, except as fantasy. Lyric, then, is what happens when mediation makes poetic presence scarce, when it makes us want it. Like Colin, lyric can only point to something already gone.

So it seems, at least, on Acidale. For Colin and Calidore all that remains is the inadequate work of rehearsal and reconstruction. Colin agrees to describe the departed dancers, but what is there to say? His explanation is disappointingly secondary—a repetition of what the narrator has already told us—and so we are left on the periphery of Colin's vision and song, removed first in space and now in time from its ecstatic center. Now there is only recollection, the after-the-fact recovery of memory and text. For Helfer, Acidale represents Spenser's own *ur-Aprill*; but if so, it is but one more frustration of the desire for originary return. The lost song attests to the power of Colin's sustaining fantasy of lyric presence even as it concedes that such presence, like the literary domain founded upon it, can never be more than an object of nostalgic longing. In its sense of its own evanescence, this late evocation of Colin's domain captures the ambivalence of relative autonomy in the literary field: a space that must exist within and yet apart from the world at large, as an aspirational future and an irretrievable past. This complex double time found a fit object in Sidney's personae, Astrophil and Philisides. Their projection of an imagined coterie past carried Colin's picture of the literary field further, framing an image of a restricted poetic elite against the field at large and, in the process, disclosing the struggles over legitimacy and distinction on which it was constituted.

CHAPTER 3

Astrophil, Philisides, and the Coterie in Print

Philisides made his home on the margins of Philip Sidney's *Arcadia*. A shepherd and a poet, he found himself relegated to the eclogues that periodically punctuated the main narrative of the romance. Even so, his isolation was mostly his own doing. Sidney's persona (the relation was evident in the name, an amalgam of "Philip" and "Sidney") was melancholy and reticent; his songs—when he could be persuaded to sing them—dealt bitterly with his disappointment in love. Like Colin Clout, Philisides resisted the attention of his Arcadian companions and, by extension, of the book's readers, seemingly concentrating Sidney's ambivalence toward the poetic career that he would famously call his "vnelected vocation."[1] All of which meant that for readers who knew Philisides, the first printed edition of the *Arcadia*, published by William Ponsonby in 1590, would have come as a shock. For he had been transformed. No longer a shepherd-poet, Philisides had vanished from the eclogues, where the poems that were once his had been assigned to other characters, or else simply omitted. Instead, he entered the romance as a knight, riding into Iberia, retinue in tow, to participate in a tournament at the court of the queen, Andromana. Evoking Sidney as he endured in the imagination of the Elizabethan public, this new, chivalric Philisides was an altogether more fitting vehicle for Sidney's public debut as an author. The book's typesetter seemed to think so: on its first appearance, the name *PHILISIDES* was rendered in capital letters (fig. 4), offered up as a typographical monument to Sidney's belated, vaunted arrival in print.

Sidney's career, like his persona's, seemed to stretch across the gap between manuscript and print, coterie and public. During his life, in the received

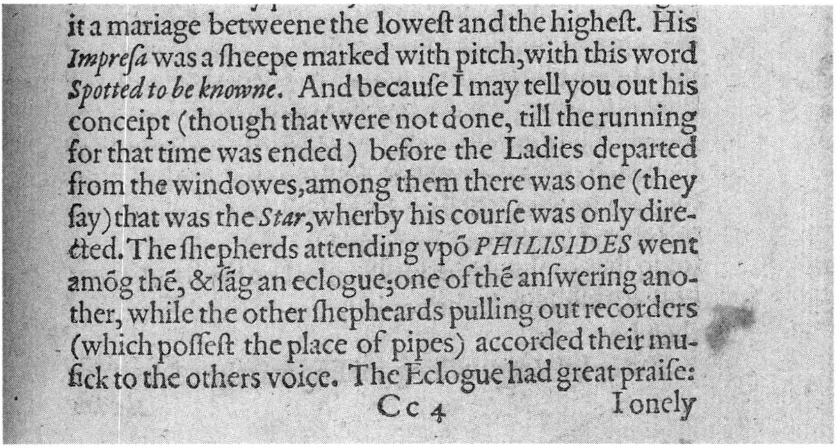

it a mariage betweene the loweſt and the higheſt. His
Impreſa was a ſheepe marked with pitch, with this word
Spotted to be knowne. And becauſe I may tell you out his
conceipt (though that were not done, till the running
for that time was ended) before the Ladies departed
from the windowes, among them there was one (they
ſay) that was the *Star*, wherby his courſe was only dire-
cted. The ſhepherds attending vpõ *PHILISIDES* went
amõg thẽ, & ſãg an eclogue; one of thẽ anſwering ano-
ther, while the other ſhepheards pulling out recorders
(which poſſeſt the place of pipes) accorded their mu-
ſick to the others voice. The Eclogue had great praiſe:
Cc 4 I onely

Figure 4. Philip Sidney, *The Covntesse of Pembrokes Arcadia* (London, 1590), sig. Cc_4^r. By permission of the Beinecke Rare Book and Manuscript Library, Yale University.

narrative, he belonged to the coterie, his readerships bounded by the walls of Wilton House, the estate of his sister Mary, the Countess of Pembroke, and by the networks of family and friends to whom his works circulated. Sidney's literary reputation, even after his death in 1586, paled in comparison to his celebrity as a courtier and soldier, and it was only with the publication of the *Arcadia* in 1590—and then, a year later, of *Astrophil and Stella*—that he began an afterlife in print. As a result, his emergence as leading literary light is usually framed as a consequence of his migration from the privacy of manuscript circulation to the exposure of print publication. Consider, for instance, the introduction to Gavin Alexander's important study of Sidney's reception: "Had he lived, his works might never have been printed: only in this way—the manuscript author entering print posthumously—could the 1590s become the decade in which Sidney dominated literary culture."[2] It is a story that the editorial fate of Philisides seems to confirm: before Sidney and his persona could enter the public space of print, their shared manuscript past first had to be set aside.

But it isn't the full story. Philisides, at least, was not content to fade away. Three years after his omission from the first edition, the second edition of the *Arcadia* (1593) brought back the original version of Sidney's persona, installing him once more in his old home, and with his old melancholy affect, in the romance's eclogues. Philisides's restoration, in turn, suggested that Sidney's print afterlife was more complicated than a steady ascent to literary glory. Popularity had indeed begun to prove as much a curse as a blessing: as Lori Humphrey Newcomb argues, the printing of the *Arcadia* and *Astrophil and Stella* brought their considerable prestige into question.[3] No longer materially scarce, Sidney could now be found in the same bookshops as the "base men, with seruile wits" at whom he had once sneered.[4] The *Arcadia*, in particular, found itself occupying a place on the crowded shelf of prose romance, alongside books like Greene's *Menaphon* and Thomas Lodge's *Rosalynde*. When Gabriel Harvey wrote that "the Countesse of Pe[m]brookes Arcadia is not greene inough for queasie stomackes, but they must have *Greenes* Arcadia," he recognized a difference between the *Arcadia* and *Menaphon* and, at the same time, suggested how small it was: Sidney may not have been Greene, but he was Greene enough.[5] For the caretakers of Sidney's legacy, then, the challenge was the securing of his distinction in the face of the ubiquity of his works and the "semiotic proliferation," in Joel B. Davis's phrase, of his name.[6] The publication of his writings thus quickly inspired attempts, as Newcomb puts it, "by the very coproducers who dragged his work posthumously into the marketplace" to construct him "as exclusive."[7]

At the heart of this project of reclamation were Sidney's fictional personae. For Hugh Sanford and Mary Sidney, who edited the second edition of the *Arcadia*, the reinstatement of the old *Arcadia*'s Philisides allowed Philip Sidney a kind of posthumous position-taking, staking out for him a place apart from the literary public in which his books circulated. But the project was not contained to Sidney's "coproducers." The editors and publishers of his books were joined by other agents with their own interests, writers eager to appropriate Sidney's prestige in order to advance themselves. For these writers, Sidney's exclusivity needed to be ensured so that they could claim their own *special* affiliation with him. Sidney's personae—Philisides and his more famous cousin, Astrophil—became touchstones for these attempts: to address or to reimagine them was to invoke a version of Sidney that was both specifically literary and attractively withholding. It is an effect evident in the title of Matthew Roydon's elegy for Sidney, "An Elegie, or Friends Passion, for His Astrophill. *Written vpon the Death of the Right Honorable Sir Philip Sidney Knight, Lord Gouernor of Flushing*," a poem first printed in 1593.[8] For Roydon, Sidney's public personage is marked by his official titles; his persona, on the other hand, encodes the more intimate "passion" of friendship. Astrophil and Philisides bore these associations because they had always mediated between a privileged in-group and a larger world of outsiders, hinting—through the lenses of Petrarchan self-reference and pastoral allegory—at a subtext of biographical secrets that they withheld from all but the most familiar audiences. As Sidney's writings reached wider audiences, first in manuscript and then in print, his personae offered themselves as a way to recover the exclusivity that his texts seemed to have lost.

This chapter explores Astrophil and Philisides's complex reframing of Sidney's public position. In doing so, it builds on a body of important work on Sidney's reception, including H. R. Woudhuysen's authoritative study of the circulation of his literary manuscripts and Joel Davis's probing analysis of the bibliographic competition that shaped the publication history of his works in print, as well as superb accounts of imitation and adaptation by Stephen Dobranski, Gavin Alexander, and Natasha Simonova.[9] As Simonova has recently argued, Sidney's works and his life alike seemed to urge continuation: attempts to rewrite or pick up the *Arcadia* (the revised version of which cut off midsentence) and Sidney's own prematurely ended life.[10] Alexander describes writing after Sidney as a practice of "prosopography," in which a dead and absent Sidney might hauntingly be brought back; Astrophil and Philisides were key instances of this impulse, resurrections of Sidney's fictions and of Sidney himself.[11] Their afterlives—sustained in a range of epigrams, elegies, epistles, and prose romances—reveal a countercurrent to Sidney's arrival in the 1590s as a public literary icon: a series of attempts to imagine Sidney as, once again, a poet of the coterie. Or, perhaps more accurately, they mark the process by which Sidney was *constructed* as a poet of the coterie (rather than the public) and of manuscript (rather than print) in the first place. For, as we will see, the careers of Astrophil and Philisides helped to articulate the oppositions that have framed Sidney's reception ever since. Roydon found his elegy incorporated into the most ambitious of the texts to rewrite Sidney's legacy when it was reprinted, along with a series of elegies by other poets, at the end of the quarto volume of Spenser's *Colin Clouts Come Home Againe* (1595). The volume convened a pastoral cast of personae in order to mourn the shepherd-poet they addressed alternately as "Astrophel" and Philisides. Inserting themselves into his personal allegory, the elegists conjured a fictional coterie centered on Sidney, constituted in print, and projected before the reading public.

Fictions like these opened up a new dimension in the complex intersections between manuscript and print cultures at the end of the sixteenth century. The distinction between the two is, in fact, one that Sidney's personae seem to frustrate at every turn. Their exclusivity (or rather the perception of it) was not a function of print circulation alone; it was central to their effect in manuscript as well. There, too, they mediated between the many and the few, distinguishing a relatively closed circle of familiars from the wider, more open networks in which the *Arcadia* was transmitted. From this vantage, the turn to print marked a shift in scale rather than in kind: a further opening of the audiences that Astrophil and Philisides had all along worked to hold at bay. But if Sidney's personae argue the continuity of manuscript and print, their afterlives also hint at the emergence of an opposition between them—an opposition rooted in a distinction between large-scale and restricted literary production, between public and coterie writing. The fictions that reimagined Astrophil and Philisides played a key role in the articulation of these dichotomies. Sidney's personae advertised their distinction in the literary field, orienting themselves against the market even as they circulated within it. As we saw in the last chapter, Colin Clout helped to bring that field into view; Astrophil and Philisides, in turn, reveal it in the process of its internal differentiation. Imagining them in the rarified space of the coterie, their appropriators presented themselves as being—like Sidney himself—separate and exclusive: a community of literary elites nestled into but set apart from the textual commons.

Sidney's Third Persons

The decision to remove Philisides from the *Arcadia*'s eclogues belonged to Sidney's old friend Fulke Greville, the editor the first edition. Sidney had written his persona's new, chivalric role in the process of revising and expanding the early "old" into the incomplete "new" *Arcadia*, the latter of which Greville and Ponsonby would guide into print. But according to a prefatory note, Sidney's revisions never reached the eclogues; Greville reported that he had altered them on his own.[12] Two of Philisides's eclogues he reassigned to other shepherds; a third poem he simply removed; two more, from the Fourth Eclogues, came after the new *Arcadia* broke off in Book 3, and hence could be omitted along with the rest of the romance.[13] Why the excisions? They may have been a consequence of Philisides's amorousness: his lovelorn melancholy sat uneasily with the stoic masculinity that Greville seemed to value in the new *Arcadia*.[14] But they were likely also a consequence of Philisides's sheer strangeness—of his awkwardness and social ambivalence, and of the esoteric personal allegory at which his presence hinted. Greville was keen to court the new audience that awaited the first print edition, even introducing chapter divisions and summaries "for the more ease of the Readers," and this was an audience, Greville might well have worried, that would have found Philisides's eccentricity alienating.[15]

Sidney's persona is, indeed, strikingly hard to get along with. In the *Arcadia*'s eclogues, he is repeatedly asked to join the other shepherds in song, but he continually fails to please them: in his first appearance, he lands in a bitter dispute between youth and age with an older shepherd; later, his partner Kala declines to sing with him, leaving him to express his alienation by singing a dialogue with himself in the form of an echo poem. Astrophil is little better: unwilling, it often seems, to fulfill the obligations of Petrarchan convention. He is quick to protest the tropes of love poetry, warning those who "poore *Petrarch's* long deceased woes, / With new-borne sighes and denisend wit do sing" that they "take wrong waies."[16] Against convention, in the most famous line of the sequence, he offers something like sincerity: "'Foole,' said my Muse to me, 'looke in thy heart, and write'" (*AS*, 1.14). Such disavowals were themselves conventional, and hence reminders of the artifice on which Astrophil and his poems rested; at the same time, they suggested that some more authentic self lay beneath his masks, and hinted at the possibility of its discovery.

Certainly both Philisides and Astrophil had their secrets. Astrophil's were the biggest and the most nearly open, with Sidney's eventually adulterous courtship of Penelope Devereux made almost explicit in sonnet 37, whose puns on her married name, Rich, recommended its omission from the earliest print editions of the sequence. It is hard to read *Astrophil and Stella* without wondering at Stella's identity, and at the love affair of Sidney's that the sonnets might encode; even contemporaries who, out of decorum or ignorance, failed to identify Stella as Rich tended to read her topically, as a version of Frances Walsingham, Sidney's wife. The traces of a personal allegory drift more subtly through Philisides's eclogues: in their references to Hubert Languet, the French Huguenot diplomat who became a mentor after meeting a young Sidney in Vienna; in the elusive figure of Coredens, who is mentioned in the Third Eclogues along with Languet, and then later, in the Fourth Eclogues, as a rival for Mira's affections; and in Mira herself, an enigmatic early version of Stella and a figure whose identity and meaning have long puzzled readers.[17]

Other questions trail Sidney's personae too: Did their respective frustrations allude to Sidney's fall from favor at court in 1579 and 1580 after his

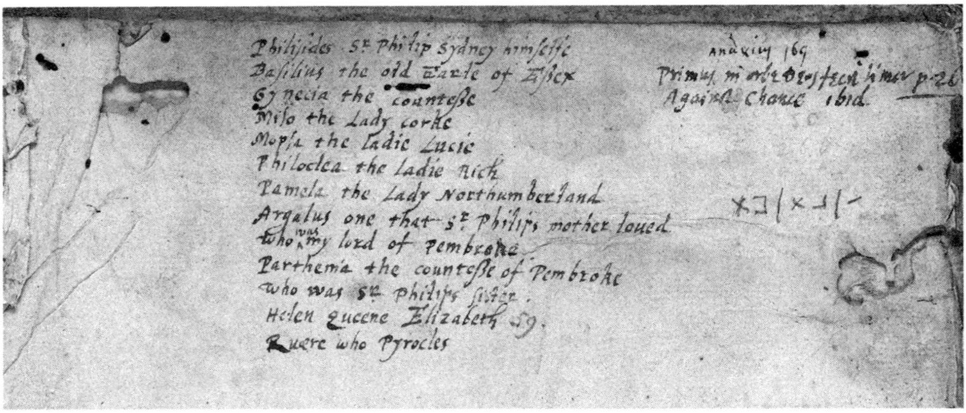

Figure 5. Henry Oxinden's key (1628) on the back page of his copy of the 1598 edition of Philip Sidney's *The Covntesse of Pembrokes Arcadia*. Ig Si14 + 590c. By permission of the Beinecke Rare Book and Manuscript Library, Yale University.

opposition to the Alençon match? Did they reflect the crumbling of his social aspirations after he lost his claim as Dudley heir in 1581?[18] Or did their fictions carry out some more sustained topical allegory? A long line of scholars—including, most notably, Annabel Patterson and Blair Worden—has read the old *Arcadia* as a covert commentary on Elizabethan politics.[19] Such readings carry on the work of seventeenth-century readers, such as Henry Oxinden and Francis Castillion, who turned out keys (figs. 5 and 6) to decode what they took to be a political *roman-à-clef*.[20] (As Stephen Dobranski's work on political rewritings of the *Arcadia* suggests, such readings reflect the political demands of their own moment as much as Sidney's.[21]) In *Astrophil and Stella*, for its part, the New Historicism found a veiled discourse on court politics, for which *eros* was merely a pretext: "Love," as Arthur Marotti's seminal essay has it, "is not love."[22] Readings along these lines can become vertiginous, for once one starts to mine the *Arcadia* or *Astrophil* for layers of hidden meaning, it is hard to say where the search for its secrets ought to end. "The very fact of penetrating any particular screen," writes Jonathan Crewe of the sonnets, "may itself become the 'proof' that it cannot have been the real screen or have concealed a real secret; there 'has' to be something more."[23]

Astrophil and Stella often seems determined to elicit this kind of disorientation. Even as Sidney slips in references to a reality hidden beneath the

203

The Interpretation of the chiefest names in Sr Phil: Sydnes Arcadia.

Sr Ph: Syd: so supposed.
Sr Ed: Dyer.
two sisters to ye Ea: of Es: sidl. Pen. Da:

Pirocles — ye Glory of fier.
Musidorus {the gifte or geuer of the Muses.
Daiphantus {Apearing fiery, euening or blessinge.
Paladius. — youthfull.
Zelman. — madde wth zeale.
Amphialus. — Compassed wth a crowne.
Philoclea. — The louer of glorry.
Pamela. — All Musicke.
Phalantus. A shininge flower.
Philoxemus. — A louer of a stranger.
Demagoras. the Gatherer of a multitude.
Timotheus. The Honor of God.
Artesia. a binder of me vnto her.
Calander. an honest & faire conditioned man.
Clitopho. a famous sound or voyse.
Basileus. — A Kinge.
Antiphilus. — Contrary to Loue.
Pamphilus. Louinge All.
Anaxius. Princely or royall.
Gynecia. — Womanly.
Philanax. a louer of ye Kinge.
Claysus {Lamentable a shepheard so called.
Strepho. — Turned.

Gero. an old ma. a shepherd.
Pas. — All.
Vrania. Heauenly.
Cosma. — Beautifull.
Nous. — the mind or spiritt.
Plangus. A kinde of Eagle.
Erona. Louely. or a louely on.
Helotes. people dwelling in marishes.
Parthenia. a Virgin, or maydenly.
Argalus {hard, or difficult to be moued; constant.
Euarchus. a good or blessed Kinge.
Andromana. Mad after a man.
Plexirtus. A scowrger or whipper.
Clinias. Auoydinge blowes.
Mastix. a whippe, or a scourger.
Miso. — Hated. or hatefull.
Mopsa {this word seemes to be deriued from Mopsus an illfauored shepheard in Virgil, but hath no proper signification.
Dametas. An Heardswayne in Virgill.
Cecropia {A woma of Athens. or a cunning woma.
Artaxia. Worthy of late.

Arcadia was written by Sr Ph: Sidney for the loue he bare vnto my Lady Penelope Deuoreux, who he wold haue married; but afterwards she married vnto my Lo: Ritche.

Figure 6. An etymological key to Philip Sidney's *The Covntesse of Pembrokes Arcadia* in the manuscript letter-book of Francis Castillion (1591–1638). Osborn fb69. By permission of the James Marshall and Marie-Louise Osborn Collection, Beinecke Rare Book and Manuscript Library, Yale University.

sequence's fiction—the puns on "Rich" in sonnet 37, an apparent allusion to the Devereux arms in sonnet 13, a reference to his father Henry's suppression of Ulster in sonnet 30—Astrophil rebukes his readers for attempting to decode the artifice. He does so most sharply in sonnet 28, a poem that raises the prospect of speculative interpretation in order to quash it:

You that with allegorie's curious frame,
   Of other's children changelings use to make,
   With me those paines for God's sake do not take:
I list not dig so deepe for brasen fame.
When I say "*Stella*", I do meane the same
   Princesse of Beautie, for whose only sake
   The raines of *Love* I love, though never slake,
And joy therein, though Nations count it shame. (*AS*, 28.1–8)

The second-person pronoun to which the sonnet is addressed distills the nervy tension that the sequence cultivates between poet and reader, presuming familiarity even as it radiates contempt: Sidney (or Astrophil) knows these curious wits all too well, he implies, but they don't know him well enough to read the poems correctly. What it would mean to read them correctly, however, is unclear. The admonition against allegorical decoding is above all a provocation, offered as it is in the face of such evident ciphers. Perhaps because of this contradiction, the prickliness of the rebuke quickly softens into something more playful. Astrophil's identification of Stella turns out to be a tautology—she is what we already know her to be, the "Princesse of Beautie" whom he loves—and so it settles nothing, her name left as a signifier of uncertain content. What begins as a denial of any subtext thus leads us, by the middle of the poem, back to the allegorical surface: whoever Stella is, Astrophil is not going to tell us, or at least not here. We reach a similar dead end in sonnet 104, where his prying companions—whose "morall notes straight my hid meaning teare / From out my ribs"—can prove only that "I / Do *Stella* Love," a conclusion that writes its own rejoinder: "Fooles, who doth it deny?" (*AS*, 104.12–14).

The common thread in the two poems is the opacity of Stella's name. Dwelling in its evocative force—"let me but name her," he declares in sonnet 55, "I well find no eloquence like it" (*AS*, 55.12, 14)—Sidney sidesteps, though he doesn't reject, the notion that the name is a veil; in doing so, he tacitly licenses the very curiosity that he scolds. Sonnet 104, in fact, seems to offer a clue of its own: as William Ringler points out, Astrophil's mention of stars that "I . . . upon mine armor beare" seems to encode a covert allusion to Sidney's own armor (*AS*, 104.10).[24] It may be, then, that the sonnets' "laborious interpreters," as Katherine Duncan-Jones calls them, were wrong not because they detected hidden meanings, but because they could do so only laboriously.[25] The sequence's ideal readers, by contrast, would simply recognize what to them would be open secrets. For those readers, Stella's name would be not a cipher but a readily legible sign; neither her identity nor Astrophil's would need any special act of readerly excavation.

If there were such readers, they were to be found in the small audience situated at Wilton House and in Sidney's exchanges with Greville, Edward Dyer, and other friends. More than Sidney's other writings, *Astrophil and Stella* seems to have been produced for a circumscribed group. "Then be they close," Sidney urges in sonnet 34, and they were; numerous copies were made of the sequence's songs, but H. R. Woudhuysen, in the most comprehensive study of the circulation of Sidney's manuscripts, argues that the sonnets reached few readers without direct ties to Sidney.[26] Their circulation therefore performed a kind of intimacy. "To be left to read or to copy the poems in Sidney's own working collection," writes Woudhuysen, "or to be given one or more by the author himself, must have been a rare and exciting privilege for his family, friends, and acquaintances"—an affirmation of their membership in his inner circle.[27] But that acknowledgment was shadowed by the sonnets' ambiguous accounts of their reception: were Sidney's close acquaintances the "envious wits" he deplored in sonnet 104? Or were Astrophil's barbs directed at outsiders, at a wider, hypothetical audience against which insiders could measure their proximity to Sidney? The likeliest answer is that the sonnets inspired both reactions—that they led Sidney's first readers, like later ones, to feel alternately confided in and left out, to see themselves as casually privy to Astrophil's secrets and to worry that they weren't.[28]

This differentiation between insiders and outsiders was not an effect of *Astrophil and Stella* alone. In the old *Arcadia*, Sidney's narrator frames the scene of storytelling by periodically addressing the "fair ladies" at Wilton; a prefatory epistle addressed to Mary Sidney describes the work as written "only for you, only to you."[29] It is a moment that seems to concentrate the divide between insiders and outsiders: in Wendy Wall's reading, the presence of Sidney's sister stands as a reflection of "the insulated world of the coterie, here shrunk to the perimeters of the sibling relationship."[30] But while this differentiation was mostly notional in the sonnets—nearly all of their early readers *were* close to Sidney—it was more concrete for the romance, which was disseminated (in at least fifteen manuscript copies) to what Woudhuysen suggests was a relatively wide body of readers, many of them surely only loosely connected to Sidney.[31] In 1586, Greville wrote to Francis Walsingham, Sidney's father-in-law, warning him of an unauthorized attempt to publish the old *Arcadia*—a version that he described as "that first w[h]ich is so com[m]on."[32] Philisides was thus more likely than Astrophil to encounter readers who would apply "allegorie's curious frame," prying into the secretive autobiographical subtext that the eclogues at once hinted at and occluded. If Sidney's sonnet sequence entertained the idea of wider exposure, his romance faced it in fact.

Much of Philisides's story, as it takes shape in the eclogues, is about his failures to make himself understood. Like Sincero, Jacopo Sannazaro's persona in his own, fifteenth-century *Arcadia*, Philisides is an unlucky lover: we learn that he has exiled himself in Arcadia (and put on a shepherd's weeds) after being spurned by Mira, his beloved, who never appears in the book. As a foreigner, Philisides becomes an object of curiosity for the native shepherds; even the duke Basilius, on his own pastoral sojourn, asks Philisides "to declare the discourse of his own fortunes" (*OA*, 159). Philisides demurs, finding the occasion "too joyful to suffer the rehearsal of his miseries" and later, when he begins to unpack his past, his attempts to do so are abortive and unsatisfying. His poem in the Third Eclogues, "On Ister bank," begins as autobiography but soon turns into an eccentric political fable; some shepherds praise it, but others respond by noting "the strangeness of the tale, and scanning what he should mean by it" (*OA*, 259). When the shepherds convene again in the Fourth Eclogues, he recites a pair of poems that mine the story of his love for Mira. In the middle of the second poem, however, he is abruptly cut off: "Philisides would have gone on in telling the rest of his unhappy adventures, and by what desperate works of fortune he was become a shepherd; but the shepherd Dicus desired him he would for that time leave particular passions, and join in bewailing this general loss of that country which had been a nurse to strangers as well as a mother to Arcadians" (*OA*, 344). At last ready to tell his story, Philisides finds that he has picked the wrong time. By this point, the shepherds' curiosity has turned to frustration. Their complaints—the "particular passions" that resist common understanding, the intensive "scanning" that his self-disclosures require—suggest a sense that Philisides's isolation is willful, that he is deliberately withholding himself from his Arcadian companions.

It makes sense, then, that arrangements of partial knowledge and limited disclosure would turn up at the heart of the old *Arcadia*, where Philisides's masking of Sidney finds a parallel in the disguises adopted by the princes

Pyrocles and Musidorus. Like Philisides, the princes are interlopers in Arcadia; like him, they are obsessive, self-transforming lovers; and like his, their stories are layered in miscomprehension and disguise. But where Philisides is seemingly inscrutable by accident, Pyrocles and Musidorus deliberately misrepresent themselves, assuming the disguises of Cleophila (an Amazon) and Dorus (a shepherd), respectively, in order to deceive Basilius, who has retreated to the country in order to protect his daughters from an oracle's enigmatic warnings of threats to their chastity. Dissimulation is what allows the princes to approach Philoclea and Pamela, but their disguises also preclude—for reasons of gender in one case and class in the other—the consummation of their courtships, and the *Arcadia*'s narrative thus becomes a drama of unveiling, with the princes attempting to reveal their true selves to their beloveds without arousing the suspicion of anyone else. The task proves too much for Pyrocles, whose cross-dressing is at once too effective and not effective enough, causing both Basilius (who believes the disguise) and his wife Gynecia (who sees through it) to fall in love with him; Philoclea, for her part, is thrust into sexual confusion by her desire for a person she believes to be a woman. Kathryn Schwarz and Julie Crawford have unpacked the homoerotic attraction that the cross-dressing Cleophila elicits; one effect of disguise, their readings suggest, is the teasing out of the secret desires of those who meet them.[33]

Musidorus has more success, partly because his disguise doesn't arouse the kind of erotic energy that his cousin's does and partly because he manages the revelation of his identity more carefully. Pretending to woo the dull, conceited shepherdess Mopsa, he compliments her in deliberately ludicrous terms, and he makes sure that Pamela is there to catch on: "The more she marked the expressing of Dorus's affection towards Mopsa, the more she thought she found such phrases applied to Mopsa as must needs argue either great ignorance or a second meaning in Dorus; and so to this scanning of him was she now content to fall, whom before she was resolved to banish from her thoughts" (*OA*, 99). Eventually he tells a story (still in the character of Dorus) about a prince named Musidorus, who had come to Arcadia, fallen in love with the duke's daughter, and disguised himself as a shepherd in order to woo her. The point is predictably lost on Mopsa, who by the end has nearly fallen asleep. Pamela, however, sees that "he meant by the tale himself, and that he did under covert manner make her know the great nobleness of his birth" (*OA*, 106). Musidorus's disguise allows him to tell his own story, with his own name, without being discovered. He can utter his secrets in company, secure in the knowledge that they will be recognized only by the right audience.

That audience is Pamela, but it is also Sidney's readers, who have been in on the secret all along. Our complicity is called upon by the book's narrator, who refers to the princes, for as long they are disguised, by their adopted names—a practice that Sidney presents as an acquiescence to their wishes: "For still, fair ladies," he writes of Cleophila, "you remember that I use the she-title to Pyrocles, since so he would have it" (*OA*, 38). It is a counterintuitive act of deference, one that implicates narrator and readers unexpectedly in the princes' ruses, as if referring to them as Pyrocles or Musidorus would somehow blow their cover. One effect of this courtesy is that the disguises can come to seem real, so that when Dorus tells the story of Musidorus it takes a moment to remember which is the "real" character and which is the faked identity. We are thus made at once naïfs and insiders, lulled into glimpsing the princes from the perspective of the Arcadians; and in leading the reader to straddle the border between public and private knowledge, Sidney makes a point of the distinction. In the middle of the third book, the princes part ways, and the narration of their farewells captures in miniature this bewildering mixture of distance and familiarity:

> "O Cleophila," said Dorus, with his eyes covered with water, "I did not think so soon to have displayed my determination unto you, but to have made my way first into your loving judgement. But, alas, as your sweet disposition drew me so far, so doth it now strengthen me in it. To you, therefore, be the due commendation given, who can conquer me in love, and love in wisdom. As for me, then shall goodness turn to evil, and ungratefulness be the token of a true heart, when Pyrocles shall not possess a principal seat in my soul, when the name of Pyrocles shall not be held of me in devout reverence." (*OA*, 175)

In a moment of such intimacy, the narrator's use of "Dorus" marks a respectful remove from the princes that the very reporting of the speech (which itself drops Pyrocles's pseudonym for his real name midstream) violates, a reminder that we are outsiders looking in. And this, in turn, brings home what it is to be in on the secret: we are Mopsa and Pamela both.

Our implication in the secrets of Pyrocles and Musidorus echoes our similar implication in those of Philisides. Like the princes', Philisides's secrets exist in the open but remain opaque to the wrong audiences—the most visible wrong audience being the Arcadian shepherds among whom he sits "as a stranger" (*OA*, 254). Who is the right audience? Sidney suggests that it is the circle of "fair ladies" whom his narrator addresses. These readers would be ready to understand the significance of figures like Coredens and Mira, would know what biographical backstory lay behind Philisides's melancholy, would recognize the strands of truth woven into the *Arcadia*'s fiction. Like the princes' disguises, Sidney's persona depends on careful opacity, on disclosures that address some readers but pass over others. In this respect, Philisides quietly divided Sidney's audience: even as the *Arcadia* moved into wider networks of manuscript transmission, those closest to Sidney would remain its most capable, and its most welcome, readers. Unlike Mopsa, however, the readers excluded from Philisides's secrets aren't allowed to forget it: the enigmatic traces of autobiography in his eclogues would have reminded outsiders—as they remind modern readers—just how much they were missing.

When Sidney revised this episode in what would become the "new" *Arcadia*, he inserted a moment where Musidorus's ruse nearly falls apart. In the midst of telling his story, Musidorus realizes that "he had (with the remembraunce of that plight he was in) forgotten in speaking of him selfe to vse the third person."[34] The line is a reminder of how complicated Musidorus's (or Dorus's) deception has become—of how hard it is to separate oneself from one's mask. The line also seems to have suggested another insertion, later in the book, by the editors of the *Arcadia*'s second edition (1593). In the process of restoring Philisides and his omitted poems, Mary Sidney and Hugh Sanford added a poem that had never before been included in the romance, an early poem known as "The lad Philisides." As an introductory comment notes, this poem (which describes how Philisides fell in love with Mira) differed from Philisides's other eclogues in abandoning the first-person voice: "To shew what a straunger he was to himselfe," the narrator reported, he "spake of himselfe as of a thirde person."[35] It is tempting to think that the insertion, and the note, were Mary Sidney's doing. If so, it marks a touching moment of collaboration between siblings, for it links Musidorus and Philisides in a shared strategy of rhetorical indirection and oblique self-disclosure ("what a straunger he was to himselfe"). At the same time, it reminds the book's readers that Sidney had been speaking of *himself* "as of a third person" all along. As a gloss in passing on her brother's uses of his persona, the comment offered exactly the kind of knowing appreciation that Sidney must have hoped Philisides, like Astrophil, would elicit from his most familiar readers.

If Men but Knew, the Halfe That He Did Write

Sidney's personae thus framed the relation between privacy and publicity as a dialectical one. The intimacy on offer in the *Arcadia* and *Astrophil and Stella* emerged precisely when they projected public attention from which to retreat—when they worried about the "envious wits" of a wider manuscript audience. Philisides and Astrophil held this prospective public at bay, and so brought it into view as the clarifying opposite of the Wilton circle. It was a shrewd strategy for controlling the reception of texts that Sidney surely knew would eventually find readers beyond those that he himself chose—a prospect acknowledged in his description, in *The Defence of Poesie*, of his "hauing slipt into the title of a Poet."[36] Indeed, although his works remained as yet unprinted, Sidney spent the 1580s slipping into wider circles of literary exposure. His works, especially the *Arcadia*, acquired new readers as they were copied and exchanged in manuscript, and references to them increasingly found their way into print. What was striking about this process of reception was how it, too, depended on a dynamic of limited disclosure: as Sidney's writings gained wider publicity without being made openly available, the perception of their exclusivity increased. Just as his personae tantalized the very readers they estranged, the advertised restriction of his texts served to heighten their allure.

Scholars have often observed that Sidney's poetry was little more than a footnote to a celebrity that in the 1580s rested primarily on other achievements. The elegies that flooded into print in 1587—including collections of mostly Latin verse from both universities—celebrated him as the perfect soldier and scholar joined in one. In the transnational Protestant communities of continental Europe, he had earned a reputation as a cosmopolitan intellectual, and at home he was widely recognized as a patron of letters.[37] The downplaying of Sidney's poetry reflected the cultural politics of the 1580s, when, as Kevin Pask argues, Elizabethan absolutism and Protestant militarism heralded a masculinized image of Sidney as the exemplary aristocrat-soldier.[38] Even so, Sidney's writing became part of his public image earlier than we tend to think. In 1580, the published letters of Spenser and Harvey linked him to a group of poets pursuing an art of English poetry in classical meters.[39] A year later, a member of the Earl of Pembroke's household, Thomas Howell, published a collection of poems, one of which praised the *Arcadia* as a "most excellent Booke, full of rare inuention."[40] After Sidney's death, such mentions became more common. Several of the Latin elegies cited his poetry, and particularly the *Arcadia*, among his accomplishments; one elegist, Richard Latewar, mourned Philisides as the poet who had guided his own literary ambitions.[41] In an elegy of his own, Angel Day celebrated the "sondry meeters" of "a book by him penned called the Countesses of Pe[m]brooks Archadia" and mourned the passing of a poet "whose honny dewes, that from his quil did passe, / with honny sweetes, aduaunst thy [England's] glorious name."[42] In still another, George Whetstone, rather confusedly praised Sidney for the *Arcadia* and *The Shepheardes Calender* alike.[43]

References like these helped to carve out a small space in the public consciousness for Sidney as a poet: they brought his poetry to the attention of readers in print even though the texts themselves remained unpublished. To come across references to the *Arcadia* without access to it must have been to glimpse a world apart—a literary community of which one could glean only traces. Whetstone's elegy emphasizes this sense of obscurity:

> If men but knew, the halfe that he did write,
> Enough to tyre, a memory so young
> Needes must they say the *Muses* in him sounge,
> His *Archadia*, vnmacht for sweete deuise:
> Where *skill* doth iudge, is held in Soueraigne price.[44]

For Whetstone, it seems, obscurity leads directly to value: if the "Soueraigne price" in which the *Arcadia* is held marks an aesthetic evaluation, it is also reflects the gap between growing demand and scarce supply. When the manuscript's readers are flattered for their discernment ("Where *skill* doth iudge"), in fact, the two modes of valuation seem to merge—skill and possession (or at least access) apparently amount to the same thing. Whetstone's own, uninitiated readers, on the other hand, are left on the outside looking in; they are asked to assent passively to a judgment they can neither participate in nor dissent from. More than anything else, printed celebrations of Sidney's poetry reminded their audience how much they were missing.

The sense of publicized exclusion was realized most powerfully in Abraham Fraunce's rhetorical manual *The Arcadian Rhetorike* (1588).[45] As a client of the Pembrokes' patronage, Fraunce evidently had access to Sidney's literary manuscripts, and he used them extensively in his manual, excerpting dozens of passages from the *Arcadia* (and a few from *Astrophil and Stella*) in order to illustrate figures and schemes. The excerpts were often substantial—enough to give his readers a rough introduction to the *Arcadia*'s plot and characters—and together they amounted to a partial unveiling. For Newcomb, indeed, the central effect of the *Rhetorike* was its capacity to "disseminate Sidney's exclusive manuscript, to open up what had been sealed."[46] Thus opened, Sidney could take his place as a national literary hero, alongside Fraunce's other source authors, Homer, Virgil, and Tasso. The august company was, as Allessandra Petrina suggests, an attempt to dignify English letters, and its implication was that the *Arcadia*, like the *Iliad* or the *Aeneid*, belonged at the head of a national canon—that it ought to be a general cultural patrimony rather than the property of a segregated elite.[47]

Even as Fraunce's manual opened up what had been sealed, however, it also hinted at how much remained closed. It did so not least by presuming a familiarity with Sidney's writings that was, for most readers, unrealistic. The first excerpt is introduced with no more than a brief tag—"Sir Philip Sydney in the 2. Act of Arcadia"—neither the text nor its form, apparently, meriting explanation. The lack of context would have brought many of the manual's readers up short, reminding them of their exclusion from the networks in which the *Arcadia* circulated: as Joel Davis points out, a key effect was thus the advertisement of Fraunce's "connectedness" to a circle from which his readers were excluded.[48] Yet the casual references also flattered readers, treating them as the insiders they weren't. It was a performance of access that played cleverly on the aspirational promise of the vernacular manuals, which offered Latin-less readers a modest introduction to humanist rhetorical training that, as Frank Whigham has emphasized, served to signal social distinction.[49] Fraunce's other sources presented another obstacle for unlearned readers, who lacked the languages necessary to read Homer or Virgil without translations. (Here a further effect was to push attention even more directly onto Sidney, whose passages were virtually the only ones in English.) Fraunce exploited a gap between educational and social haves and have-nots, in other words, by reproducing it—presenting his readers with languages they did not know and a text to which they did not have access. Sidney's standing as an elite, coterie author was thus central to his utility: the tantalizing destination the *Rhetorike* dangled before its audience was membership in the kind of community for which the *Arcadia* really was common knowledge.

When the first editions of the *Arcadia* and *Astrophil and Stella* were published over the next few years, then, their effect was not to introduce Sidney to the reading public, at least not in any absolute sense. His authorial name, along with substantial samples of his writing, was already there. But the printed editions did alter a powerful configuration of cultural capital, and one that

Sidney's personae, by projecting an opposition between insiders and outsiders, had enforced. If the indirect, esoteric subtexts of Astrophil and Philisides marshaled a distinction between smaller and larger networks of manuscript circulation, Whetstone and Fraunce reproduced that distinction in print: they circulated not the works themselves but the perception of their exclusivity. The effect was to fashion a literary celebrity for Sidney that did not render him "common"—a celebrity that depended on a refusal of publicity. The paradoxical goal of the first editions of the *Arcadia* and *Astrophil and Stella*, then, was to capitalize on the very exclusivity they dissolved.

Thus the stationer Thomas Newman—in the pirated, and quickly suppressed, first edition of *Astrophil and Stella* (1591)—framed his book as at once a vehicle of rare goods and an act of liberation: "I was moued to sette it forth, because I thought it pittie anie thing proceeding from so rare a man, shoulde bee obscured, or that his fame should not still be nourisht in his works, whom the works with one vnited griefe bewailed."[50] The volume's preface was written by Thomas Nashe, who used Sidney (as we will see in the next chapter) to position himself as mediator between the print marketplace and the more rarified cultural air that—he was keen to suggest—lay beyond it. Nashe played up the distance between Sidney and his counterparts in print: Astrophel's entrance "in pompe," he wrote, in a striking theatrical metaphor, promised to end "the Sceane of Idiots" that preceded him and inaugurate a golden age: "*Tempus adest plausus aurea pompa venit.*"[51] If his arrival thus promised to ennoble his new readers, however, it also depended on them. Astrophil could hardly be "Englands Sunne" if he remained unread by the wider public: "The Sunne for a time, may maske his golden head in a cloud: yet in the end, the thicke vaile doth vanish, and his embellished blandishment appeares."[52] But the risk was that his allure might not survive his emergence through the clouds. Once Sidney's texts were as ubiquitous as his name, they could no longer carry the same aura of inaccessibility.

Arcadian Communities

The loss of that aura meant that Sidney's writings were no longer qualitatively different from the other texts—prose romances especially—that filled the print marketplace. As Newcomb has shown, romance was both widely popular and worryingly lacking in prestige, its emerging association with female readerships reflecting a "slide down the social register."[53] In Bourdieu's terms,

Sidney had undergone a shift in position: despite the difference in their class dispositions, Newcomb points out, he had come to share a position in the literary field with Robert Greene—a sign, she adds, of "the volatility of the field."[54] As a result, the distinction of Sidney's texts now had to be actively asserted.

This was a process that began with the second edition of the *Arcadia*, published in 1593 under the supervision of Mary Sidney and Hugh Sanford. Sanford's prefatory epistle was scathing in its attack on Greville's first edition, noting that the "spottes wherewith the beauties thereof were unworthely blemishd" had persuaded Sidney's sister to step in.[55] Greville's editing, however, wasn't particularly error-ridden, and Sanford's complaint reads as a stalking-horse for something deeper. Its real goal, suggests Joshua Phillips, was "to restrict the *Arcadia* to a very specific type of interpretive community"—one that seemed to exclude the reading public whom Sanford invidiously compared to cattle interloping in Arcadia.[56] Not only did such a pose elevate Sanford himself; as Joel Davis suggests, it also argued "aristocratic friendship" as the book's proper setting, an argument bolstered by the "fabrication" of Mary Sidney's new role as Philip's literary successor.[57] Shrewdly encoding social exclusion as moral sentiment, Sanford insinuated that not every reader was worthy of Sidney's romance: "If it be true that likeness is a great cause of liking, and that contraries inferre contrary consequences: then it is true, that the wortheles Reader can neuer worthely esteeme of so worthye a writing: and as true, that the noble, the wise, the vertuous, the curteous, as many as haue had any acquaintaunce with true learning and knowledge, will with all loue and deareness entertaine it, as well for affinity with themselues, as being child to such a father."[58] The worthiest reader, of course, was Mary Sidney, and whereas Greville had made a point of bringing the book to a print audience, Sanford argued that it belonged instead to her. The romance, he wrote, was "now by more than one interest *The Countesse of Pembrokes Arcadia*: done, as it was, for her: as it is, by her."[59] An echo of Philip Sidney's dedication of the book to his sister as written "only for you, only to you," the line reclaimed it for the coterie to which, Sanford was quick to insist, it had first belonged.

Predictably, Sanford and Mary Sidney began by removing the chapter divisions and summaries that Greville had introduced for the "more ease" of his readers.[60] But it was their restoration of Philisides that most powerfully realized this project of reclamation. They reversed each excision of the persona, reinstating a dialogue between Philisides and Geron in the Second Eclogues and returning to him two poems—an echo poem in the Second Eclogues and

"On Ister Bank" in the Third—that Greville had given to other shepherds.[61] (A sharp reader, even without access to the *Arcadia* in manuscript, might have noticed something amiss in the first edition: Fraunce had included the echo poem in *The Arcadian Rhetorike*, attributing it not to the shepherd Lamon—as Greville did—but to Philisides.)[62] Sanford and Sidney's revisions meant that two different versions of Sidney's persona now occupied the same text: Philisides still appeared as the chivalric challenger at Andromana's tournament, but he was now also, once again, the melancholy, retiring shepherd-poet. The results could be confusing. In 1621, a linking narrative by William Alexander began being printed with the *Arcadia* in order to bridge the gap between the end of the revised text and the resumption of the story in Book Three of the old *Arcadia*.[63] Alexander's addition paid tribute to Sidney by having Philisides the knight die of a wound suffered in battle—a thoughtful gesture, but one that would have left readers surprised when, later in the book, Philisides returns, singing "The Lad Philisides" in the eclogues as if nothing had happened.

The reluctant singing of the Philisides whom Sanford and Mary Sidney restored must have read as a reticence not only toward his fellow shepherds, but also toward his readers—as a desire to keep his own counsel even as he became public. In this sense, he had the force of what Bourdieu would call "position-taking," of a claim made on a position in the literary field, and the symbolic capital that came with it.[64] Sidney, of course, could no longer take a position himself; instead, his persona absorbed the responsibility, his self-isolation and esotericism staking out for the *Arcadia* (and for Sidney) a position with the exclusivity that it seemed to have lost. This relocation could hardly be effected materially: there was little hope of restricting the circulation of the *Arcadia* once it was in print. The posture of restricted production thus could only be a posture, asserted and performed but never realized objectively. Sanford's epistle bears the marks of the frustration felt by Sidney's coproducers: when he tries to delimit the *Arcadia*'s readership on moral grounds by arguing that "worthless" readers can never "esteem" such a work, the attempt exposes the impossibility of delimiting it in any more robust way. The restoration of Philisides advanced the cause more subtly, for it not only ascribed the book's new ambivalence toward public attention to Sidney himself (reflected in his persona) but also located that ambivalence within the *Arcadia*. Philisides, from 1593 on, became a way to discover a private Sidney in his most public text—or even a sign that the text was at some level not a public one at all.

But it was not only Sanford and Mary Sidney who found in his personae a way to claim a position for him apart from the public. Sidney had other posthumous collaborators too: writers who were interested in appropriating his prestige for their own purposes, and so also concerned to reassert his distinction in the face of popularity. Philisides and Astrophil accordingly became, like Colin Clout, touchstones for poets who wished to claim a place alongside them. To retrace their wanderings is to explore the history of Sidneian imitation and adaptation recently charted by Gavin Alexander and Natasha Simonova. But my focus is at once narrower and broader than theirs: narrower in that I am concerned with the immediate reception of Sidney's personae in the 1580s and 1590s, and broader in that I am interested less in the fate of the *Arcadia* or *Astrophil and Stella*—or even Sidney himself—than in the uses to which his personae were put. Like Colin Clout, and like Greene's ghosts, Sidney's personae assembled imagined communities around them. In the previous chapter, we saw how Colin encoded the formation of a literary field, or a domain of poetry. Sidney's personae belong to the same story of literary institutionalization; indeed, the "world apart" that Colin helped to anchor was in many ways conceived in their image, as a distinctly Arcadian literary sphere. It was a space that relied on the logic of symbolic affiliation—on the possibility of writing oneself into Colin's story, or into Astrophil's or Philisides's. But it also depended on the logic of difference. For Bourdieu, a literary field is defined by the struggles that shape it, the contests for legitimacy that establish and enforce (and are in turn motivated by) the structure of positions. The complex rewritings of Sidney's personae encode these struggles, and in doing so they shed light on the gradual articulation of a literary field. What they reveal, more specifically, is an emergent opposition between two subfields: what Bourdieu calls the "field of large-scale cultural production" and the "field of restricted production." The latter is oriented by its rejection of the former, and of the mass audience it courted; in the field of restricted production, Bourdieu writes, "producers produce for other producers."[65] Evoking exclusivity in public, Astrophil and Philisides were positioned to enforce just such a distinction.

Early citations of Sidney's personae tended to invoke the persona in order to find a literary Sidney beneath his other identities. Richard Latewar, one of Sidney's Oxfordian elegists, wove Philisides into the refrain of his poem: "*Dicite Philisidem mea carmina, dicite vatem* [Tell of Philisides, my songs, tell of the poet]."[66] Latewar evinces an interest in Sidney's poetry that is rare in the university elegies, and a familiarity with the *Arcadia* that is unmatched in them. He regrets not knowing Sidney personally, but he claims, with a charming modesty, an indirect mentorship: "*Ille meos sublime modos tentare, paremq[ue] / Imparibus docuit famam affectare Camaenis* [He taught me to stretch my rhythms aloft, and to aspire with my unequal muses to equal fame.]"[67] As a gesture of affiliation, the poem measures its own limits: Latewar knows the books, not the man. But the book's limited circulation gives the claim force: to know the *Arcadia* was to know a Sidney that not many did. Matthew Roydon struck a similar note in his elegy, which was first published in the miscellany *The Phoenix Nest* (1593) but circulated in manuscript for several years before it was printed. As Latewar had used Philisides, so Roydon used Astrophil to express an intimacy that Sidney's public titles resisted—but also to invoke Sidney specifically as a poet whom "the Muses taught . . . [to] sing, to write, and say."[68] Barnabe Barnes—last seen writing Colin Clout into his own Arcadia—made space for Astrophil too:

Sing sing (*Parthenophil*) sing, pipe, and play:
  This feast is kept vpon this plaine
Amongst *th'Arcadian* shepheard's euery where
For *Astrophill's* byrth-day: sweet *Astrophil.*
Arcadies honour, mightie *Pan's* cheefe pride:
Where be the Nymph's, the Nymphes all gathred bee
  To sing sweet Astrophil's sweet prayse.[69]

And Spenser himself began the *envoi* of *The Ruines of Time* (1591), a poem largely devoted to the commemoration and consecration of Sir Philip Sidney, by hailing the "Immortal spirite of *Philisides*, / Which now art made the heavens ornament, / That whileome wast the worlds chiefst riches."[70] In each case, the use of Sidney's persona balanced commemoration and affiliation; to cite one of them was to show that one knew how to invoke Sidney as a fellow poet.

Barnes's evocation of a distinctly Arcadian pastoral hints at its role as an organizing myth for English literary culture. It was a myth that found its most substantial expression in a pair of romances by John Dickenson—the same writer who would go on to resurrect Robert Greene in *Greene in Conceipt* (1598). Dickenson's *The Shepheardes Complaint* (1592 or 1593) and *Arisbas* (1594) followed Sidney's example not only in their mixture of prose and verse but also in their Arcadian settings.[71] Dickenson announced his acts of homage with prefatory comments celebrating Sidney ("the whitest Swanne & sweetest of Apolloes musicall birdes," a preface to *Arisbas* called him), and he carried them out in the model of alternating poetic recitations that Dickenson borrowed from the *Arcadia*'s eclogues.[72] Narrative in each book takes a backseat to other concerns, offering a space for experiments in quantitative verse, for instance, and allowing Arcadia to become a kind of literary dreamscape—a space, in Alexander's striking description, "where authorial personae detach from their bodies, like the shadow in Hans Christian Andersen's tale, and develop a life of their own."[73]

It was fitting, then, that one of the poems recited by *Arisbas*'s title character (like Musidorus a prince disguised as a shepherd) would take the name "The worth of Poesie." The poem tells the story of laurel tree poisoned by Envy and wasted away by Ignorance until Fame arrives to nurse it back to health. By the end of the poem, literary order is restored: "The Lawrell flourisht in her former hue: / Fame bade Desert for euer there remaine / With light and sound, to shield a Poets due, / By safe defence from wrongs that might ensue."[74] Arisbas's allegory charts a familiar, periodizing arc, and the prose that follows the poem drives the point home, noting that, although Arisbas "aymde his conceipt at the merits of *Grecian* and *Romane* labors onely," the work of modern poets across Europe were "likewise registred in that holy refuge of such happy reliques."[75] Even—indeed especially—the work of English poets:

> But in *Albion* the wonder of Ilands louely *Thamesis*, fairest of the faire *Nereides* loues sea-borne Queene adoring, vaunts the glory of her maiden streames, happy harbor of so many Swans, *Apollos* musical birds, which warble wonders of worth, and chaunt clear pleasures choise in seuerall sounds of sweetnesse, pleasant, passionate, loftie, louely, whose matchlesse notes, the faire Nymph keeping tyme with the billowing of her Chrystall waues, carrying to the *Ocean* with her ebbe, doth there echo them to her astonisht sisters which assemble in those vast flouds by timely confluence.[76]

The exemplary case, of course, was Sidney, who had brought Arcadia to England and made himself its outstanding inhabitant. Now he was continually memorialized by the shepherd-poets whom he had left behind and to whom he had bequeathed the literary territory of Arcadian pastoral. "*Arcadians* doe him his deserued right," Dickenson wrote in *The Shepheardes Complaint*, "And on his Tombe greene Laurel-branches spread, / Which while he breath'd on earth, adorn'd his head."[77] The literary world that Sidney had written into being, Dickenson's pastorals intimated, consisted in large part of the rehearsing of his memory.

For all that, however, Sidney is notably hard to find in Dickenson's Arcadia. At least his name is: it appears only once in *The Shepheardes Complaint* (in a Latin form, "Sidnaeia") and not at all in *Arisbas*.[78] Indeed, Dickenson's epistle to "the Gentlemen-Readers" at the beginning of *Arisbas* makes a point of refusing to name the object of its glowing praise: "If you demaund whom I meane, euen he it is to whom I wil ascribe no other titles, the[n] the world hath allotted, though I cannot duly affoord them as he deserues them."[79] Even in the Arcadian world he had fashioned, Sidney remains somehow invisible.

Dickenson concealed Sidney in part by relying on his persona. Unwilling to name him in the prefatory epistle, he instead identifies Sidney with a couplet: "Sweet Astrophil the solace of my pen, / Wonder of worth, and Peere of peerlesse men."[80] The use of Sidney's persona seems to suit Dickenson's careful pose of modesty, allowing him to identify Sidney obliquely rather than directly; it lets him pass over the various "other titles" that the world "hath allotted" and address Sidney in the particular role of poet. Dickenson is thus able to encounter Sidney, to address him, with a familiarity that would otherwise be impossible. He becomes, indeed, something like the shepherds of his fiction, taking residence in Arcadia and like them "memorizing the worth of *Astrophell*."[81] For Dickenson, the name "Astrophell" hails a Sidney who is, like Latewar's and Roydon's, at once specifically literary and unusually private. For Dickenson, however, Sidney had already become a literary celebrity—he was no longer just an aristocratic and military one—and as a consequence the evasion of his public personage came with new stakes. It was now a retreat from his *literary* fame: a suggestion that, in spite of it, his works ought to remain private, the province of a kind of personal acquaintance. To be sure, Dickenson's vision of an Arcadian England only affirmed Sidney's cultural centrality. But Dickenson's pastoral was a meditation, above all, on the challenge of finding a relation with Sidney—and a way of articulating it—in the face of his newly monumental literary presence. Both celebrating that presence and attempting to escape it, Dickenson turns to Astrophil in order to discover a version of Sidney that he can make his own.

Dickenson's pastorals evince the same ambiguities that lie beneath most of Astrophil's and Philisides's appearances in the 1590s. On the one hand, they are, with Colin, the sponsors of an Arcadian myth that grounds a literary field in its full breadth; on the other, they are invoked precisely because they pull Sidney away from his public self and toward a kind of poetic privacy. They allow the community of writers to imagine itself as a world apart, that is, even as they mark a carefully delimited place within it. Performances of intimacy were for this reason central to their afterlives. Roydon's poem made this especially clear, with its title announcing the division of its attentions between

Sidney and Astrophil, public figure and friend. Roydon's poem continually reminded its readers how much and how little they knew Sidney, and tantalized them with hints of what it would mean to know him better:

> You knew, who knew not Astrophill,
> (That I should liue to say I knew,
> And haue not in possession still)
> Things knowne permit me to renew,
> Of him you know his merit such,
> I cannot say, you heare too much.[82]

Roydon's use of the second person teases the poem's readers, who "knew" even if they "knew not"—who knew, perhaps, *that* they "knew not Astrophill." The first person, on the other hand, claims a greater intimacy with Sidney, a friend whom Roydon "knew" and once had "in possession." The poem's audience, hearing once more about a man whose achievements they know already, are in one light cast, with Roydon himself, as Sidney's familiars; in another, they remain outside the parentheses that mark off the genuine intimacy (or so Roydon suggests) of actual friends.

It is hard not to hear in Roydon's "who knew not Astrophill" an anticipation of Spenser's question in Book 6 of *The Faerie Queene*: "Who knowes not *Colin Clout*?"[83] Spenser certainly would have known Roydon's poem, printed as it was in 1595 alongside Spenser's own elegy for the poet whom he, too, called Astrophil. Sidney had loomed over Spenser's literary career from its beginning, standing as the dedicatee of *The Shepheardes Calender* (1579) and as the most illustrious member of the Areopagus, the putative coterie that Spenser and Harvey heralded for their experiments in quantitative verse. If Spenser had cultivated Sidney's patronage, he also may have found in him an unexpected literary rival—a poet whose posthumous literary celebrity gave him the laureate prestige that Spenser had sought for himself. Their fates as poets were, in any case, now intertwined. Both the *Arcadia* and *The Faerie Queene* were published in 1590 by William Ponsonby, and thereafter, as Richard McCabe observes, Spenser and Sidney "(formerly related as dedicatee and dedicator) would appear from the same press as authors of equal cultural status."[84]

In the years between the publication of the two installments of *The Faerie Queene*, Spenser's poetry circled back more than once to the problem of Sidney's enduring legacy. *The Ruines of Time* (1591) wove a lamentation of Sidney's loss into a meditation on the instability of every form of fame and power except poetry—the poem's mourning of the "immortal spirite of *Philisides*," Spenser suggested, would preserve him more surely than any physical monument ever could. Harnessing the immortality topos, Spenser seemed to imagine himself to be fulfilling the duty of a poet toward a patron; in the poem's dedication to Mary Sidney, he called her brother "the Patron of my young *Muses*."[85] But "Astrophel" (1595) presented a rather different Sidney—less a benefactor owed the honor of poetic remembrance than a fellow poet, a departed member of the community gathered to mourn him.[86] "For he could pipe and daunce, and caroll sweet," Spenser wrote, "Emongst the shepheards in their shearing feast . . . And layes of loue he also could compose, / Thrise happie she, whom he to praise did chose."[87]

The book that introduced Spenser's "Astrophel" to the world was an eccentric one. William Ponsonby had appended the elegy, along with a series of elegies for Sidney by other poets, to his quarto edition of *Colin Clouts Come Home Againe*; at the end of the poem, a new page presented the title of "Astrophel. A Pastorall Elegie vpon the death of the most Noble and valorous Knight, Sir *Philip Sidney*," and the dedication to Sidney's widow, Frances Walsingham. After "Astrophel" came "The Doleful Lay of Clorinda," a poem that scholars have attributed alternately to Spenser and to Mary Sidney, who appears here (whether or not by her own doing) in the pastoral guise of Clorinda.[88] A series of elegies by other writers followed: first a pair of poems usually attributed to Sidney's friend Lodowick Bryskett (the latter is signed with the initials L. B.), then Roydon's poem, and finally two elegies that had been published with Roydon's in *The Phoenix Nest*—the first believed to be by Raleigh and the second by Dyer or Greville.[89] The elegies are thus not a natural sequence: they were written by different poets, at different times, and for different audiences. But Ponsonby's book shapes them into something like one. Printed together, they become a dialogue: a series of discrete poems that gain strength by their collection, their presentation as a communal celebration and lamentation.

Spenser's "Astrophel" roots itself in a reanimation of Sidney's Arcadian pastoral. "A Gentle Shepheard borne in *Arcady*," it begins,

> Of gentlest race that euer shepheard bore
> About the grassie banks of *Hæmony*,
> Did keepe his sheep, his little stock and store.
> Full carefully he kept them day and night,
> In fairest fields, and *Astrophel* he hight. (*CC*, sig. E_4^r)

Spenser's opening makes clear how the elegy will remember Sidney, retrieving his biography by way of his fictions—fictions that immediately merge with each other, as the Petrarchan Astrophil (and later Stella, too) are absorbed into the pastoral world of the *Arcadia*. The strategy was taken from Roydon, who likewise had set his poem in Arcadia: his narrator discovers an unnamed man grieving Astrophil in a natural amphitheater of trees and animals and birds. Remembering Sidney as a synthesis of his personae brought his literary activity to the foreground: presented in early accounts of Sidney's life as ancillary to his public achievements, his writings now became the lens through which those achievements (and even his death) were understood. Indeed, invoking Astrophil and Philisides signaled that he was, before anything else, a poet. Finding Sidney as Astrophil, and in Arcadia, served as a particularly literary homage, and a way of sustaining and continuing his fictions after his death. Like Dickenson's *Arisbas*, their poems invoked Arcadia out of a doubled instinct of preservation and self-assertion: Sidney's invented world had to be kept alive so that they could encounter him in it.

Or, at least, so they could encounter each other. Pastoral, as Paul Alpers has argued, is conventional in the particular, nearly lost sense that it *convenes*, that it is a form concerned with "the idea of coming together."[90] In the "Astrophel" elegies, pastoral convention is called upon to turn a series of independent, separately written poems into a collective ritual of mourning. Spenser's own poem is as much a framing narrative as a discrete elegy. After telling the story of Astrophel's life (a rewriting of real events in Sidney's life in the register of myth) from his childhood up to the point where he is gored by a "cruell beast," the poem pauses around his prone body, which becomes the focus of the poem's conclusion (*CC*, sig. F_2^v). A group of shepherds cares for his wound; Stella sits at his side as he dies; and the gods transform the lovers into a flower. Then shepherds from around Arcadia gather to mourn. All of "Astrophel," it turns out, has been a preparation for the exchange of poems that will comprise the rest of the book. First comes Clorinda, Astrophil's sister, singing "a dolefull lay, / Which least I marre the sweetnesse of the vearse, / In sort as she it sung, I will rehearse" (*CC*, sig. F_4^v). Then "another swaine" takes his turn—Bryskett in the person of Thestylis—and when that poem is done,

full many other moe,
As euerie one in order lov'd him best,
Gan dight themselues t'expresse their inward woe,
With dolefull layes vnto the time addrest. (*CC*, sig. G_3^r)

By the end of Bryskett's poems, the additions from *The Phoenix Nest* can be assimilated straightforwardly. Incorporated into the pastoral fiction that Spenser has fashioned, they are transformed from a set of discrete and disparate poems into something whole, the collaborative work of a group of like-minded Arcadian shepherds.

Membership in that group meant taking on a persona of one's own. Mary Sidney became Clorinda, and Bryskett became Thestylis; in the second of his poems, "A pastorall Aeglogue upon the death of Sir *Philip Sidney Knight, &c,*" Bryskett recast himself as Lycon and fashioned a dialogue with Spenser's Colin.[91] Their responsive "pastoral Aeglogue" turned on a refrain that invoked Sidney's other persona: "*Philisides* is dead." The line became the prompt for each of Colin's and Lycon's responsive songs. "*Philisides* is dead," sings Colin at one point,

O lucklesse age;
O widow world; O brookes and fountains cleere;
O hills, O dales, O woods that oft haue rong
With his sweet caroling, which could asswage
The fiercest wrath of Tygre or of Beare. (*CC*, sig. H_4^r)

To grieve for Philisides (rather than Sidney) in the persona of Lycon or Colin (rather than Bryskett or Spenser) was to find one's way into Sidney's personal allegory, to enroll oneself in the same story that their elegies perpetuated. The select company thus enrolled began to look like the kind of coterie for which Philisides had been crafted. It was no surprise that Sidney's sister, as Clorinda, was the group's lynchpin, granted pride of place with her "doleful lay" coming first after the framing narrative of "Astrophel." This new coterie, the arrangement implied, would be built around the person who had anchored Sidney's original one.

The Coterie in Print

The "Astrophel" elegies thus aimed at a reclamation of the privacy of the coterie. But we might wonder how much the imagined community fashioned in the elegies was an excavation, and how much it was, instead, a retrojected fantasy. It is easy to see Dickenson's and Spenser's fictions—and the more modest citations of Astrophil and Philisides across a range of poems—as versions of an inherited model, renovating the manuscript coterie as a useful fiction in print. It may be more accurate, however, to see the coterie as something more complicated: an image of restricted production summoned by the struggle for distinction in an emergent literary field—summoned, that is, by the demands of position-taking in the present. From this perspective, the afterlives of Sidney's personae reveal not the effects of the divide between manuscript and print, or between coterie and public, but its genesis. To read them is to witness a moment in the differentiation of "manuscript culture" from "print culture"—in the process by which they came to be imagined as opposites.

This was, in any event, a project in which the elegists found themselves working alongside Sidney's coproducers. Like Hugh Sanford and Mary Sidney, they claimed him—or claimed to reclaim him—as a poet of the coterie, insisting that his works belonged to a sphere of restricted cultural production. William Ponsonby's role as publisher suggested the alliance of interests. As the owner of the *Arcadia*'s title, he had an interest in protecting Sidney's reputation; as the publisher of *The Faerie Queene*, however, he also had an interest in cultivating Spenser's. Those interests happily aligned in *Colin Clouts Come Home Againe* and the "Astrophel" elegies, where the fantasy of an exclusive Sidney allowed Spenser to figure himself as a restricted producer. This fascination with exclusivity is, as we saw in the last chapter, central to the eclogue that gave the volume its name. Colin's account of his journey to Cynthia's court includes a catalogue of poets whom he identifies, as he did Elizabeth, with pseudonyms: Harpalus, Corydon, Alcyon, Palin, Alcon, Palemon, Aetion. Left undecoded, the names stand as riddles to any reader who doesn't already hold the key, and as a result the literary world of the court appears to the book's readers as one open only to initiates.[92] The series culminates with one final name: "All these, and many others mo remaine, / Now after *Astrofell* is dead and gone: / But while as *Astrofell* did liue and raine, / Amongst all these was none his Paragone" (*CC*, sig. C_2^v). The inclusion of Astrophil, the only readily legible pseudonym on the roster, conferred authority on the pseudonymous circle that the poem described. At the same time, it reeled Sidney back into the world of a segregated elite, investing "Astrofell" once again with an aura of exclusivity.

It was an effect that the book's pastoralism reinforced. Pastoral lyrics had long situated themselves at a distance from whatever they projected as the real world, their "green worlds" marking off a space in which the concerns of poetry could take precedence over those of political and social actualities (or in which those actualities could be examined from a critical distance).[93] Spenser drew on this sense of withdrawal, using the *locus amoenus* of pastoral to imagine Sidney's recovery in a cloistered community of literary peers. Dickenson did much the same in *Arisbas*, figuring in Arcadia the image of a literary collectivity complete in itself:

> It is the custome of *Arcadians* to rest in some shade when Sommers scortching heate annoyes them. Being shrowded from the Sunne, they spend the time in discoursing on their owne or their fellowes fortunes, Shepheards I meane, men of their owne profession, whether natiue in *Arcadia* or no: as in memorizing the worth of *Astrophell*, praising the perfections of *Phillis*, lamenting the losse, commending the loyaltie of *Amyntas*, mourning the death, yet misliking the disdeine and pride of *Amaryllis*, pitying the distresse of the forlorne Shepheard, the vnhappy admirer, though happy herauld of her worth.[94]

Amyntas and Phillis, as Alexander points out, are characters associated with Thomas Watson—Amyntas, indeed, was used as a name for Watson—while Amaryllis seems to be a persona for Dickenson himself.[95] Mingling them with Astrophil, *Arisbas* produces a pastoral hodgepodge that can serve as a meeting ground for real writers and the fictions they had produced. If Sidney's Arcadia, like so many pastoral worlds, was a space of prodigious poetic production, Dickenson turns it into something more. His shepherds are not merely poets; they are poets by "profession." Spenser similarly addresses himself to his fellow poets—those shepherds, he writes, "that wont on pipes of oaten ride, / Oft times to plaine your loues concealed smart"—insisting that "To you alone I sing this mournfull verse . . . To you I sing and to none other wight" (*CC*, sig. E_4^r). This is poetry, he insists, that has been written for the poets whom the volume gathers; it is a work of restricted production in Bourdieu's sense of the term—poetry produced for an audience of fellow producers.

Crucial to both Dickenson's and Spenser's pastoral accounts of literary production is the projection of a world without text, and hence without publication. Spenser is careful to frame the collection's poems as orally sung and only later "rehearse[d]" in his transcriptions (*CC*, sig. F_4^v). Sidney's own poetry is likewise imagined to have existed only in his "sweet caroling," as Bryskett's Colin terms it in "A pastoral Aeglogue." His death, the elegies suggest, marked a final silencing of his songs, which can be preserved only in the sorrowful knowledge of their having passed from the world: "Alas," Bryskett's Colin laments, "who now is left that like him sings? / When shall you heare againe like harmonie? / So sweet a sownd, who to you now imparts?" (*CC*, sig. H_4^r). Clorinda even warns the gathered shepherdesses that it would be somehow wrong to reproduce his poetry: "Ne euer sing the loue-layes which he made, / Who euer made such layes of loue as hee?" (*CC*, sig. G_1^v). The exception to the rule of orality comes in Bryskett's eclogue, in an inscription "engraued by his hand," on a nearby tree, of Stella's name. Here, at least, is some durable relic of Philisides's (or Astrophil's) verse, and it inspires in Bryskett's Colin a vision of a future when the tree's "sacred branch" would provide crowns of honor to poets and emperors both (*CC*, sig. H_4^r). But even this inscription remains just a riddle—not a poem but a name, a pseudonym that demands prior knowledge. In imagining Sidney as, to the last, a poet of the coterie, the "Astrophel" elegies simply leave out the fact of his posthumous publication and popularity. The poems must have read as an uncanny counter-history, with Sidney's death marking the end rather than the beginning of his literary career.

But if Sidney himself had died, Bryskett's poem suggested, the poets gathered to memorialize him were ready to perpetuate his coterie. In his final response to Colin, Bryskett's Lycon moves from Philisides's carols to the songs of the shepherds whom he leaves behind:

> *Philisides* is dead. O happie sprite,
> That now in heau'n with blessed soules doest bide:
> Looke down a while from where thou sitst aboue,
> And see how busie shepheards be to endite
> Sad songs of grief, their sorrowes to declare,
> And gratefull memory of their kynd loue.
> Behold my selfe with *Colin*, gentle swaine
> (Whose lerned *Muse* thou cherisht most whyleare)
> Where we thy name recording, seeke to ease
> The inward torment and tormenting paine,
> That thy departure to vs both hath bred;
> Ne can each others sorrow yet appease. (*CC*, sigs. H_4^r–H_4^v)

One of the passage's functions is to describe the kind of genealogical transmission of authority that Raphael Falco has argued was the dominant concern of Spenser's relation to Sidney in the 1590s, with the latter's mantle passed on to the poet whom in life he had "cherisht most."[96] But its more powerful effect is the articulation of a community of poets under the aegis of Philisides and the organizing control of Colin Clout. By adopting their own personae, the volume's poets claim (or the volume claims for them) an affiliation with Sidney, along with all the authority that derives from it. And in his absence, Sidney's coterie becomes *their* coterie. His death, almost a decade earlier, had been the occasion for a massive public funeral; now the deaths of Astrophil and Philisides prompt a different kind of ritual, a convocation of "busie shepheards," or, as Dickenson had phrased it, of "men of their owne profession." Spenser and his fellow poets meet and mourn Sidney in an Arcadia they have lovingly reconstructed for him—a space of privileged remove, apart from and above the reading public in which *Colin Clouts Come Home Againe* in fact circulated.

For the book was, after all, printed and sold—it was designed for public consumption. There was no actual coterie, at least not the one that the volume evoked. The poems gathered in it had been written separately from each other, by authors who didn't anticipate their eventual collection under the banner of Spenser's "Astrophel"; the poems from *The Phoenix Nest*, indeed, were already in print. What the volume's performance of communal lamentation allowed, beyond the comforts of imagined companionship, was the projection of a fiction of self-contained literary community before the collection's actual audience, the book-buying London public. It was a fiction that needed that public, a community that existed only insofar as the book's readers participated in imagining it. Yet the imagined coterie also needed those readers to register their exclusion, to recognize the distinction that the elegies for Sidney implicitly claimed for Spenser and his fellow poets.

The rewritings of Sidney's personae in the 1590s thus brought the coterie into print as a fiction of a particularly circumscribed imagined community. It was a community that depended on the intimation of aristocratic elitism, but one that translated class exclusivity into the literary exclusivity of poets writing for one another, in what appeared, in the "Astrophel" elegies and in Dickenson's *Arisbas*, as an autonomous Arcadian world. Garth Bond has noted a similar effect in Ben Jonson's imagined scenes of reception, where his "rare poemes aske rare friends": in appealing to the coterie, Bond argues, Jonson asserted his poems' rareness to the print audiences who read them.[97] Like Jonson, Astrophil and Philisides seemed to herald a scene of manuscript circulation for readers in print. In this sense, we might say, they reproduced the hierarchical relation often attributed to the two mediums—the prestige of manuscript circulation against the vulgarity of print—within the print public. But perhaps it is better to say that the differential logic of the literary field encouraged the *production* of that relation. The coterie as it appears in the afterlives of Sidney's personae points up an emergent opposition between restricted and large-scale literary production. For Bourdieu, the emergence of this oppositional relation is the key moment of autonomization: only when the subfield of restricted production rejects large-scale production (and its commercial logic) can a literary field arrive at its own, internal criteria of legitimacy.[98] The coterie of Astrophil and Philisides expressed this conceptual opposition: it was conjured into being as a virtual space to be positioned against the marketplace at large—and to be installed, retrospectively, as their original home.

It was in Sidney and his personae that these fictions found their grounding: the peculiar opacity of Astrophil and Philisides—their ability to mediate between insiders and outsiders—provided the writers who would seize on them with a way to reimagine exclusion and affiliation in print. Gavin Alexander has argued that the wave of responses to and imitations of Sidney's writings in the late sixteenth and early seventeenth centuries depended on poets who could claim some genuine acquaintance with him. "Relating to Sidney," he writes, "seemed to require a personal connection."[99] This, at least, was the fiction. Affiliation mattered, but it could be constructed. (It could also be deconstructed: in the midst of the savage pamphlet quarrel that will occupy much of the next chapter, Thomas Nashe mocked Gabriel Harvey for "parret[ing] . . . in print" Sidney's purported favor.)[100] Sidney's third persons, his strange and elusive personae, became a source for the fantasies of affiliation that proliferated around him in the 1590s as much because they were alienating as because they were inviting. To write oneself into Astrophil's and Philisides's world was to insinuate a special kind of literary kinship with Sidney, and hence to stake a joint claim for Sidney's literary distinction and for one's own.

CHAPTER 4

Pierce Penilesse and the Art of Distinctions

Philisides and Astrophil were creatures of distinctions, marked by the imperatives of discrimination and difference. Their appearances probed, and were put to the work of asserting, the differences between restricted and mass production, between elite and popular writing, between manuscript and print, between poet and hack. Distinctions like these were much in demand in the 1590s, as the *Arcadia* and *Astrophil and Stella* rubbed shoulders with a growing pamphlet industry. With the flood of new publications came worries about the stability of old hierarchies. Sidney himself had deplored the "seruile wits" who cared only to be "rewarded of the Printer," blaming them for the disrepute into which he argued poetry had fallen, and others agreed, suggesting that the sheer scale of literary production had made it difficult to tell good books from bad, and that the reading publics to which the marketplace catered had tilted aesthetic taste—and consumer demand—toward the latter.[1] The anathematic grounds of this discourse, of course, reflected the positional struggles that underpinned it: in Bourdieuian terms, debates over literary legitimacy are inextricably bound up with the struggle for symbolic capital in the literary field. We saw in the last chapter how personae were drawn into, and in turn shaped, attempts to delimit that field. This chapter turns to the logic of distinction itself—a logic that the form of the persona both enabled and, in revealing ways, confounded.

Few writers were more forceful in their attacks on the literary field than Thomas Nashe. For Nashe, writing in 1589 as a newcomer to London's literary scene, the indiscriminate appetites of the city's readerships had corroded the mechanisms of literary discrimination. It was an environment, he complained, in which "an Egge that is full, beeing put into water sinketh to the bottome, whereas that which is emptie floateth aboue."[2] The problem of discrimination preoccupied Nashe in the early years of his public career, and it became a central concern of his notorious quarrel with Gabriel Harvey. The quarrel was striking not least in how little the two sides differed on the issues at its heart. Harvey shared Nashe's bleak assessment of the print marketplace, likewise lamenting what he took to be a breakdown of literary distinctions. "Iudgement," Harvey declared in 1593, in a passage that either man could have written, "is the wisest reader of Bookes; and no Art of distinctions, so infallible, as grounded Discretion: which will soone discerne betweene White, and Blacke: and easely perceiue, what wanteth, what superaboundeth; what becommeth, what misbecommeth; what in this, or that respect deserueth commendation; what may reasonably, or probably be excused; what would be marked with an Asteriske, what noted with a blacke coale."[3] Harvey's unfurling oppositions frame reading as practice of careful discernment, coded in terms that combine the moral and the aesthetic. Deciding "what becommeth" and "what misbecommeth" is a project of maintaining the categories one invokes, of protecting a sense that some books deserve praise and some don't—and that there are legitimate criteria that might distinguish them. Maintaining and applying these criteria is a matter of careful reading, and the passage is most revealing in the authority it confers upon the readers whose asterisks and black coals carve out the worthy and unworthy from the texts they read. At stake throughout Nashe's and Harvey's exchanges was the question of what exactly this "Art of distinctions" might look like, and—more importantly—who might possess the "grounded Discretion" necessary to wield it. For while they might agree on the need for such an art, each was bent above all on asserting himself as its legitimate practitioner. Their quarrel thus spun off its own problem of distinction: the question of just what it was that separated the combatants.

It was in and through these nested crises of distinction that Pierce Penilesse, Nashe's eccentric, outrageous alter ego, emerged as a recurring character in the literary world of the 1590s and early 1600s. Begotten in the 1592 pamphlet *Pierce Penilesse His Supplication to the Diuell*, Pierce immediately began to wander. He made his way first into *Kind-Harts Dreame*, the pamphlet (1593) in which Henry Chettle imagined the ghostly return of Robert Greene; in Chettle's text, Pierce found himself the addressee of Greene's letter from the grave. More borrowings came later, in a series of sequels that continued the story begun in Nashe's original: a story in which Pierce, a desperate young writer, writes a supplication (in the form of a moral satire on the seven deadly sins) to the devil. Thomas Middleton's *The Blacke Booke* (1604), the anonymous *The returne of the knight of the poste from Hell* (1606), and Thomas Dekker's *Newes from Hell Brought by the Diuells Carrier* (1606) all featured responses from the devil. And in between was Nashe's quarrel with Harvey, an ongoing controversy that put Pierce front and center—so much so that Harvey's most substantial contribution appeared in 1593 under the title *Pierces Supererogation or A New Prayse of the Old Asse.*

Pierce was thus every bit as mobile and detachable as the personae considered in the foregoing chapters. Like Greene's ghost, like Colin Clout, like Philisides and Astrophil, Pierce's hold on his readers was a function of his peculiar autonomy—of his existence beyond Nashe's, or anyone else's, apparent control. Yet Pierce also bore a distinctively complex relation to Nashe himself. Colin and Philisides could be met as substitutes for Spenser and Sidney; or, rather, as specifications of their literary selves, selves with whom Matthew Roydon, John Dickenson, Michael Drayton, and Barnabe Barnes might claim a poetic affiliation. Pierce troubled this sort of substitution, submitting it to a running, and ambiguously ironic, vein of reflexive play—the complexity of which multiplied as Pierce was himself appropriated and reimagined. It is only in Pierce, that is, that the question of the precise relation between writer and persona, rather than that between persona and reader or rewriter, emerges as central. As we will see in the coda, this shift would prove a significant moment in the later development of the persona, and of its relation to the figure of the author.

The story of Pierce's reception, despite or perhaps because of his multiple incarnations, is one of largely unresolved contradiction. In the words of Nashe's modern biographer, Pierce was "Nashe's *persona*, his public image," and critics have often read Pierce's desperate poverty and literary frustration as reflections of Nashe's own position and attitude.[4] "The very title of *Pierce Penilesse*," wrote G. R. Hibbard a half-century ago, "is both an indication of the straits to which he was reduced and of the spirit in which he faced his difficulties."[5] More recently, Laurie Ellinghausen has described Nashe's pamphlet as "semiautobiographical," observing the parallels between Pierce, the "poor, embittered learned man who makes a bargain with the devil," and Nashe, "the frustrated scholar *cum* writer for pay . . . who is compelled to adjust to a new socioeconomic reality."[6] Yet if Pierce is at times taken as a nearly transparent self-representation, he is just as often read an object of satire—an "ironic exposé," in the words of Jennifer Richards, "of the hypocrisy and financial self-seeking of 'moral' authors," or a parody, in Mike Rodman Jones's account, of moral satire in the Protestant ploughman tradition.[7] The most influential of these ironic readings belongs to Lorna Hutson, who calls Nashe's persona "a bankrupt fool, ingenuously confessing the emptiness of the moralizing posture on which a successful bid for patronage depends."[8] This divergence is a symptom of deeper disagreements about Nashe's place in Elizabethan literary culture: whether he was a fundamentally conservative defender of a moralizing civic humanism or an antagonist of traditional forms of authority, for instance, or whether he was a writer for patronage or commercial profit.[9] These debates have left Pierce in decidedly uncertain territory: a persona who is neither Nashe's public self nor his ironic other, and who is also both at once.

But this ambiguity is hardly the invention of modern readers. On the contrary, the uncertainty of Pierce's relation to Nashe was the central reason for his enduring hold on the imaginations of Nashe's readers and fellow writers. Nashe himself was playfully elusive in his treatment of his persona, pointedly declining either to embrace Pierce as his double or to clarify their difference from each other. In *Haue with You to Saffron-Walden*, his final reply to Harvey, Nashe appears in the guise of "Piers Respondent" while, at the same time, fielding questions from his interlocutors addressed to "Tom" (*TN*, 3:25). Despite the playful tone, however, the distinction between author and persona—or lack thereof—was a matter of some urgency in such a fiercely *ad hominem* controversy. Harvey in particular was bent on determining Pierce's status, whether by insisting that the persona was a mere mask, separable from Nashe himself, or by arguing that Pierce was a vehicle of autobiographical confession. In either case, the question of Pierce's identity became the stalking-horse for a socioliterary attack—an attack on Nashe's stylistic inferiority, on his brash presumption, or on his mercenary relation to print.

The controversy between Nashe and Harvey is by now widely recognized as a contest for authority in the new discursive spaces opened by the growth of the book trade. "At stake for both Harvey and Nashe," writes Alexandra Halasz, who has done more than any other critic to shape this consensus, "is the position of the orator, of oratory, in a discursive field no longer delimited by institutional sites of high literacy and audiences whose rank and status could be predicted."[10] But if rhetoric, with its university pedigree, lies behind this contest, it is itself transformed by its collision with the eccentric pamphlet forms whose popularity Halasz documents—and by the similar uncertainty of its discursive cousin, poetry. Accordingly, I trace the quarrel's stakes to a perceived breakdown of literary categories more broadly: to the oft-asserted loss of hierarchies of prestige and discriminations of merit. Pierce found himself at the heart of the quarrel because he was, from the beginning, a personified act of self-assertion—of position-taking—in the Elizabethan literary field. Through Pierce, Nashe fashioned a position for himself at once within the field in need of regulation and at a critical distance from it. Over the course of the quarrel, however, Pierce came to embody the very crisis of judgment that Nashe bemoaned. If the power to distinguish "what becommeth" from "what misbecommeth"—learning from ignorance, good from bad—rested on the ability to discern more fundamentally "between white and black," then the stubborn ambiguity of Tom-Penniles (as Harvey would call him) argued the futility of any such discriminations. Nashe and Harvey's struggle over the lost art of judgment was thus realized most forcefully in their competing attempts to determine the complex relation between person and persona.

An Undiscerning Judgment

In a prefatory epistle to his theological pamphlet *The Lamb of God*, published in 1589, Richard Harvey—younger brother of Gabriel—paused an invective against Martinist reformers to rebuke "one *Thomas Nash*." Although Nashe had likely written pseudonymous anti-Martinist screeds himself, Harvey accused him of being a version of his enemy: "[He] taketh vppon him in ciuill learning, as *Martin* doth in religion, peremptorily censuring his betters at pleasure, Poets, Orators, Polihistors, Lawyers, and whome not? and making as much and as little of euery man as himself listeth."[11] The jab took aim at a preface that Nashe, in his public debut, had written earlier the same year for Robert Greene's pastoral romance *Menaphon*. Aside from praise for a handful of contemporary writers (Gascoigne, Spenser, Thomas Watson), the preface was a hatchet job, a broadside against the inkhornism, the bombast, the "home borne mediocritie" that Nashe found in his counterparts in print (*TN*, 3:316). For Richard Harvey, the brash newcomer evinced "the rash presumption of this age, that euery man of whatsoeuer qualitie and perfection, is with euery man of whatsoeuer mediocrity, but as euery man pleaseth in the aboundance of his owne swelling sense."[12] It was a criticism that oddly reproduced Nashe's own dismissal of the presumptuous mediocrities of the age—the diagnosis might be correct, Harvey suggested, but Nashe was in no position to make it—and in this respect it foreshadowed the paradoxes of his brother's contributions to the ensuing controversy.[13]

Mediocrity is a theme to which Nashe's early writings obsessively return. Part of the problem, he argued in the preface to *Menaphon*, was the proliferation of "drowping wits" in a growing print marketplace (*TN*, 3:313). He puts the point most bluntly near the beginning of the *The Anatomie of Absurditie*, comparing the "vnlearned Idiots" of print to "she Asses, who bring foorth all their life long; euen so these brainlesse Bussards, are euery quarter bigge wyth one Pamphlet or other" (*TN*, 1:9). Nashe invokes the familiar metaphor of literary procreation in order to debase it, reducing writing to brainless, brutish reproduction. As troubling as the buzzard-writers, however, are readers who "swallow all draffe without difference" ingesting (in the debasing of a familiar metaphor for reading) without the capacity of distinguishing taste (*TN*, 3:313).[14] If taste offered one language for a lost mode of aesthetic discrimination, commodity metal provided another. "So farre discrepant," he writes, "is the idle vsage of our vnexperienced and illiterated Punies from this prescription, that a tale of Ioane of Brainfords will, and the vnlucky frumenty, will be as soone entertained into their Libraries as the best Poëme that euer *Tasso* eternisht: which, being the effect of an vndiscerning iudgment, makes drosse as valuable as gold, and losse as wel-come as gaine" (*TN*, 3:314). Here poetic quality finds its way into an analogy with economic value, an analogy that supplies its own theory of what the consequences of the confusion of true worth might be. To have an "undiscerning judgment," Nashe hints, is to condemn oneself to a kind of cultural poverty, hoarding dross and ignoring gold. The more worrying implication is that the cultural capital of golden learning and wit could simply disappear, that literary commodities might be left without any aesthetic economy (and hence any value) at all.

It is hard to know just how seriously to take these complaints. That Nashe and Richard Harvey could stake out nearly identical positions suggests the convenience of the pose: in attacking the degradations of the print, each could offer himself as the clear-eyed outsider ready to restore order. The pose depended largely on their status as university graduates. Both Harvey and Nashe had taken degrees at Cambridge (the former serving for a time as university praelector in philosophy, before decamping for a rectorship in Kent), and their rhetoric played up the distance between the university and the print marketplace.[15] Nashe's preface to *Menaphon* begins with a salute "to the gentlemen stvdents of both vniversities" and an appeal to their sympathy: "Cvrteous and wise, whose iudgements (not entangled with enuie) enlarge the deserts of the learned by your liberall censures; vouchsafe to welcome your Scholler-like Shepheard with such Vniuersity entertainment as either the nature of your bounty or the custome of your common ciuility may afford" (*TN*, 3:311). The unentangled judgment of these colleagues stands as the horizon of his argument, their "liberall censures" providing the perspective from which the "ideot Art-masters" whom Nashe attacks can be recognized as frauds (*TN*, 3:311). If scholastic authority measures the failures of print, however, it is also constructed through and against them.

And ultimately it is Nashe, more than his readers, who needs this oppositional authority. "Reade fauourably," Nashe urges his colleagues near the end of his preface, and "I will persecute those idiots and their heires vnto the third generation, that haue made Art bankerout of her ornaments, and sent Poetry a begging vp and downe the Countrey" (*TN*, 3:324).

But the opposition between university and print marketplace was largely a fabricated one. Nashe and Greene, so often taken as representative figures of Elizabethan print culture, were representative not least in their possession of Cambridge degrees: university men predominated in published texts across genres—including the bombastic tragedies and the satiric poetry that Nashe singles out for blame in the preface to *Menaphon*. Writers found in print a medium that enabled the wider projection of institutional authority and prestige, circulating sermons (to take one staple of the book trade) written by university-trained preachers and published under the church's imprimatur to growing public readerships. Yet the growth of the book trade did not leave the university, or the church, untouched. Print may have amplified scholastic authority, but in situating the circulation of discourse in an emergent market, as Halasz argues, the publishing industry also eroded its monopoly on intellectual legitimacy.[16]

In declaring a crisis of literary discrimination, Nashe was diagnosing this relocation—a relocation that required new ways of establishing discursive authority and allocating prestige. He was not alone in doing so. Ben Jonson was similarly caustic in *Timber, or Discoveries* (1641), his posthumously published commonplace book. "*Nothing* in our Age," he wrote, "is more preposterous then the running *Iudgements* upon *Poetry*, and *Poets*; when wee shall heare those things commended and cry'd up for the best writings, which a man would scarse vouchsafe, to wrap any wholsome drug in."[17] Among Nashe's contemporaries, William Webbe made the argument most directly. He offered his own critical treatise, *A Discourse of English Poetrie* (1586), as a work "whereby I thinke wee may not onelie get the meanes which wee yet want, to discerne betweene good writers and badde, but perhappes also challenge from the rude multitude of rusticall Rymers, who will be called Poets, the right practise and orderly course of true Poetry."[18] For Webbe, as for Nashe, the circumstances of print publication had destroyed the available mechanisms of intellectual judgment and provided none to replace them. Overrun by the "rude multitude," poets were no longer distinguishable from hacks; what's worse, there were apparently no means of discernment at hand—no "art of distinctions," to recall Gabriel Harvey's phrase, by which the field might be reorganized, divided into the categories of "good" and "bad." And without such an art, Webbe insists, it was impossible to say who ought to "be called Poets," or even—most disturbingly—what the "right practise" of poetry really was.

Nashe's worries echo Webbe's closely, right down to the anxiety about the title of "poet": in the *Anatomie*, he attacks the "babling Ballets" that "obtaine the name of our English Poets, and thereby make men thinke more baselie of the wittes of our Countrey" (*TN*, 1:23–24). But for all their complaints about the difficulty of telling good from bad, Webbe and Nashe seem to have little trouble making such distinctions. On the contrary, their treatises are premised on the same foundational opposition between true poets (or, in its variant form, true scholars) on the one hand and, on the other, the "unlearned idiots" and "rusticall Rymers" who have overrun them in print. If it is tempting to take Nashe and Webbe at their word—to read their treatises as ingenuous accounts of the structural changes in circulation born of print—it is also wise to be cautious. Indeed, Nashe's barbs about "vnlearned idiots" and "bable bookemungers" serve to invent the very print marketplace that he bemoans, an invention that furnishes his critique with an object and provides a foil for the articulation of his own position (*TN*, 1:11). Only once he has fabricated an image of print—once he has conjured it as a space of chaotic disorder in need of regulation—can he then enter it, secured by his gestures of opposition to the public he addresses. It is an invention, or an objectification, that in some ways anticipates modern writing on the history of the book: an early version of the critical reification that is "print culture."

For Nashe, the chaos of print was in large part a function of what he (like many of his peers) described as a decline of patronage. "Beleeue me, Gentlemen," Nashe writes in the opening pages of *Pierce Penilesse*, "ther is not that strict obseruation of honour, which hath beene heeretofore. Men of great calling take it of merite, to haue their names eternizde by Poets; & whatsoeuer pamphlet or dedication encounters them, they put it vp in their sleeues, and scarce giue him thankes that presents it" (*TN*, 1:159).[19] Diminished generosity, Nashe complains, came in tandem with a loss of discrimination, as patrons accepted "whatsoeuer pamphlet" might be dedicated to them without giving real support to anyone. Deprived of the support of patrons, writers were increasingly left to depend on the fees they could earn selling their manuscripts to stationers; and consumers, Nashe was quick to point out, were particularly indiscriminate arbiters of value.[20] Output and novelty, he suggests, were their primary concerns—hence the success of the "brainlesse Bussards" who produced new pamphlets "euery quarter," and the struggles of the finer wits who did not.

Nashe's self-serving account was, unsurprisingly, short of the full picture. In his recent study of early modern patronage, Richard McCabe traces the fruitful interactions of patronage and the market: writers relied on patronal affiliation to counter the taint of commercialism, while a new merchant class (what McCabe calls the "aristocracy of trade") eagerly sought the prestige of patronal status.[21] By emphasizing the disruption of the patronage system, however, Nashe was able to insist that the role of discriminating authority had shifted from patron to writer—where, of course, Nashe himself sat waiting to take it up. In a key passage of the *Anatomie*, he describes the task of discrimination as one incumbent on men of learning in particular: "I trust that there is no man so simple, who can discerne wisedome from folly, and knowledge from ignorance, but his mother wit wil afford him so much vnderstanding, that there is necessary vse of learning in euery calling, bringing praise to them that possesse it, and shame to them that want" (*TN*, 1:38). Here Nashe makes explicit the connection between the pamphlet's general fascination with the practice of making discriminating judgments—wisdom from folly, black from white, dross from gold—and its particular concern with the recovery of a workable model for the articulation of literary and social distinctions.

But the most striking aspect of the passage is its frank circularity: if learning and wit are in need of praise, it is the learned and witty who are tasked with their discernment.[22] In the absence of a robust patronage system, Nashe claims the recognition of intellectual and literary value, and the distribution of the corresponding prestige, as the responsibility of the intellectual class—his fellow university men, now cast as the arbiters of their own worth.[23] Of course, the idea that a shift from patronage to market economy would enfranchise this class flies in the face of Nashe's forcefully argued opposition between hacks and university wits, insiders and critical outsiders. The contradiction was particularly acute in Nashe's preface to Thomas Newman's 1591 first edition of *Astrophil and Stella*, where, even as he mocked print rhymers, he positioned himself as Sidney's conduit into the medium. "Put out your rush candles, you Poets and Rimers," he wrote, "and bequeath your crazed quaterzayns to the Chaundlers; for loe, here he co[m]meth that hath broke[n] your legs" (*TN*, 3:330).[24] Beneath Nashe's fulsome praise for Sidney, as Arthur Marotti argues, is a subtler argument for a reorientation of cultural authority—an argument "that the educated 'Gentlemen' who will buy and read Newman's pamphlet are the real socioliterary center of the culture," and that Nashe was their mediator.[25]

Nashe's ambiguous, contradictory relationship to print publication evinces the strain of competition in London's emerging literary field. In presenting himself as Sidney's fit arbiter, Nashe staked his claim to what Bourdieu calls "the monopoly of literary legitimacy": the power "to say with authority who are authorized to call themselves writers."[26] Bourdieu's insight—that an aesthetic judgment is always also a social assertion, a bid for the authority to say who is and is not a legitimate writer—should have a familiar ring, for William Webbe had made much the same point. To discern "betweene good writers and badde," in Webbe's account, was implicitly to answer the question of who could properly "be called Poets"—indeed it was to police the definition of literature, to say what "the right practise . . . of true Poetry" truly was. In this sense, Nashe's fight for critical distinctions was a form of self-assertive position-taking. And as Richard Harvey's rebuke of Nashe for "censuring his betters" makes clear, self-assertions like this one were invariably contested: one person's legitimate authority was another's pretension. Like so much else in the Elizabethan literary field, Nashe's own position was a matter in need of discerning judgment.

Taking Positions

Pierce Penilesse His Supplication to the Diuell begins on familiar territory. "Learning," Nashe writes early in the pamphlet, "is rated after the value of the inke and paper: and a Scriuener better paid for an obligation, than a Scholler for the best Poeme he can make; [and] euery grosse braind Idiot is suffered to come into print, who if hee set foorth a Pamphlet of the praise of Pudding-pricks, or write a Treatise of *Tom Thumme*, or the exployts of *Vntrusse*; it is bought vp thicke and threefold, when better things lie dead" (*TN*, 1:158–

59). Here is perhaps Nashe's tidiest summary of Elizabethan print culture, an account of a world that suffers fools and flattens rightful hierarchies and rewards no one. In begetting Pierce, Nashe gave these concerns—and the positional struggle they encoded—a local habitation and a name. He had staked his public image on a particular idea of the print marketplace; now he brought it to life.

Pierce was born, Nashe explains, of the dearth of patronage awaiting young scholars. In the pamphlet's opening pages, the narrator vainly seeks support for his "vulgar Muse" and slides, "in prime of my best wit," into poverty (*TN*, 1:157). At last he catches wind of "a certaine blind Retayler called the Diuell"—"a greedy pursuer of newse," we are told, and "and so famous a Politician in purchasing, that Hel (which at the beginning was but an obscure Village) is now become a huge Cittie, whereunto all countries are tributary" (*TN*, 1:161). Nashe's narrator wastes no time: "These manifest coniectures of Plentie, assembled in one common-place of abilitie, I determined to clawe Auarice by the elbowe, till his full belly gaue mee a full hande, and lette him bloud with my penne (if it might be) in the veyne of liberalitie: and so (in short time) was this Paper-monster, *Pierce Penilesse*, begotten" (*TN*, 1:161). Nashe's devil is an odd blend of patron and publisher, at once a "priuy Benefactor" and a blind retailer whose buying and selling have made Hell a city as bustling as London. In some respects, the devil resembles the book-buying readers whom the retailers of print served: like them, he has a voracious appetite for news, and, like them, he is frustratingly elusive—invisible despite being omnipresent.[27]

This reading public, moreover, could be reached only thanks to the interventions of publishers and printers and booksellers; so too the devil is accessible to Nashe's narrator only through a mediating agent. After a search that takes him to the Westminster law courts, then across town to the Royal Exchange, he goes home defeated: "I . . . like a carelesse malcontent, that knew not which way to turne, retired me to Paules, to seeke my dinner with Duke *Humfrey*" (*TN*, 1:163). Duke Humphrey's tomb, R.B. McKerrow notes, was "a common rendezvous of gallants and . . . of persons who went in fear of arrest for debts," because of its location on the cathedral's land provided immunity.[28] But Paul's churchyard was also the center of the book trade, and it is here that Pierce finally finds the devil's Knight of the Post. The proffering of the book to the devil's agent is thus enacted as a kind of sale, conducted via a middleman and carried out in sight of the booksellers' stalls.

Like the devil, who is both patron and purchaser, Pierce plays two roles at once: while "Pierce" refers to the desperate writer who addresses the devil, it also names the supplication that he writes. Pierce is both author and text, person and commodity—an ambiguity compounded in early editions that tend to render both the book title and personal name in italics. It is this odd doubleness that Nashe's account of Pierce's conception crystallizes, combining material object and prodigious organism in the phrase "Paper-monster." Both text and person, Pierce lives within the processes of print dissemination, with sexual reproduction emerging, in Melissa Hull Geil's reading, as a metaphor for the mass production of books.[29] He is thus a figure in whom the calculated distance of the *Anatomie* seems to drop away. Nashe may have begun his career by attacking a reification of print culture, but in offering Pierce as a surrogate he takes a seemingly different tack, adopting the guise of a writer so deeply absorbed into the economy of print as to become one of its vendible commodities. In this sense, Pierce marks an acknowledgment of the paradoxical status of Nashe's gestures of opposition, which always reflected his implication in the marketplace he decried.

Yet it is not at all clear that Nashe ought to be identified with Pierce, a character whose identity is always elusive. Pierce's name links him to the descendants of Piers Plowman—and thus to a tradition of popular, corporate identity—but perhaps, as Mike Rodman Jones argues, only to invert it, ironically turning a "stern Protestant figure," and a Marprelate avatar, "into an embittered, bad-tempered wit."[30] His surname is no simpler: so oddly generic, in fact, that it might apply to any of London's almost invariably (so Nashe implies) poor young writers and thus one that can slip away from Nashe even as he coins it. Pierce's slide from significance befits a name that, as David Landreth observes, plays with barrenness, with the pennilessness of an empty "purse." "This marginality of matter reduced to the threshold of nonexistence—to being as little as possible—is," Landreth argues, "the condition of Pierce's demoniac persona."[31] It is his status as a cipher, reflecting versions of his readers while eluding their attempts to pin him down, that allow him, for David J. Baker, to commodify early modern anticonsumerism and, in the process, to expose his audience to the contradictions of their own desires.[32]

Pierce's defining emptiness may be why attempts to pin down his relation to Nashe seem doomed to fail. To read Pierce as Nashe's mouthpiece is to risk missing the irony that so often suffuses the moral tract that Pierce gives to the Knight of the Post; on the other hand, to take him, with Jonathan Crewe, as a case of Nashe "playing the fool" is to ignore his bouts of vehement earnestness.[33] For Hutson, Nashe's satire runs into trouble in those moments when he slips out of character—which is to say, when he allows his own voice to blur with Pierce's. If Nashe is "occasionally in earnest," Hutson writes, such moments point to an "inconsistency within Nashe's own conception."[34] But it is more likely that these inconsistencies are not slips at all. Rather, they are instances of the strategic indeterminacy that characterizes Pierce from the moment of his begetting. As Georgia Brown suggests, in a reading that gets at the fluidity and unpredictability of Nashe's self-presentation, Pierce's appearances function as "an endless game of partial veiling and unveiling" that reveals Nashe even as it withholds him.[35] Not simply insider nor outsider, pamphlet nor person, Nashe nor anti-Nashe, Pierce's rhetorical value lies in his ability to be both terms at once.

The effects of Pierce's congenital ambiguity are felt most powerfully in the defense of poetry that, for several pages, overtakes his supplication's account of wrath. Pierce's response to "the enemies of Poetrie" begins on a familiar Nashean note: their failing, he observes, is their inability to distinguish good writing from bad. "Those are they," Pierce declares, "that tearme our best Writers but babbling Ballat-makers, holding them fantasticall fooles that haue wit, but cannot tell how to use it" (*TN*, 1:192). In the lines that follow, Pierce singles out one group of antagonists for particular opprobrium: the preachers whose sermons occupied the same shelves in the bookstalls as sonnets and romances, indeed dominating the speculative market for printed texts.[36] The sense of rivalry is inescapable in Pierce's rebuke: "Should we (as you) borrowe all out of others, and gather nothing of our selues, our names should bee baffuld on euerie Booke-sellers Stall, and not a Chandlers Mustard-pot but would wipe his mouthe with our wast paper. Newe herrings, new, wee must crye, euery time wee make our selues publique, or else we shall bee christened with a hundred newe tytles of Idiotisme" (*TN*, 1:192). Pierce's first-person plural pronouns here ground a performance of solidarity that is, in a sense, the polemical fruit of his cultivation of the role of insider. The opposition between *you* and *we* hardens the distinction between the two professions; or, more accurately, it insists by opposition that poetry *is* a profession comparable to divinity. This coalition of writers is held together by their shared subjection to a consuming public that demands the constant production of novelty. In the *Anatomie*, Nashe had sneered at the "vnlearned idiots" of the print market. Now, by contrast, "Idiotisme" is a label that threatens all writers, Pierce included; and it is a label, he suggests with a newfound generosity, that is unfair to all of them. The breadth of Pierce's *we*, in fact, depends on his refusal to make certain distinctions: all writers, regardless of genre or status, are subject to the whims of the market, which demands new herrings even from old arts.

It is in the shadow of this surprising statement of professional allegiance that Pierce sets his positive statement of poetry's virtues: that it has led the English to "aspire to a richer puritie of speech," that it inspires soldiers, that it celebrates virtue and chastens sinners (*TN*, 1:193). If this is a rather bland platform, that is because Pierce seems less concerned with defining poetry than with policing the profession's borders. Hence his attention to discourses that border on and compete with literary writing—first sermonizers and then, in a passage that follows soon after, the "lay Chronigraphers, that write of nothing but Mayors and Sheriefs, and the deare yere, and the great Frost," whose traffic in almanacs and local histories leads Pierce to draw another opposition. It is not these "chronigraphers," he writes, "that can endowe your names with neuer dated glory: for they want the wings of choise words to fly to heauen, which we haue: they cannot sweeten a discourse, or wrest admiration from men reading, as we can, reporting the meanest accident. Poetry is the hunny of all flowers, the quintessence of all Sciences, the Marrowe of Witte, and the very Phrase of Angels" (*TN*, 1:194). This last sentence, the closest Pierce comes to an intrinsic definition of poetry, is the culmination of an argument made by extrinsic negation—an argument constituted by the distinctions, drawn with other discourses, that identify poetry's specific boundaries. The force of these distinctions rests in Pierce's presentation of himself as a consummate insider, a partisan concerned above all to define and protect the place of imaginative writing in the wider field of print.[37] Once again, Pierce's map of English letters is governed by its pronouns—by the continual tension between what "they want" and what "we have."

Yet the professional unity that these pages evoke does not last long. Perhaps inevitably, Pierce's need to draw distinctions soon turns inward, to those writers whose claims to the title of poet are finally revealed to be illegitimate: "Alas poore latinlesse Authors, they are so simple they know not what they doe; They no sooner spy a new Ballad, and his name to it that compilde it: but they put him in for one of the learned men of our time" (*TN*, 1:194). Here, as the third person forcibly displaces the first, the hierarchical discriminations that Pierce has held at bay rush back in—the distinctions drawn around Latinity, the slurs against ballads and cheap print. In one sense, the development reveals Pierce's performance of solidarity to be a charade: here, at last, is what he truly thinks of his fellow writers. On the other hand, his foregoing defense of print writers was arguably never as generous as it seemed. For Bourdieu, any attempt to articulate a definition of poetry, or of the writer, is an attempt to claim authority for oneself: "There is no universal definition of the writer, and analysis never encounters anything but definitions corresponding to a state of the struggle for the imposition of the legitimate definition of writer."[38] In these terms, Pierce's defense of poetry—even at its most collegial—is a fundamentally competitive move, an attempt to lay hold of the criteria by which poets should be defined and evaluated as his own. It should be no surprise, then, that the sense of struggle would eventually come to the fore, or that in the process Nashe would come as close as he ever does to removing his mask. In a passage that immediately follows Pierce's discussion of poetry, Nashe launches into a scalding attack on Richard Harvey, who "hath named me expressely in Print . . . and accused me of want of learning" (*TN*, 1:195). The oppositional discourse that courses through Pierce's defense of poetry here takes its most honest form, that of open confrontation between individuals.[39]

For Nashe, Pierce's tactical value lay in his indeterminacy. As a creature of the print market, Pierce claimed the standing of an insider, of someone who might legitimately speak for London's unfairly maligned (and impoverished) poets. At the same time, the ironic distance that periodically intervenes between writer and persona affords Nashe the role of outsider, of critical onlooker. Pierce's indeterminacy is, from this perspective, the indeterminacy of the literary field itself, a field that flickers into being—conjured by Pierce's forceful first-person plural—as often Nashe needs it to. If Pierce's pennilessness makes clear just how urgently and materially interested he is in the status of poetry, his teasing emptiness conversely elicits a paradoxical sense of absence, and hence disinterest, framing him as a nobody offering a view from nowhere. The latter may enable the critical judgment that Nashe is concerned to exercise, but it is the former that allows that judgment to situate itself within the discourse of literary legitimacy—precisely unlike those divines who, because they cannot recognize poetry's specific value, blindly condemn *all* poets. Nashe's discourse of literary distinction requires Pierce's peculiar blend of proximity and distance, implication and remove.

And there should be no doubt that such a discourse is what Pierce (or Nashe) is after. It is telling that the attack on poetry's critics occurs in the midst of Pierce's account of wrath, for wrath is a sin, as he explains, that "respecteth no degrees nor persons, but is equally armed agaynst all that offende him" (*TN*, 1:187). By contrast, it is in the section on pride—a vice obsessed with degrees—that Pierce finds a solution to poetry's woes. His surprising conclusion is that pride is not necessarily a bad thing: in Denmark, he observes, the lack of mechanisms for social advancement means that there is no incentive for soldiers to demonstrate their worth.[40] The consequence—"a discontented idlenesse" for those without prospects (*TN*, 1:179)—might evoke Pierce's own plight, and in fact the discourse promptly turns to cultural production: "So in Armes, so in Artes; if titles of fame and glory be proposed to forward minds, or that soueraigntie (whose sweetnes they haue not yet felt) be set in likely view for them to sore too, they will make a ladder of cord of the links of their braines, but they will fasten their handes, as wel as their eies, on the imaginatiue blisse which they already enioy by admiration" (*TN*, 1:180). The problem, as Nashe had explained in his epistle to the printer, is that no such titles—much less the financial benefits they might carry—were forthcoming in a world where learning "is rated after the value of the inke and paper." No wonder, in such a world, that frivolous pamphlets proliferate "when better things lie dead" (*TN*, 1:158–59). Only once good writing is materially distinguished from bad might the pride of "forward minds" produce the kind of poetry that would be a true credit to England.

Pierce himself is a parable of what happens when forward minds fall into idleness, and it is never fully clear whether he is a gifted wit denied opportunity or a writer whose abjection is more or less deserved. Consider this ambiguous glimpse of self-evaluation, offered immediately after his scorning of cheap balladeers and the undiscerning readers who praise them. Having ridiculed the inability of his peers to recognize true wit and learning, Pierce demurs on the subject of his own ability—"For my part," he writes, "I do challenge no praise of learning to my selfe"—only to offer a bit of Latin that seems designed to solicit precisely such praise: "yet haue I worne a gowne in the Vniuersitie, and so hath *caret tempus non habet moribus*." And then, suddenly, he is nakedly boasting: "But this I dare presume, that, if any *Mecænas* binde me to him by his bounty, or extend some round liberalitie to mee worth the speaking of, I will doo him as much honour as any Poet of my beardlesse yeeres shall in *England*" (*TN*, 1:195). The quick turn from humility to arrogance is typical of Pierce, whose rhetorical register can flip back and forth from word to word. Indeed, even Pierce's bragging cannot help undermining itself. His profession of poetic ability, for one thing, comes off as troublingly mercenary—in the next breath, he promises, less nobly, to rail against anyone who denies him support. But the giveaway is Pierce's ostentatious Latin, which turns out, on closer inspection, to be gibberish, a bit of early modern *lorem ipsum*.[41] Having disparaged "poore latinlesse Authors," Pierce turns out to be one himself.

The unraveling contradictions of this self-description are the stuff of which Pierce is made. He is always an unsorted mixture of sincerity and irony, wit and folly, Pierce and Nashe. In the passage above, Nashe's presence is barely concealed—it is of course his university degree to which Pierce refers. Yet Nashe's coming out from the shadows, far from clarifying the register of Pierce's rhetoric, further confuses it, for it submits Nashe's comparatively prestigious biography to the same play of irony as Pierce's penniless desperation. It is because the two are never fully separable that Pierce's performance as a creature of the print market, a paper-monster born from a pamphlet, is so persuasive: nothing in the pamphlet is as full-throated as its defense of writers against the critics of poetry. On the other hand, the skeptical irony that always follows Pierce is a function of their never being fully identifiable with each other. If Pierce is in the first place an emblem of the literary field in print, he thus also stands as a figure of oppositional difference. An earnest insider and a critical outsider, Pierce articulates a principle of legitimacy that seems at once to inhere within the print marketplace and to derive from beyond it.

But this ambiguity also rendered Pierce an embodiment of the confusion he lamented. For all of his confident discriminations—the separation of poets from divines and "chronigraphers," of *true* poets from Latin-less authors—Pierce's discerning judgment founders on the subject of his own person. The relation between Nashe and Pierce, that is to say, emerges in Nashe's text as a boundary point where the cultivation of a distinguishing critical judgment fails—as a figure, indeed, who unsettles the very idea of stable judgment. Nashe's persona was for this reason a standing provocation, tempting readers into making distinctions—between poet and hack, or author and persona—that would inevitably be misinterpretations. Such a temptation, of course, served to reinforce the position of authority to which Pierce had surreptitiously laid claim: in baiting misreadings, Pierce could contrive to leave Nashe alone in the know. The joke was, in this sense, on the reader. Near the end of the book, Nashe finally sets aside his persona and speaks in his own voice.[42] He addresses his alter ego directly: "Now, *Pierce peniles*, if for a parting blow thou hast ere a tricke in thy budget more then ordinarie, bee not daintie of it, for a good Patron will pay for all." For a moment, the speech seems to promise clarification; here, perhaps, Pierce might be found out, his relation to Nashe finally resolved. Instead, it turns out to be a final misdirection. "I," Nashe playfully exclaims, "where is he?" (*TN*, 1:241). It is only an accident of typography that gives Nashe's exclamation the appearance of a personal pronoun. But the result is a fortuitous allegory of Nashe's relation to his persona: *he* is nearly reduced to *I*, only to escape, at the last moment, back into ambiguity.

With Critique Pen

When Robert Greene's ghost appeared in Henry Chettle's *Kind-Harts Dreame*, he came bearing a message for Pierce Penilesse, an account of the attacks that had surfaced after his death. "In my graue was I scarse layde," he reports, "when Enuie (no fit companion for Art) spit out her poyson, to disturbe my rest."[43] Pierce, Greene's ghost observes, had suffered as well: "Now, in the blooming of thy hopes, thou sufferest slaunder to nippe them ere they can bud."[44] The wrongs to which Greene's ghost refers are left vague, but it is not hard to guess their source. Months or perhaps weeks earlier, Gabriel Harvey had published his own pamphlet, *Foure Letters, and Certaine Sonnets*, attacking in its pages both the recently deceased Greene and the lately arrived Thomas Nashe—in the latter case, springing to the defense of his brother Richard.[45] In doing so, he had unsuspectingly written himself into the widening story of Greene's and Nashe's personae, a story that turned Pierce into a character whose domain extended beyond the pages of Nashe's original text. The quarrel between Nashe and Harvey was in this sense an especially tense example of the collaborative rewritings that sustained so many Elizabethan personae. Like Greene's ghost, Pierce provoked a distinctive (if a very different) style of reading: a bewildering compound of naked *ad hominem* railing and the critical "art of distinctions" that Harvey so dearly prized.

Foure Letters began the quarrel in earnest, and Nashe responded quickly with *Strange Newes*, alternately titled *The Apologie of Pierce Pennylesse*.[46] Possibly regretting the intensified hostilities, Nashe then offered an apology and an overture for peace in the preface to his next long work, *Christes Teares ouer Jerusalem* (1593). By the time the apology reached Harvey, however, his latest attacks—*A New Letter of Notable Contents* (1593) and the long, eccentric *Pierces Supererogation* (1593)—were already at press, and Nashe responded by removing the apology in later editions of *Christes Teares*. Georgia Brown is one of many to suspect the interference of John Wolfe, Harvey's printer, who would have had every incentive to publish the *New Letter* early in order to capitalize on the controversy.[47] Three years would pass before Nashe had his final say in the debate in the pamphlet *Haue with You to Saffron-Walden* (1596), deliciously subtitled *Gabriel Harueys Hunt Is Vp*. Having ground to a halt thereafter, the quarrel was ended by fiat in 1599, when John Whitgift and Richard Bancroft, respectively the Archbishop of Canterbury and the Bishop of London, prohibited the publication of a list of books, mostly satires, that included "all nasshes bookes and D Harvyes bookes," ordering as well that existing copies be burnt.[48]

The quarrel is, if nothing else, a striking artifact of literary criticism. Its invectives were carried out on largely stylistic grounds, in increasingly pointed barbs about inkhorn novelty and scholastic pedantry. Nashe, in a representative insult, mocked the "misbegotten bodgery" of Harvey's "Hermaphrodite phrases" (*TN*, 1:265). Harvey, for his part, castigated his opponent's "vnsauory slaumpaump of words."[49] Like Nashe, Harvey was interested in regulating the disorderly, often disreputable literary productions of English print writers, of whose "monstrous newfanglednesse" Greene and Nashe were the primary exhibits. "The world is full inough of fooleries," he wrote of Greene's romances in *Foure Letters*, "though the humor be not feasted with such luxurious, and riotous Pamphlets."[50] And like Nashe, Harvey was concerned to distance himself from the abuses he documented. He deplored, with an irony that increased with each insult, the age's "Spirit of Contradiction," and he took care to strike a pose of scholarly detachment (*FL*, sig. E_3^r). In the commendatory sonnet that closes the text, Edmund Spenser praises Harvey as "a Looker-on / Of this worldes Stage" who notes "with critique pen / The sharpe dislikes of each condition" (*FL*, sig. K_2^r).

Indeed, Harvey had much in common with his antagonist, another writer bent on imposing order on a recalcitrant literary field. Both were from modest, though not poor, families. Both were graduates of Cambridge; Harvey, several years older, had taken his master of arts degree and, despite failing in his candidacy for the position of university orator, remained "one of the most noteworthy and most widely known of the members of his University."[51] They shared, in other words, what Bourdieu calls a disposition—the complex of class background, education, and socialization that shapes an individual *habitus*—and their particular criticisms of the literary field in many ways reflected their similarity.[52] Both disdained the ballads and news broadsides that constituted the lower end of the print market; both revered Sidney and Spenser; both insisted on the need for stronger mechanisms of aesthetic discrimination, for a more parsimonious definition of poetry.[53] To the extent that their enmity evinces the narcissism of small differences, it was typical of struggles for authority in the literary field. We should read their battle, then, not as the "conflict of principles"[54] that has often been sought in a seemingly empty quarrel, but rather as conflict of positions—as a contest over the position of orator in print, as Halasz argues, or over the "status of professional authorship" at a moment of incipient professionalization, as Brown maintains; or, as I suggest, over the monopoly of literary legitimacy.[55]

Pierce Penilesse was implicated in this struggle in more than one way. In the first place, he was an embodiment of the position that Nashe sought to claim, indeed a performance of position-taking, and as such he was bound to become a point of contention. More subtly, because he was neither simply identical with Nashe nor safely distinct from him, Pierce became a test case for the discriminating judgment that Harvey hoped to cultivate. Harvey's pamphlets circle back to Pierce again and again, bestowing on him the kind of verbal inventiveness more often associated with Nashe: "Better a man without money, then money without a man," he writes in *Foure Letters*, "Pennilesse is not his purse but his minde: not his reuenue, but his resolution" (*FL*, sig. E_1^r). The force of the line lies in the witty distinctions that allow Harvey, with arch moral disapproval, to put Pierce in his place.

The evident relish with which he draws such distinctions is a reminder of Harvey's predilection for Ramist method, a revision of the *trivium* that swept through Cambridge in the 1580s.[56] Ramist dialectic was an art of careful division and subdivision, of distinctions between classes and kinds: its characteristic form is the bifurcating tree, branching from universal categories through particular genera to the multiplicity of individual species. Harvey's "art of distinctions" is animated by the same dichotomizing impulse: to separate "what becommeth" from "what misbecommeth," black from white, Pierce's purse from Pierce's mind. Reading in these terms is a matter of careful selection, and of constant vigilance to one's own categories, categories threatened acutely by Nashe's antic, chaotic prose.[57] For Harvey, mastery over Nashe and Pierce required a program of discipline-by-discrimination, of the sort of careful interpretation that might force writer and persona into clarifying shape.

The impulse to submit Pierce to this discrimination is realized most powerfully in the lists and genealogies that proliferate in Harvey's pamphlets. Harvey introduces Pierce with an insult by association, calling him the "sworne brother" of Robert Greene, and he is immediately used to ground what becomes, in Harvey's fertile imagination, a monstrous literary family caught between fiction and reality: "Alas," Harvey writes, "he is pitifully bestead, that . . . is constrained to make woefull *Greene*, and beggarly *Pierce Pennylesse*, (as it were a Grasshopper, and a Cricket, two pretty musitians, but silly creatures) the argumente of his stile" (*FL*, sig. G_2^r). It is Pierce's standing as a fully textual creature—albeit one of uncanny vitality—that leads Harvey into the aesthetic arguments of style, and it is his status as a derived version of Nashe himself that spurs Harvey's concern with imitation and originality, likeness and difference. Perhaps because they manifest the portability of authorial style, personae typically ground Harvey's rosters of literary affiliation. In *Pierces Supererogation*, for instance, a mention of the "Braggadocio" who "truly intitle himselfe, Pierce Penniles" sets off a list of imitators—"Nash, the Ape of Greene, Greene the Ape of Euphues, Euphues the Ape of Enuie, the three famous mammets of the presse"—that moves from persona to proper name and back again (*PS*, sigs. S_3^v–S_4^r). We have already encountered the most fascinating of Harvey's genealogies: the garden of English letters in which Sidney and Spenser "budd" as flowers of art and witt, "till the one begane to sprowte in M. Robart Greene, as in a sweating Impe of the euer-greene Laurell; the other to blossome in M. Pierce Pennilesse, as in the riche garden of pore Adonis: both to growe to perfection, in M. Thomas Nashe" (*PS*, sig. C_1^r). The striking inversion of Pierce and Nashe, with the latter springing from the former, evokes the monstrous confusion wrought by Greene, Nashe, and their ilk—a company of weeds, Harvey suggests, that thrive in the chaotic disruption of literary order.

Harvey's genealogies conjure the literary field as a system of monstrous resemblances, of likeness uncannily reproduced from one writer (or persona) to the next. If that reproduction is a function of slavish imitation, it is paradoxically coded in the terms of prodigious biology—of grasshoppers and sprouting flowers. This may be why Nashe appears as Pierce's offspring: he has begun to leech his persona's irreducible indeterminacy, emerging in Harvey's account as a figure at once derivative and "singular," unoriginal and disturbingly newfangled.[58] Genealogy is a way of conceiving of likeness for Harvey, but it is also a way of asserting difference. At the end of his description of the garden of letters, Harvey remarks that Roger Ascham, Sidney, and Spenser had "a kind of smooth, and clenly, and neate, and fine elegancy," but "nothinge liuelie, and mightie, like the braue *vino de monte*"; such vitality awaited Nashe, whose "frisking penne began to playe the Sprite of the buttry, and to teach his mother-tongue such lusty gambolds, as may make the gallantest French, Italian, or Spanish gagliards to blushe, for extreame shame of their ideot simplicitie" (*PS*, sig. C_1^r). Harvey's valorization of Nashe is, needless to say, ironic: the understatement of Sidney's and Spenser's "elegancy" is set against the comic exaggeration of Harvey's mocking praise of Nashe, praise that he delivers in a parodic imitation of the latter's frantic prose. But parody is a risky business. For Harvey, the danger is that the force of imitation and resemblance might overtake his argument of aesthetic distinction. Mocking his opponent's style by reproducing it, he risks rendering himself the Ape of Nashe—the latest member of his own parade of fools. At some level, Harvey may have realized this himself: the "troubling yet pleasurable flourishes" of his railing, suggests Maria Micaela Teresa Prendergast, can be read as disclosing an eroticized recognition of likeness.[59]

The point is not simply that Harvey had much more in common with his opponent than he was willing to admit, though this was surely true. Rather, it is that Harvey's fascination with Pierce Penilesse—and by extension, his interest in drawing genealogies and countergenealogies of the literary field—was a symptom of his desire to distinguish himself from an opponent whom he in many ways resembled. In the literary garden, the distinguishing of author from persona is a game played against our recognition of their equivalence, a way of discovering difference out of likeness. Later in *Pierces Supererogation*, Harvey takes the act of division and distinction a step further, dividing Pierce, Penilesse, and Nashe into discrete grammatical entities: "Pierce, the hoggeshed of witt: Penniles, the tospot of eloquence: & Nashe, the verye inuentor of Asses" (*PS*, sig. F_4^r). Here the recognition of identity (Pierce is Penniles, and both are in some sense Nashe) grounds a performance of discrimination, the parceling out of a single literary style into the discrete categories of wit, eloquence, and invention. The line reveals Harvey to be, as Gerard Passannante describes him in another context, "that rarest of things: a Ramist with a sense of humor."[60] Its euphuistic excess—quite unlike the plain style often associated with English Ramism—discloses the satisfactions of methodical play in its witty production of difference.

Such differentiation turns out to be Harvey's strategy more generally in *Foure Letters*. Although that pamphlet begins by using Pierce's unscrupulous desperation to discredit Nashe, conflating author with persona, Harvey soon moves to distinguish them—reading Pierce, in Stephen Hilliard's paraphrase, as "a disreputable persona adopted by the proper young man Nashe because of Greene's bad example."[61] "It was not thy person, that I any-way disliked," Harvey avers, "but thy rash, and desperate proceeding against thy well-willers" (*PS*, sig. G_1^r). These were sins that he was willing to forgive, confirming the reversal by omitting Pierce from another of his lists, a roster of the "professed Sonnes" of the Muses, "*Edmond Spencer, Richard Stanihurst, Abraham France, Thomas Watson, Samuell Daniell, Thomas Nash*, and the rest: whome I affectionately thancke for their studious endeuours, commendably employed in enriching, & polishing their natiue Tongue, neuer so furnished, or embellished as of late" (*FL*, sig. F_4^v). In order to find his way into this special company, Harvey implies, Nashe must first put away the childish rashness of his erstwhile persona; by rejecting one line of literary affiliation, he might be admitted into another. The gesture is an attempt, albeit a patronizing one, to restore the collegiality that ought to obtain between two men with so much in common. It is the closest Harvey comes to recognizing his own image in Nashe. Yet in salvaging Nashe's better self, Harvey also paradoxically finds a way to insist on his difference from his opponent: to separate Pierce from Nashe, after all, is to draw precisely the kind of distinction that Harvey wants to assert between Nashe and himself—a distinction between the poet and the print hack, the scholar and the manic neologizer, the public-minded intellectual and the specialist in private grievance.

For his part, Nashe was unwilling to accept such a condescending overture—and eager to point out the similarities that Harvey was at pains to banish. In *Strange Newes*, his immediate reply to *Foure Letters*, Nashe impishly declares that the "Deuils Oratorship, which he ascribeth to *Pierce Pennilesse*, me thinks had beene a fit place for his Doctorship," a quip that pokes fun at Harvey's failed bid for the position of university orator at Cambridge (*TN*, 1:268).[62] Later, in revisiting the origin story of Pierce's supplication, Nashe adds a new twist. When Pierce brought his foul papers to Paul's Church, Nashe explains in *Strange Newes*, it was "the Ape Gabriel" (a telling reciprocation of Harvey's earlier insult) who took them up and "made mops and mows at them beslauering the outside of them a little" (*TN*, 1:306). Replacing the Knight of the Post, Harvey emerges—in a representation that must have enraged him—as, like Pierce, a natural denizen of the grubby center of bookselling London. Indeed, Nashe casts him as at once the most voracious and the most idiotic consumer of cheap print. Slobbering on the manuscript, Nashe writes, Harvey "coulde not enter into the contents, which was an ase beyond his vnderstanding" (*TN*, 1:306). Against Harvey's attempt to distinguish Nashe from Pierce, Nashe responds with the clever suggestion that there was very little to separate Pierce and Harvey. They were equally creatures of the pamphlet market.

Pierce thus provided a mirror for both of the quarrel's participants, an image of the role of writer either to cleave to or reject. In part, this had to do with Pierce's ability to connect the particulars of style to the competition for literary legitimacy: if Nashe's persona was an emblematic case of the writer in print, he was equally an embodiment (at least in Harvey's eyes) of Nashe's monstrous, newfangled prose. Engagement in the controversy accordingly left one doubly at risk of becoming like Pierce, either by falling into the overheated language of invective or by laying bare one's ambition. For Harvey, these were symptoms of excess, of superfluous, wasted intellectual energy. In a key passage from his next pamphlet, he suggests that Pierce was the concrete form of such "supererogation":[63] "Well, my maisters, you may talke your pleasures of Tom Nash; who yet sleepeth secure, not without preiudice to some, that might be more ielous of their name: but assure your selues, if M. Penniles had not bene deepely plunged in a profound state of extasie of knauery, M. Pierce had neuer written that famous worke of Supererogation, that now stayneth all the bookes in Paules-churchyard and setteth both the universities to schoole" (*PS*, sig. D_1^v). It is the act of writing such works, Harvey suggests, that transforms "Nash" inexorably into "Pierce." The implication for his own situation lingers uneasily in the background. By this point, Nashe was not the only writer to have polemics littering Paul's churchyard. Becoming Pierce, moreover, now seemed a worryingly permanent metamorphosis: "Nashe," Harvey wrote some pages later, "wil carrie a tache of Pierce to his graue" (*PS*, sig. E_4^r). Perhaps it was anxiety about the "tache" that Harvey was earning for himself that precipitated his change of strategy in *Pierces Supererogation*: where before he had granted a difference between Pierce and Nashe, Harvey now sought to bind Nashe to the persona whom he enigmatically termed Nashe's "mothers sonne" (*PS*, sig. V_4^v).

Harvey's new insistence on the inextricable entwinement of "Tom-Penniless" implied the retraction of his earlier praise of "Thomas Nashe," whom he no longer admitted into the heady poetic company of Sidney and Spenser (*PS*, sig. I_3^r). The idea of Nashe's literary excellence, indeed, is one that Harvey quietly disowns, attributing it instead to Nashe's own pretensions:

> He disdaineth Thomas Delone, Philip Stubs, Robert Armin, and the common Pamfletters of London, eue[n] the painfullest Chroniclers tooe; bicause they stand in his way, hinder his scribling traffique, obscure his resplendishing Fame, or haue not Chronicled him in their Catalogues of the renowned moderne Autors, as he meritoriously meriteth, and may peraduenture be remembred hereafter. But may not Thomas Delone, Philip Stubs, Robert Armin, and the rest of those misused persons, more disdainfully disdaine him; bicause he is so much vayner, so little learneder, so nothing eleganter, then they; and they so much honester, so little obscurer, so nothing contemptibler, then he? (*PS*, sigs. Aa_1^r–Aa_1^v)

A year earlier, Harvey had "chronicled" Nashe in his own catalogue of renowned authors, but here he pointedly refuses to grant any distinction between Nashe and "the common Pamfletters of London." His list of negated comparisons—"so little learneder, so nothing eleganter"—systematically denies Nashe's every claim to special wit or eloquence, allowing him to be exceptional only in his vanity.

In supposing himself worthy of better company, Nashe reveals himself to be not only vain but also a poor arbiter of his true worth, arrogating (a pun that is surely at work in Harvey's attacks on Pierce's "supererogation") a position that is not properly his. Hence Harvey's jabs at the self-interestedness of Nashe's fixation on literary judgment—the accusations that "singular Penniles" wished to be "Preferrer of his owne Vertue, or Iudge of his owne cause" (*PS*, sig. V_3^v). In such lines, Harvey identifies Pierce as directly as possible as a strategy of position-taking, a figure of self-advancement disguising itself as a vehicle of judgment and discernment. The effect is to strip Nashe of the doubled insider-outsider position that he had attempted to establish through Pierce. Harvey allows him only the claims of the insider, of the writer "thrise-affectionatly bounden to the Right-honorable Printing-house, for his poore shifts of apparell" (*PS*, sig. V_3^v). With Nashe thus dismissed, Harvey can offer himself as the rightful arbiter of literary worth. His authority is now constituted on the discrediting identification of Nashe with Pierce, a conflation that underwrites Harvey's careful separation of himself from them. Only he, safely distanced from the common pamphleteers, can pass judgment on them. "It is little of Value," he intones haughtily toward the end of the text, settling into the role, "either *for matter, or manner*, that can be performed in such perfunctory Pamflets" (*PS*, sig. Dd_3^r).

Piers Respondent

It should be clear by now why Nashe's persona played such a pivotal role in his quarrel with Harvey. Not only did Pierce serve as the visible face of Nashe's self-assertion, he also embodied the crisis of discrimination—discrimination of literary value and, at the same time, of social position—that lay at the heart of their quarrel. For Harvey, determining Pierce's status was urgently necessary, both because doing so was a way to determine by proxy his own relation to his opponent and because it was a way demonstrate his possession of the "grounded discretion" that, as he argued in *Pierces Supererogation*, characterizes the "wisest reader[s]." Realizing what was at stake, Nashe responded by encouraging the sense that Pierce was a riddle who would inevitably foil Harvey's attempts to solve him.

Nashe's calculated ambiguity reached its height in his final involvement in the controversy, the 1596 pamphlet *Haue with You to Saffron-Walden*. At times, his approach is continuous with *Strange Newes*'s insinuations that Harvey was not as different from his object of scorn as he might wish. Early on, Nashe mocks his opponent's fixation on Pierce, accusing Harvey of stealing "the name of *Piers Pennilesse*"—which had, of course, appeared in the title of Harvey's most recent attack—in order "to help his bedred stuffe to limpe out of *Powles* churchyard" (*TN*, 3:35). Here Harvey emerges as one of the "obscure imitators" that Nashe had warned of in the second edition of *Pierce Penilesse*, laying claim to the persona in a craven play for sales (*TN*, 1:153). In general, however, *Haue with You*'s tactics are less direct, borne out in a meta-narrative every bit as involved as the origin story that frames *Pierce Penilesse*.

The premise of *Haue with You*, like that of Nashe's earlier pamphlet, is a fiction of textual mediation. Rather than the Knight of the Post, Nashe now presents his text-within-the-text—an overdue response to Harvey—to a group of friends shortly before it is to go to press. "I pry thee (in honestie)," one of his companions urges, "if thou hast anie of the papers of thy Booke about thee, shew vs some of them, that, like a great Inquest, we may deliuer our verdit before it come to the *Omnigatherum* of Towne and Countrey" (*TN*, 3:32). Nashe's anticipation of the book's public reception, vividly captured in the Anglo-Latin portmanteau, suggests how significant it was that his quarrel with Harvey had played out not merely before their university peers but before a broad consumer readership.[64] Yet Nashe evokes this readership in order to evade it, appealing instead to a decidedly more intimate audience: the pamphlet unfolds as the reading aloud of the manuscript to a cast of assorted friends, punctuated by their periodic interjections. Just as Philisides and Astrophil emerge as figures of coterie privacy over and against the publicness of their texts, so too the manuscript—and the circle of familiars—become meaningful for Nashe when positioned against the pressures of the public. Here, too, the division between manuscript and print is an emergent, constructed one; in this case, it is designed as a way to characterize, and hence control, publicity. The disciplinary effect is strengthened by the form of the conversation: a mock-legal "inquest," convened in order to render a "verdit" on manuscript and author. Accused in *Pierces Supererogation* of aspiring to be "the judge of his own cause," Nashe thus responds with a fiction of forensic deliberation in which he assumes the new role of defendant—and, given that his "papers" are an extended attack on Harvey, the role of prosecutor as well.

Haue with You's inquest made literal the judicial metaphor that always lurked behind Nashe's or Harvey's evocations of judgment, or discrimination, or discernment. The participants in the trial are extravagantly named personae, apparently covers for Nashe's friends, "men which haue dealt with me in the same humour that heere I shaddow":

> *Inprimis, Senior Importuno,* the Opponent.
> The second, *Grand Consiliadore,* chiefe Censor or Moderator.
> The third, *Domino Bentiuole,* one that stands, as it were, at the line in a Tennis-court, and takes euerie ball at the volly.
> The fourth, *Don Carneades de boone Compagniola,* who, like a busie Countrey Iustice, sits on the Bench, and preacheth to theeues out of their own confessions (*TN*, 3:20–21)

Nashe completes the cast in the person of "Piers Pennilesse Respondent," the writer whose text stands under examination. Legal jargon is never far from the dialogue: when Piers presents a letter purportedly written by Harvey's boyhood tutor, Don Carneades asks of Consiliadore, "What is your censure, you that bee of the common counsaile; may this Epistle passe or no without a demurre or prouiso?" (*TN*, 3:69). Such gestures, like the *dramatis personae*, mark the text as a travesty of actual legal proceedings and, by extension, a send-up of Harvey's earnest commitment to the judgment of the wise reader.[65] Yet Nashe uses the form for more than parody, designing the inquest to sharpen his criticisms of his opponent. When, for instance, Consiliadore interjects that "I would not wish thee so to upbraid him with his birth"—an insult Nashe uses often—"which if he could remedie it were another matter," Nashe responds by distinguishing (however disingenuously) between his mockery of Harvey's birth and Harvey's arrogance in pretending to "forget the house from whence he came" (*TN*, 3:56). Later, the panel addresses Harvey's suggestion that an anonymous gentlewoman was ready to publish her own attack on Nashe and promptly dismisses it: the lady, Consiliadore declares, is a fiction, "a mere coppy of his countenaunce" (*TN*, 3:111).

Some of Nashe's verdicts are more directly literary. It is in *Haue with You*, indeed, that Nashe works most strenuously to differentiate his aesthetic commitments from Harvey's, whose judgment he describes as uniquely undiscerning. Harvey's own poetry, Piers Respondent reports, had "made the price of wit and Poetrie fall with him, when hee first began to be a fripler or broker in that trade" (*TN*, 3:61). Harvey also frequently recommended poets to his publisher, John Wolfe, and invariably bad ones: "were their stuffe," Piers observes, "by ten millions more . . . barbarous than balletry, he would haue it prest vpon *Wolfe*, whether he would or no, and giu'n it immortall allowance aboue *Spencer*" (*TN*, 3:89). Nashe's particular example is Barnabe Barnes, whose "Philistine Poem of *Parthenophill* and *Parthenophe*, which to compare worse than it selfe, it would plague all the wits of *France*, *Spaine*, or *Italy*" (*TN*, 3:89).[66] Barnes's case makes clear the degree to which Harvey's evaluations were stained by cronyism: in 1593, he had written verses praising Harvey and attacking Nashe that appeared at the front of *Pierces Supererogation*. Harvey's authoritative judgments are thus discredited, exposed as the products of self-interest or, worse, of simple bad taste.

For all of the trappings of judicial certitude, however, Nashe's pamphlet is in large part a performance of uncertainty. Consider, for example, the mock "life" of Harvey that comprises the middle third of *Haue with You*. A send-up of the biographies often supplied in early modern editions of ancient authors, the life was a response in kind to Harvey's invidiously biographical reading of Pierce, padded out with presumably invented tales of Harvey's vanity and belligerence as a boy and university student. It is in this section that Nashe fakes the letter from Harvey's tutor, who describes his former charge as "distractedly enamourd of his owne beautie" (*TN*, 3:68). Such details accord with Nashe's running critique of Harvey's vanity, but they are also jokes and, possibly, traps—attempts to bait Harvey into earnestly rebutting the lies and thereby publicly missing the point. The pamphlet is in general happy to carve out a space between fiction and truth, its slanders never quite asserted as fact even as Piers (mostly facetiously) insists on his honesty. In a different section, Nashe assembles an oration from scraps of Harvey's actual writings. When he alerts his interlocutors to "here expect the cleare repurified soule of truth, without the least shadow of fiction," the promise is neither sincere nor merely ironic: the oration *is* a true picture of pedantry, but one fragmented and reassembled for effect (*TN*, 3:42).

This sort of teasing ambiguity is the underpinning of *Haue with You*'s forensic structure—an "inquest" that is not an inquest, officiated by the fictional doubles of real people. Piers's interlocutors are crucial to the effect of this ironic performance, for, if they are part of the ambiguous tissue of Nashe's fiction, they are also his coconspirators, participants in the game of oblique self-presentation. Much of their purpose is simply to be a knowing audience:

to get the jokes that Harvey might be expected to take literally, and thus to ratify Nashe's wit while playing his opponent for a fool. As a fiction of reception, the inquest thus modeled for *Haue with You*'s readership a way to grasp the pamphlet's complicated game. But it also offered an image of a smaller community of winking insiders whose very separation from the public "omnigatherum" ensured Nashe's privileged position. For Nashe's readers—and most of all for Harvey—the eccentric play-acting of Piers and company was bound to remain at some level incalculable.

And there was nothing more incalculable than Pierce/Piers himself, who remains to the last a riddling cipher. "Whatever else *Have With You* may be about," observes Hutson, "it is definitely not concerned with reinstating the 'good name' of Thomas Nashe. No attempt to dissociate Thomas Nashe from the taint of Pierce Penilesse is ever made."[67] But neither did he simply embrace his persona. In a particularly enigmatic aside, Nashe writes that "many a faire day agoe haue I proclaimed my selfe to the worlde *Piers Pennilesse*, and sufficient petigrees can I shewe to prooue him my elder brother" (*TN*, 3:31). It is hard to say just what Nashe's confession (or is it a declaration?) might mean. The line begins by announcing their identity ("I proclaimed my selfe . . . *Piers*"), only to deny it in the next breath; it insists on their difference, but only by conceding that they are brothers. Like the pamphlet's "Harvey," an amalgam of truth and fabrication, Piers and Tom form a confusing and unsorted whole. The relation between author and character, between real and virtual persons, hangs in the balance, but Nashe cannot summon the energy, or more likely does not wish, to settle the question.

News from Hell

After the publication of *Haue with You*, the quarrel fell silent. By 1599, with the promulgation of the Bishops' Ban of that year, it was forcibly ended, and two years later Nashe was dead. Among the works destined to remain unwritten was the sequel to *Pierce Penilesse* contemplated nearly a decade earlier: "If my leisure were such as I could wish, I might haps (halfe a year hence) write the returne of the *Knight of the Post* from hel, with the *Deuils* answer to the *Supplication*" (*TN*, 1:154). Harvey's answer had intervened before the Nashe could write the devil's, but the quarrel had the same effect in at least one respect: it turned Pierce into a serial character, a figure who would endure in London's bookstalls in spite of the Ban and after Nashe's death. In the first decade of the seventeenth century, a series of imitators issued versions of the sequel that Nashe never wrote—the return of Knight of the Post with the devil's response to Pierce.

As a group, these various returns to Nashe's story were acts of homage characterized by an embrace of their model's penchant for self-parody and ironic deflation. Thomas Dekker, writing in 1606, began *Newes from Hell Brought by the Diuells Carrier* with deliberate echoes of *Pierce Penilesse*, describing books as "Paper-monsters" that are "sure to be set vppon, by many terrible encounters."[68] Inserted into Dekker's dedicatory epistle to a potential patron, Sir John Hamden, Dekker's echo invokes Nashe's complicated relation to the patronage economy—an economy that, like Nashe, Dekker sends up even as he participates in it. In the body of Dekker's text, this sense of collegial alliance is even clearer. The story begins with the news that the devil has grown so frustrated with the scholars in his employ that he has sworn Pierce (another poor scholar) would never "get a good word at his handes." "I hearing this," reports Dekker's narrator, "and fearing that the poore Suppliant should lose his longing, and bee sent away with *Si nihil attuleris*, resolued (euen out of my loue to *Pierce Pennylesse*, because he hath beene always a companion to Schollers,) to doe that for nothing, which a number would not for any money."[69] In seeking employment of his own with the devil, Dekker's narrator becomes Pierce's inside agent, working to influence the answer to the supplication from the end of its reception. He also becomes Pierce's double, working for the same patron and even foregoing payment: his only compensation, he insists, will be Pierce's stipend. To write a reply to *Pierce Penilesse*, Dekker suggests, was not simply to intervene in his reception, but also to become a version of Pierce oneself. It was the same lesson that Harvey had learned the hard way.

The devil's-reply pamphlets as a group were quick to acknowledge their debt to Nashe, professing as much affection as Harvey did enmity. In *The Returne of the Knight of the Poste from Hell*, published just before *Newes from Hell* in 1606, the anonymous author described Nashe as "mine intimate and neare companion . . . one with whome I communicated both my loue, mine estate, and my studies, and found euer out of his disposition an equall, or if possible a more feruent sympathie of like community and affection."[70] As this passage indicates, *The Returne* lacks *Newes from Hell*'s ironic wit—a deficit that Dekker points out in describing the pamphlets as arrows "of two contrary flights."[71] Thomas Middleton's *The Blacke Booke* (1604), on the other hand, was very much in Nashe's vein. In the most striking scene of Middleton's pamphlet, the devil finds Pierce (in a passage discussed at the beginning of this book) lying drunken and filthy in a London tiring-house. Neil Rhodes has suggested that this passage, with its remarkable evocation of Pierce's misery is, "the first attempt in English prose actually to visualise what it is like to be down and out in a large city."[72]

Humiliation, of course, is for Pierce an odd form of homage: what drives the description is its grotesquerie, its morbid specificity, and this style is borrowed almost wholesale from Nashe, whose presence as interlocutor prevents the passage from slipping into the vindictiveness of Harvey's sneering account, in a comparable scene from *Foure Letters*, of Robert Greene's death. Middleton's visit to Pierce's quarters is, in fact, a return to the scene of his begetting: along with Pierce himself, Lucifer finds "the old Copy of his Supplication in foule written hand which my blacke night of the Post conueyed to Hell."[73] Jeffrey Todd Knight takes "the centrality of the text" in this scene as a sign of the bibliographic orientation of continuation as a genre—a genre rooted, in his account, in the material practices of compilation and recombination through which early modern printed books were made.[74] But the text that Lucifer finds is not a copy of the published pamphlet; it is its earliest manuscript draft. Middleton's expansion of the fictional world that Nashe had crafted is thus drawn back to its origins—to the scene of writing in which Pierce was first begotten. In *Haue with You*, the presentation of the manuscript draft had distinguished Piers Respondent's familiars from his public audience. The dynamic is much the same in *The Blacke Booke*: here, too, Lucifer's discovery of Pierce's foul papers is a gesture of a kind of intimacy, inscribing in miniature Middleton's debt to Nashe.

The self-conscious irony of this passage thus realizes the kind of literary companionship that Nashe had imagined in *Haue with You*. Where Harvey strained to determine Pierce (and by extension Nashe), first by dissociating persona from author and then by insisting on their identity, Middleton and Dekker—like Piers Respondent's jury—are clued in from the beginning to Nashe's play of identities and drafted as collaborators. Their winking participation in Nashe's complexly ironic self-presentation points up the misreading that lay behind Harvey's earnest invective. Bent on determining Pierce, on resolving him into Nashe, Harvey instead revealed his inability to draw the distinctions—between author and persona, fact and fiction, poet and hack, good writing and bad—that mattered so much to him. In this sense, Pierce embodied the crisis of literary judgment that lay behind the quarrel between Harvey and Nashe, for Nashe's persona both tempted and frustrated these distinctions. Nashe's trick—and eventually Middleton's and Dekker's—

was to refuse to draw them and, in doing so, to intimate a mastery of Pierce's ambiguous self-presentation that lay beyond reductive clarification.

So it was no coincidence that Dekker would make mention of Harvey in his own pamphlet's most enigmatic description of Pierce Penilesse. Early in the story, having decided to become the devil's scholar, Dekker's narrator pauses to invoke a pair of muses. The invocation is of a piece with Dekker's parodic self-dramatization, beginning with a grandiose address to that original underworld traveler, Orpheus. Then it turns to Dekker's more proximate inspiration:

> And thou, into whose soule (if euer there were a *Pithagorean Metempsuchosis*) the raptures of that fierie and inconfinable *Italian* spirit were bounteously and boundlessly infused, thou sometimes Secretary to *Pierce Pennylesse*, and Master of his requests, ingenious, ingenuous, fluent, facetious, *T. Nash*: from whose aboundant pen, hony flow'd to thy friends, and mortall Aconite to thy enemies: thou that madest the Doctor a flat Dunce, and beat'st him at two sundry tall Weapons, Poetrie, and Oratorie: Sharpest Satyre, Luculent Poet, Elegant Orator, get leaue for thy Ghost, to come fro[m] her abiding and to dwell with me a while, till she hath carows'd to me in her owne wo[n]ted ful measures of wit, that my plump braynes may swell, and burst into bitter Inuectiues against the Lieftennant of Limbo, if he casheere *Pierce Pennylesse* with dead pay.[75]

Harvey had by this point been silent for a decade, yet he remains, for Dekker, Nashe's and Pierce's irreplaceable foil. Against Nashe's ambiguous, paradoxical self-presentation, his indiscernible blend of the "ingenuous" and the "facetious," Harvey could hardly come across as anything but a "flat dunce." Nashe and Pierce, on the other hand, remain unresolved doubles of each other. The most striking aspect of Dekker's invocation may be its inversion of the priority of author and persona: Nashe is presented not as Pierce's begetter, but instead as a secretary in his service—a writer doing the bidding of a character who has at last outgrown him. For Dekker as for Nashe, Pierce was destined to remain a cipher, continually reframing his relation to his author without ever allowing its resolution and, in doing so, reserving the authority of judgment, and the art of distinctions, for Nashe's hand-picked jury of friends and followers.

Coda

Nashe's uncertain relation to his "elder brother" reflected the enigmatic terms of Pierce's existence. Pierce was a vivid personification of writing: a way of imbuing texts with presence, of turning them into persons. But the personality that Pierce offered was personality reduced to a paradoxical minimum. Thomas Nashe was indisputably real: he was a person who might find himself banished to Yarmouth (as he was, in 1597), who might have his books proscribed by the censor (as they were, in 1599). Pierce was not. He had no obligations, no needs, no life apart from his life in the pages of the texts that invoked him, and in this sense, despite his peculiarly personal charisma, he was something less than an integral person. It is a paradox that lies at the heart of the term *paper monster.* Read straight, the label registers the sensational agency of books come to life. But read aslant, its force becomes unexpectedly deflationary, an insistence on the *mere* textuality of its object—of a persona that is, in the end, not quite real. Pierce may be the animating personality of the pamphlets in which he appears, but he is also an abstraction: a reduced and delimited self that, unlike "Tom Nash," obtains only in the world of literary exchange.

This tension appears, in a slightly different form, in each of the foregoing chapters. For if personae were called on to animate the texts they inhabited—if they promised their readers the thrill of personal contact—they were also asked to pare away the trappings of extraliterary personality, to delineate a form of identity that was specific to and coterminous with its medium. The burden of this work is especially clear in the afterlives of Philisides and Astrophil, personae who tantalized their readers with the prospect of initiation into an intimately personal allegory even as they enforced a distinction between Sidney as public figure and Sidney as poet. Thus Matthew Roydon could balance the name "Philip Sidney" against the persona "Astrophill," the latter taught by the Muses to "sing, to write, and say," while John Dickenson could imagine a convocation of poets—"men of their owne profession"—gathered in Arcadia to "memoriz[e] the worth of *Astrophell*."[1] In moments like these, the persona pulled forward a particular aspect of Sidney's public self, marking it off and thus rendering it available for the specifically literary fellowship that Roydon and Dickenson wished to claim. Sidney may have been especially in need of such specification, but a similar dynamic underwrote Colin Clout, who came to anchor a community of shepherd-poets cast in his own language of pastoral pseudonym. Colin in fact seemed to encode the paradox of Elizabethan personation, his fiction of personal presence continually running up against the fact of its mediation. And if Colin thus served as a reflection on the mediation of personality, so too did Robert Greene, whose afterlife made ghostly haunting an allegory for the peculiar evanescence of those persons known only as names printed on the posts of Paul's walk—persons that were at once effects of textual circulation and its distinctive agents.

This last description is one that we are likely to associate with another figure: the author. After all, authors have always been something more and less than ordinary persons. As Foucault observed, in an essay that has underwritten the study of authorship ever since, an author is above all a discursive formation, a "function" of literary reception. "It would seem," Foucault wrote, "that the author's name, unlike other proper names, does not pass from the interior of a discourse to the real and exterior individual who produced it; instead, the name seems always to be present, marking off the edges of the text, revealing, or at least characterizing, its mode of being."[2] So whereas the blue-eyed Parisian Pierre Dupont—Foucault's example of a real individual—remains Dupont even if we discover that his eyes are not blue or that he is not from Paris, Homer and Shakespeare depend in a more absolute way on their defining attributes—on the body of works they organize. Authors, as Alexandra Gillespie glosses Foucault, "mediate the place of a fictional text in the world. They assign themselves, and they are repeatedly reassigned, responsibility for textual production and they accrue reward and censure accordingly."[3] Personae find themselves at the same discursive interstices—at the meeting points between textual insides and outsides, between composition and reception—and they mark a similarly delimited form of literary identity. It seems clear, then, that the history of the persona bears on the longer history of the author. They are cousins, or even (like Pierce and Tom Nash) brothers. But what should we make of their kinship?

The persona's ascendance came at a period of transition for the author function—a period in which a complex system of authorial roles derived from medieval hermeneutics gradually gave way to a concept of the author as possessive agent. As A. J. Minnis has shown, the *auctor* was closely tied in medieval literary theory to *auctoritas*, and hence to a sense of pastness: "No 'modern' writer could decently be called an *auctor* in a period in which men saw themselves as dwarfs standing on the shoulder of giants, i.e. the 'ancients.'"[4] When Chaucer presented himself as a "compiler," rather than an *auctor*, he was operating within one of the lesser roles left to moderns. Yet Chaucer, as Gillespie observes, was soon invested by his readers and imitators with the more prestigious status of author. His laureation reflected what Roger Chartier describes as a more general shift of literary categories under the influence of increasingly ambitious modern languages: "The trajectory of the author can be thought of as a gradual change in the way texts in the vernacular were regarded, attributing to them a principle of designation and election that had long been characteristic only of works that were referred to an ancient *auctoritas*."[5] As classical *auctoritas* was absorbed by emerging vernacular traditions, it largely retained the aura of pastness. In *Greenes Vision* (1592), the dreaming narrator watches the approach of "two ancient men," Chaucer and Gower: "their visages were wrinckled, but well featured, and their countenances conteyned much grauitie."[6]

But while Chaucer and Gower enter Greene's dream-vision as latter-day *auctores*, it is Greene himself who is identified as an "author"; indeed, the final section of the narrative offers "The Authours answere to *Gower* and *Chawcer*."[7] Greene's authorship is not rooted—at least not in any simple way—in his authority. He is an author in the more straightforward sense that he is the book's writer; or rather, to get the grammar of possession right, the book is his: it is *Greenes Vision*. The distance between the *auctoritas* of Chaucer and Gower and the authorship of Greene points to a secondary shift in the author function—a shift from the *auctor* as past authority to the writer as discursive agent in the present. To see authors as beings in a living discursive field was, as Foucault argued, to render them susceptible to legal action and, as Joseph Loewenstein and others have shown, capable of sustaining claims to intellectual property. Thus, for Loewenstein, authorship emerged as "a form of public agency . . . distinguished by possessiveness," thanks to the competing proprietary claims of publishers, which foregrounded the "proper-ness" of books and so cultivated "the sense that a printed book is proper to a writing self."[8] If this agency, this sense of a writing *self*, arose as an accident of industrial competition, however, it also depended on the imaginative resources of the author-as-character. As we have already seen, the publishing frenzy that followed Greene's death routed disputes over stationer's rights to copy through the vexed question of just what belonged to Greene. And to answer that question was to be drawn back into the fiction of prodigality and repentance that Greene had woven into and around his books. The external determination of authorial identity, it turns out, is not so easily separated from the internal forms of its representation.

Personae, needless to say, did not "invent" the author. Yet their rise was in crucial ways linked to the changing terms of the author function in early modern England. Poised between the imaginative practices of literary characterization and the social determinations of textual identity, personae occupied the territory that was to become the author's, and, even as they ceded it, they helped to articulate authorship as a form of agency in a living field of literary production. The interactions of persona and author took two different, and in broad terms successive, forms. In the first stage, the persona took part in the conceptual formation of the author, allowing the latter to be imagined as a form of virtual identity in a virtual public. In the second stage, the direction of influence was reversed: as the author function solidified, the persona was reconceived in the terms of self-reflexive irony, as a form of characteristically authorial metafiction. The following sections consider the first effect by examining *Englands Helicon*, a lyric miscellany published in 1600, and the second through a reading of Democritus Junior, the eccentric alter ego of Robert Burton in *The Anatomy of Melancholy* (1621).

The Names of Poets

When the stationer Nicholas Ling gathered the poems that would comprise *Englands Helicon*, he included several stanzas of ballad-meter verse from the second book of Anthony Munday's *Primaleon of Greece*, published four years earlier. Munday's poem was apparently popular—it survives in several manuscripts and was published in other collections of songs and poems in the seventeenth century—but for Ling it was an awkward choice: *Englands Helicon* was a miscellany devoted to pastoral poetry, and *Primaleon* was a chivalric romance. To be sure, nothing marked Munday's poem, on its own, as being *not* pastoral, but there was little to identify it with the anthology's theme. So Ling made two rather odd revisions. One was the attribution that followed the poem, which assigns the verses not to Munday but instead, more colorfully, to "Sheepheard Tonie." The other was the omission of the heading that had introduced the lines, in *Primaleon*, as "Prince Edwards third song in the

Garden to Princess Flerida."[9] In its place, Ling introduced a new heading that addressed the lines "To *Colin Cloute*."[10]

The interpolation of Spenser's persona is at first glance hard to figure. After all, there was little reason to link Munday and Spenser, two very different writers. But Colin's arrival makes more sense in the context of *Englands Helicon* as a whole, for Ling's volume is filled with a cast of pastoral characters—characters like Tityrus and Coridon and Rowland and Amintas—who wander through the book's pages, greeting, praising, grieving, and singing for each other. Colin himself appears several times: early in the volume, he mourns "Astrophell" in lines taken from Spenser's elegy, and later, in an excerpt from Peele's *Aragynement of Paris*, he returns as an "enamoured Sheepheard" singing his "passion of loue."[11] What is striking about his appearance with Shepherd Tonie, however, is that Colin has no obvious business here; he has, at least, no poem to offer in response. For Ling, it seems, the value of Spenser's alter ego lies elsewhere, in the fiction of pastoral fellowship for which he had long since become a symbol—a fiction evoked simply by Colin's presence as silent addressee.

Ling's fascination with personae disclosed a broader concern with literary personality. It was a concern with a complex background in the lyric miscellany, a form specially implicated (because of its reliance on multiple authorship) in questions of attribution and authorial agency. By the time Ling published *Englands Helicon*, the printed miscellany was nearing the end of a long period of popularity, stretching back to 1557, when Richard Tottel had published *Songes and Sonettes*, the volume that introduced the poems of Henry Howard, Earl of Surrey, and Sir Thomas Wyatt to print. Tottel had divided his volume on the principle of authorship, devoting discrete sections to Surrey, Wyatt, Nicholas Grimald and "Uncertain Auctours."[12] And yet one can read pages at a time in *Songes and Sonettes* without coming across an author's name: the book's presentation, suggests Matthew Zarnowiecki, "tend[s] towards a levelling of authorship and style" under the rubrics of genre and theme and the guiding presence of "The Lover," the figure who appears throughout the volume as nameless speaker.[13] In the miscellanies that sought to capitalize on Tottel's success—*Songes and Sonettes* was a bestseller, going through ten editions by 1585—the author often took a backseat to another, equally shadowy figure: the miscellaneous compiler. In some cases, print anthologies were derived directly from manuscript miscellanies. Richard Edwards's miscellany, for instance, formed the backbone of *The Paradyse of Daynty Deuises* (1576), the prefatory epistle of which describes its contents as "collected togeather, through the trauell of one, both of woorship and credite, for his priuate vse: who not long since departed this lyfe."[14] *The Phoenix Nest*, published in 1593, presents itself as "set foorth by R. S., of the Inner Temple *Gentleman*."[15] In emphasizing the act of collection, these books work to mitigate the social risks associated with publication, which threatened gentlemanly poets with what Tottel had invidiously called the "swinelike grossnesse" of the common reader.[16] The emphasis was also an advertising strategy: in framing collecting as a private pastime for the well-to-do, the miscellanies courted readers with the allure of access to an exclusive, elite social world.[17]

In a sense, the history of sixteenth-century poetry in print tracks the intersecting careers of the collector and its budding counterpart, the author. In the middle of the century, as Elizabeth Heale demonstrates, the role of collector provided a convenient pretext for the author wishing to protect his "well-framed, masculine authorial self" from the effeminacy of amorous verse: thus George Gascoigne framed his *A Hundreth Sundrie Flowres* (1573) as an anthology collected by a certain H. W., containing the work of multiple writers.[18] But by the 1590s, compilers could make the opposite move, collecting under a nominal author poems by various, unattributed writers, as in *The Arbor of Amorous Devices* (1597), a collection attributed to Nicholas Breton, or, most notoriously, in *The Passionate Pilgrim* (1599), whose title page claimed Shakespeare as its sole author. The arrival of *Englands Helicon* thus came at a moment of growing attention to the author, which it reflected in its thorough commitment to attribution. The anthology's attributions are occasionally imprecise: two poems reprinted from Tottel's "uncertain Auctours" section, for instance, are assigned without explanation to Surrey, who seems to have absorbed an author function for *Songes and Sonettes* as a whole. But they are also exhaustive. Every poem in the anthology is given an attribution of some sort—even anonymous poems are signed with the tag "Ignoto." And when errors were made, corrections (at least in some cases) followed. In several extant copies, five of the signatures are covered with cancel slips, four of them replacing names with "Ignoto" and a fifth changing an attribution from Sidney to Breton.[19] Interpretations of the cancel slips have varied: the slips that replaced the initials "S. W. R." (Sir Walter Ralegh) under two poems have often been thought to reflect his desire for anonymity, although their authorship remains uncertain. "The cancel slips," judges Marcy North, "might represent a corrected misattribution, an unknown name, or affected courtly modesty."[20]

Englands Helicon is, in short, a text filled with authors—with named authors, misnamed authors, pointedly unnamed authors. It is also a text at pains to understand what kind of person an author is. The anthology's place in the history of authorship rests not only on its practices of attribution but on Ling's prefatory epistle (itself ambiguously credited to "L. N.").[21] The epistle is a striking document, one conceived under the pressure of an unusual convergence of competing interests. Unlike earlier miscellanies, which largely published hitherto unprinted lyrics, "more than three quarters" of the poems in *Englands Helicon* had already been published elsewhere.[22] As a result, a number of stationers could insist that the rights to poems printed in the anthology properly belonged to them. It was a possibility that Ling was eager to forestall: "Nowe, if any Stationer shall finde faulte, that his Coppies are robd by any thing in this Collection, let me aske him this question, Why more in this, then in any Diuine or humaine Authour: From whence a man (writing of that argument) shal gather any saying, sentence, similie, or example, his name put to it who is the Authour of the same."[23] The answer depends on a clever sleight of hand. Although Ling begins by acknowledging the stationer's proprietary concerns (his desire to protect his "copy"), he responds as if the charge is plagiarism: an offense against authors. The switch momentarily leaves Ling on firmer ground, able to defend his borrowing as a version of commonplacing. But in appealing to the rights of authors, Loewenstein observes, Ling "temporarily forget[s] what side his bread is buttered on"—that is, on the side of the stationer's monopoly on copy.[24]

Indeed, this enfranchisement of authors introduced problems of its own. For instance: did Ling need their permission to (re)print their poems? Was he obliged to attribute verses to their authors? Conversely, was he obliged to *conceal* the identities of poets who preferred to remain anonymous? In addressing these questions, Ling finds himself speaking of poems as the property of poets: "If any man hath beene defrauded of any thing by him composed, by another mans title put to the same, hee hath this benefit by this collection, freely to challenge his owne in publique, where els he might be robd of his proper due."[25] The language of property and theft endows the poets of *Englands Helicon* with a claim on the poems in the anthology that might supersede Ling's own claims. After all, if a poet can claim public acknowledgment as "his proper due," the authority over publication seems to have been transferred to him. Yet Ling's formulation ingeniously allows the poet's claim to arise only once his poem is published. An author can protest misattribution, but he cannot protest publication, for his due consists in the attribution "in publique." (The cancel slips that followed the initial printing show practice modifying theory, with the repeated insertion of "Ignoto" seemingly acknowledging a right to remain anonymous, but not to block publication.) Ling's authors are a special kind of person: they are enfranchised—indeed, they come into being—only when they are brought before the volume's public readership in print. *Englands Helicon* thus frames itself as a synecdochal public, a textual commons in which authors could lay claim to the acknowledgment of readers that is their "proper due."

In this public, Ling suggests, the grounds of status and identity are different. In a bid to reassure scandalized gentleman-poets, he writes: "Further, if any man whatsoeuer, in prizing of his owne birth or fortune, shall take in scorne, that a far meaner man in the eye of the world, shal be placed by him: I tell him plainly whatsoeuer so excepting, that, that mans wit is set by his, not that man by him. In which degree, the names of Poets (all feare and dutie ascribed to her great and sacred Name) haue been placed with the names of the greatest Princes of the world, by the most autentique and worthiest iudgements, without disparagement to their soveraigne titles."[26] Ling's argument is not that the poetic arena constituted by his anthology is not competitive or differential (it is), but rather that it entertains a quarantined form of competition. In this arena, the pertinent value is wit, and those who enter assume a carefully delimited identity—an identity removed, if only in theory, from questions of class position and family lineage. Anthony Munday and Robert Greene are in these pages the equals of Philip Sidney and Fulke Greville; or, at least, they are equals until they can be distinguished on the basis of their wit. To appear in *Englands Helicon* as an author was to become a specifically literary person, and to occupy a specifically literary space.

From this perspective, the effect of Ling's pastoralism, and of the personae that fill the anthology, becomes clearer: they animated the public space that he imagined *Englands Helicon* to be, transforming it into a *locus amoenus* inhabited by shepherd-poets greeting, praising, and mourning each other. When Shepheard Tonie addressed Colin Clout, the miscellany became a community in which personae might meet each other—in which Drayton's Rowland, Sidney's Astrophil, and Watson's Amyntas move among Coridon, Damon, Phillis, Tityrus, and the rest of the book's swains. In their interactions, the volume's readers could glimpse the appearance of a poetic domain (like the one traced in Chapter 2), a field constituted in public but delimited by its special barrier to entry: the adoption of a specifically literary identity. This domain was an imaginary space, but it was woven in complex ways into the operations of the book trade: fashioned not only by poets but also by their mediators, and offered as a way of conceptualizing the proper place of poets in a world of textual reproduction. Ling encourages readers to connect personae to authorial names: the former appear in the headings that introduce poems ("Rowlands *Song in praise of the fairest* Beta") and the latter in the signatures that follow them ("Mich. Drayton").[27] And some figures—"Shepheard Tonie," of course, but perhaps also a certain "Ro. Greene"—themselves cross categories, merging author and persona. The conjunction reveals the relation between Ling's authors and his personae. The paradoxical existence that he grants the author—an existence only in public and in print—becomes real through the fiction that enacts it: the fiction of shepherds who exist to sing to each other.

Democritus Dixit

At first glance, Ling's miscellany and Robert Burton's sprawling treatise *The Anatomy of Melancholy* make odd company: on the one hand, an idyllically pastoral collection of brief and largely familiar lyrics; on the other, a work of unending, forbiddingly erudite, tonally discordant prose. But the categorical differences between the books make their similarities more striking. Both were open-endedly revisable: a second edition of *Englands Helicon* appeared in 1614 with a number of newly added poems; Burton, of course, made of the *Anatomy* a life's work, tirelessly adding to the text as it made its way through six editions (the last, in 1651, published eleven years after his death). In orientation, both are anthological: one a miscellany and the other a cento that, Burton tells us, "I have laboriously collected . . . out of many Authours."[28] And for both, the form of the anthology presses questions of authorial personhood. In *Englands Helicon*, those questions center on the authors whose poems Ling (re)printed: what rights do they have, and what status can they claim? In the *Anatomy*, they arise in the tension between the text as macaronic patchwork and the teasing seriocomic personality—by turns solicitous and standoffish—that Burton crafts around himself. Here, then, was a further difference: for Ling, the persona had provided the imaginative equipment with which to conceive of the author; for Burton, writing two decades later, the author has become something like a background condition of literary production, and the persona a tool for its ironic manipulation.

To be sure, Burton seems happier to hide from than live with his authorial self. If he is, like Michel de Montaigne, himself the subject of his book—

"I haue," he acknowledged in a line added to the second edition, "put my selfe vpon the stage"—his name turns out to be surprisingly hard to find.[29] It did not appear on the title page of any of the five editions that were published in his lifetime, nor on that of the posthumous edition of 1651. Burton did sign a "Conclusion to the Reader" appended to the first edition, but when the conclusion disappeared in later editions, his name went with it. And when, in the second edition of 1624, a portrait of the author adorned the book's elaborate new title page, the name that appeared beneath it was "Democritus Junior." The persona, an antic successor to the laughing philosopher, was from the beginning an overt and self-conscious performance. "Gentle Reader," begins the *Anatomy*'s long, digressive preface, "Democritus Junior to the Reader," "I presume thou wilt be very inquisitiue to knowe what personate Actor this is, that so insolently intrudes vpon this common Theater, to the worlds view, arrogating another mans name, whence hee is, why he doth it, and what hee hath to say?"[30] Burton (should I say Democritus?) takes for granted the reader's curiosity: how could we not want to know who is addressing us? We are curious, of course, about the role that he has chosen to play, the name he has arrogated. But we are also—or so Burton thinks—curious to know the author, this "Actor" who personates Democritus. As the "visard" under which "I haue masked my selfe," Democritus intercepts the inquisitive attentions of the *Anatomy*'s readers; and yet he is always severable, an identity that might be rescinded or a performance that might be stopped, should Burton ever wish to address his curious readers himself.[31]

The figure of Democritus was well suited to the uncertainties that came with the role. In the first place, Democritus embodied the much-observed tension between critical detachment and implication in Burton's account of himself: Democritus's laughter, like that of Erasmus's Folly, reflected a cynical remove from the foolishness of others, but it also hinted at his own madness.[32] By dividing the author across two selves, Democritus Junior added to the effect: Burton's movement from one voice to another, into the persona and back out, risks the suggestion of discomposure. In a revealing aside, Burton ducks the objection that he has been too "phantastical" by appealing to his split personality: "'Tis not I, but *Democritus*, *Democritus dixit*: you must consider what it is to speake in ones own or anothers person, an assumed habit and name; a difference betwixt him that affects or acts a princes, a philosophers, a magistrates, a fooles part, and him that is so indeede; and what liberty those old Satyrists haue had, it is a *Cento* collected from others, not I, but they that say it. . . . If I doe a little forget my selfe, I hope you will pardon it."[33]

The clarification is, of course, thoroughly ambiguous: if, in one breath, "Democritus speaks," in the next Democritus is reduced to "an assumed habit" to be spoken through; and if the distinction urges us to separate Democritean antics from the sober "I" who merely tries them on, it might worry us that in the disguise "I do . . . forget myself." But the passage's most interesting detail is the juxtaposition of this excuse with another: the self-effacing multiplicity of the cento form. In the shift from "not I, but *Democritus*" to "not I, but they," the play of authorial reflexivity seems momentarily a distraction. If the point of the *Anatomy*, as Drew Daniel argues, is the experience of its structure—its endless patchwork of authorities—then the focus on Burton and Democritus is a red herring, a symptom of our addiction to individuality even in a text that refuses it. Ours, but also Burton's: the *Anatomy*'s "transpersonal assemblage" is here set against his own intricate games of personation, even as the two converge as ways of forgetting oneself.[34]

In turning to Democritus, indeed, Burton reproduced his anatomy's citational method. His persona is itself an invocation of antique authority, and indeed Democritus occasionally pops up as just another of the *Anatomy*'s quotable ancients. In this sense, his presence seems to frame the author as an absent center, yet another site of deferred authority. Then again, Democritus is also the figure against whom the practice of citational gathering itself breaks down. In one of his several explanations of his alter ego, Burton observes that Democritus had written a lost work on melancholy—a project that he, as Democritus Junior, is determined "to imitate, and because he left it vnperfect, to prosecute and finish in this Treatise."[35] The entire *Anatomy* would seem to be a footnote on Democritus—a referral to an authority whose wisdom Democritus Junior merely reproduces—were it not for that authority's absence: Democritus's own anatomy of melancholy is the text that Burton cannot quote. Authorial personation is thus revealed to be an alternative form of citational assemblage, or perhaps as the point at which citation fails, or else, somehow, as both at once. Democritus is the prosopopoetic answer to and, at the same time, the ironic engine of the *Anatomy*'s dispersal of agency—an especially loquacious because especially imperiled author function.

The ironies of the part that Burton (in a suggestively elusive hesitation) "affects or acts" work to master, to hold off, to undermine, or to escape the fact of authorship. In this sense, they are the rhetoric of an author concept that seems not to emerge from the text's mercurial persona but to be its salient background: Burton's every attempt to escape into his alter ego—"Not I, but *Democritus*"—is legible because we are conditioned to demand that the "I" speak. This is the irony of metafiction, which has been ever since a doubled response to the intractable fact of authorship: at once an evasion of the pressures of being an author and an act of opportunistic self-reference, the reflexive gesture of an "authored" work. Democritus is likely to strike us as more nearly modern than the personae discussed in the foregoing chapters, because he is more thoroughly bound up in the ironic play of a distinctively authorial reflexivity. And yet: Democritus Junior's hold on Burton's imagination, and on his readers, seems finally to exceed his ironic distance, to outgrow even a book as all-encompassing as the *Anatomy*. Before long, he, like Pierce and Philisides and Greene's ghost, was a persona on the loose. In 1647, two royalist pamphlets were published under the name Democritus Junior. A third appeared under the name of "Democritus natu minimus" (Democritus the youngest), who introduces himself as the successor to the author of the *Anatomy* and posing, like his predecessor, as "a criticall observer of Times and Persons."[36] Democritus thus outlived Burton, who had died seven years earlier. But he also died with him. Burton's funerary bust in Christ Church Cathedral is accompanied by an epitaph that memorializes the author in the name of his persona: "Paucis notus, paucioribus ignotus, hic jacet Democritus Junior, cui vitam dedit et mortem Melancholia" (Known to few, unknown to fewer, here lies Democritus Junior, to whom Melancholy gave life and death).[37] The inscription seems almost to recall Colin Clout: who knows not Democritus Junior?

Reading Personally

The passage from *Englands Helicon* to *The Anatomy of Melancholy* discloses an important shift. In Ling's miscellany, the persona provides the imaginative framework by which the author as specifically literary agent becomes conceivable; in Burton's treatise, personation is presumptively authorial—a mask that the book's ubiquitous "I" holds at a strategic distance. It is a reversal that goes some way toward explaining the life of the persona form after the end of the sixteenth century. Personae, of course, have not disappeared. Far from it: one could take this book as the first chapter in a much longer history of metafictional author-characters, a history that would move from Democritus Junior to Mr. Spectator, to Robinson Crusoe and Yorick, to Prufrock and Stephen Dedalus and Nathan Zuckerman. But what did gradually disappear was the persona as *anything other* than metafiction. The consolidation of the modern author left personae to operate as simulacra: as reflexive fictions, games of riddling self-reference, ironic inversions of the ideology that Carla Benedetti calls *authorialism*.[38] And the broader range of responses that personae once inspired—sympathy and concern, love and contempt, voyeuristic fascination and reverential admiration—went elsewhere: to the character and to the author.

What gave personae their special charisma, after all, was the feeling that reading is, in some meaningful way, personal. That feeling is still with us: it is what animates the desire, oft-heard in classrooms and book groups, to "relate" to texts or characters or authors. For academic critics, however, it has become a suspicious instinct. Writing recently in *The Novel: A Survival Guide*, the novelist and critic Tim Parks lamented the continuing sway the "biographical fallacy." An amalgam of W. K. Wimsatt and Monroe Beardsley's intentional fallacy and Roland Barthes's "death of the author," the biographical fallacy warns against what we might call *personal reading*: against interpretations that take texts to be expressions of their authors' inner selves, or reflections of their lives. Parks' complaint is in part the response of an artist who knows how deeply his life is woven into his own books. But it is also the response of a reader who knows what it is like to be pulled into conversation with the writers of the books one reads. Parks sketches one such reader, a woman who returns periodically over many years to the novels of Philip Roth, so that eventually Roth has—in a very real sense—"entered her life." Parks comments:

> I am not saying that this experience, where text and biography are now inextricably mixed is *preferable* or *superior* to the one-off encounter with a fine novel about whose author we know nothing; I am simply inviting you to consider that this is the experience of reading that many people have and that drives the market for fiction, particularly serious fiction. We involve ourselves in ongoing relationships with writers and position ourselves in relation to them and the kind of stories they tell, much as we position ourselves in relation to the people we meet and know. Writing and reading are part of the immensely complex business of being ourselves.[39]

When we read, Parks suggests, we don't care about author-functions; we care about authors. As the protagonist of Michel Houellebecq's *Submission* puts it: "to love a book is, above all, to love its author: we wish to meet him again, we wish to spend our days with him."[40]

Although his polemic is broadly aimed against professional criticism, Parks's attention to the attachments that books inspire has already begun to gain purchase within the field. If we have reached the "limits of critique," as Rita Felski suggests, the answer is a shift away from its cool skepticism and toward wonder and absorption—the experiences that explain "why we are drawn to art in the first place."[41] It is in large part the pursuit of these affects that lies behind a resurgent interest in literary character, a category often viewed with critical suspicion precisely because of the intense feelings characters elicit. In the opening pages of *Why Do We Care About Literary Characters?*, Blakey Vermeule describes a graduate seminar on J. M. Coetzee's *Disgrace* derailed by her students' disgust for the novel's protagonist, a literature professor forced to resign after an affair with a student. Her impulse is to return the discussion to the safer terrain of form, away from "the literary-critical fallacy of talking about a fictional character as though he were a real person."[42] But on reflection Vermeule decides that her worries had been misplaced: disavowing the feelings that characters elicit, she writes, "deprives us of access to one of the most powerful human imaginative capacities: the power and lure of fantasy."[43] More modestly, doing so ignores the tenaciously gossipy interest we take in literary persons: the voyeuristic curiosity that pulls us ever further into *Clarissa* or *Pride and Prejudice* (or, indeed, the contemporary *Twilight* and *Harry Potter* series).

If caring about characters—feeling for them, identifying with them, fretting over them, despising or abhorring them—is one of the primary ways in which readers attach and respond to texts, Parks suggests that we approach authors on similar terms: as persons we might come to know through their books. This is perhaps most obvious in the steady rise of the popular memoir, but it is true as well in the world of "serious" literary fiction: few books in recent years have attained the prominence and the prestige of Karl Ove Knausgaard's frankly autobiographical fiction or the Neapolitan novels of Elena Ferrante, a pseudonymous author whose identity has been the subject of feverish lit-world speculation. Like characters, authors provoke fascination and obsession, sympathy and trust, doubt and suspicion; in a real sense they *are* characters, subject to—and brought to life by—the narrativizing speculations of readers who ask "What would Jane Austen do?" or imagine Shakespeare in love.[44]

I have dwelled on these personalizing styles because they are, I suspect, versions of the same readerly fascination that animated early modern personae. Seeming to leap out of whatever texts contained them, floating free in the literary world of the 1580s and 1590s, personae were walking artifacts of reader attachment. Their paradox, indeed, is that they were at once the causes and the effects of that response: each reading and each rewriting gave them fresh life, and their charisma new force. To be accosted by Greene's ghost was to be frightened and thrilled, and then to look forward to his next haunting return; to meet Philisides was to be at once drawn in and held at arm's length—it was to catch a glimpse of an exclusive circle that one might (if bold enough) try to write oneself into; to bump into Pierce Penilesse was to be pulled, with disgust or fascination (or both), into his seamy pamphlet underworld. Personae were, in short, products of reading as much writing—they were sustained and made new by the affective investments of their readers. What arose from that investment was an identity to identify with, a person to imagine a literary world around.

The rise of the author did not disperse personal reading, even if it gradually displaced the persona; instead, it absorbed the forms of personal reading, indeed was increasingly constrained by them. Thus Burton, arriving at the end of the story this book tells, can be found turning the persona-form against the demand it once answered, reclaiming it as a tool with which to deflect an attention now focused squarely on him. From then on, the investments of personal reading would settle on the author—our latest and most systematic means of finding other selves in the books we read. Authors, we might say, are personae by another name: they are likewise fictions, abstractions conjured into being, and into serial life, by those who imagine them. And if authors are in this sense invented characters—if they are fictions we take to be real—the vitality of Elizabethan England's paper monsters makes clear that they are no less powerful for it.

NOTES

INTRODUCTION

1. Thomas Nashe, *Pierce Penilesse His Supplication to the Diuell*, in *The Works of Thomas Nashe*, ed. R. B. McKerrow, 5 vols. (1904–10; repr., Oxford: Basil Blackwell, 1958), 1:161.

2. Thomas Middleton, *The blacke booke* (London, 1604), sigs. D_1^r–D_1^v.

3. Gabriel Harvey, *Pierces Supererogation or A New Prayse of the Old Asse. A Preparative to certaine Larger Discourses, intituled Nashes S. Fame* (London, 1593), sig. C_1^r.

4. For a detailed account of *persona*'s etymology and of the history of its usage, see Geoffrey W. Gust, *Constructing Chaucer: Author and Autofiction in the Critical Tradition* (Basingstoke: Palgrave Macmillan, 2009), 4–28.

5. On the history of the persona as a tool of modern literary criticism, see Robert Elliot, *The Literary Persona* (Chicago: University of Chicago Press, 1982), 3–18. But see also Gust's overview of classical and medieval "persona theory," antecedents of sorts for New Critical uses of the concept. Gust, *Constructing Chaucer*, 4–36.

6. The implied author, a term coined by Wayne C. Booth, distinguishes the historical person of the author (as well as the narrator) from the authorial personality suggested to readers by a fictional text. See Booth, *The Rhetoric of Fiction* (Chicago: University of Chicago Press, 1961), 71–76, 211–21.

7. See the first, third, and fourth definitions of *personate* in *Oxford English Dictionary*, online ed., s.v. "personate (*v.*)," accessed December 21, 2014, http://www.oed.com/view/Entry/141493.

8. Paul de Man's well-known discussion of prosopopoeia in "Autobiography as De-Facement" emphasizes the figure's rhetorical ambivalence. On the one hand, prosopopoeia expresses a desire for presence—it is, he writes, "the fiction of an apostrophe to an absent, deceased, or voiceless entity, which posits the possibility of the latter's reply and confers upon it the power of speech." On the other, it points up the *impossibility* of this entity really speaking: "Death is a displaced name for a linguistic predicament, and the restoration of mortality by autobiography (the prosopopeia of the voice and the name) deprives and disfigures to the precise extent that it restores"; see de Man, "Autobiography as De-Facement," in *The Rhetoric of Romanticism* (New York: Columbia University Press, 1984), 75–76, 81. While for de Man this frustration is an essentially transhistorical feature of language, I suggest that it is felt particularly acutely at moments—like the end of the sixteenth century—when media shift confronts readers with the fact of mediation. For a historical overview of theories of prosopopoeia and personification, see James J. Paxson, *The Poetics of Personification* (Cambridge: Cambridge University Press, 1994), 8–34.

9. George Puttenham, *The Art of English Poesie* (London, 1589), sig. Dd_2^v.

10. The prevalence of such fictions surely owed much to early modern pedagogical practices. As Lynn Enterline has shown, "habits of personification—from advanced lessons in the techniques of prosopopoeia to other exercises in grammar and translation—permeated school training in rhetorical skill at every level of instruction." Enterline, *Shakespeare's Schoolroom: Rhetoric, Discipline, Emotion* (Philadelphia: University of Pennsylvania, 2011), 7. Enterline's nuanced account of the ways in which the practices of the Latin schoolroom shaped the literary and dramatic construction of passion and subjectivity leads her to lament "the heuristic pallor of the term *persona*," observing that "acts of poetic ventriloquism, in this period, could be at once profoundly moving and deeply enigmatic" (29). If it is possible to quibble with Enterline's insistence that the persona-concept and complex subjectivity are incompatible, the point nonetheless helpfully clarifies my use of the term here. For my concern in this book is not the subjectivity-effect of Elizabethan personae; rather, it is precisely their susceptibility to *objectification*, their tendency to be treated as concrete and detachable fictions.

11. Such figures are the subject of Robert Durling's classic study *The Figure of the Poet in Renaissance Epic* (Cambridge, Mass.: Harvard University Press, 1965).

12. Geoffrey Chaucer, *The Canterbury Tales*, in *The Riverside Chaucer*, ed. Larry Benson (Boston: Houghton Mifflin, 1987), frag. A, lines 21–22.

13. On Chaucer's early reception and the construction of poetic authority, see Seth Lerer, *Chaucer and His Readers: Imagining the Author in Late-Medieval England* (Princeton: Princeton University Press, 1993); Alexandra Gillespie, *Print Culture and the Medieval Author: Chaucer, Lydgate, and Their Books 1473–1557* (Oxford: Oxford University Press, 2006).

14. John Lydgate, *The Siege of Thebes*, ed. Robert R. Edwards (Kalamazoo: Medieval Institute Publications, 2001), line 92.

15. On fifteenth- and sixteenth-century Plowman texts, see Sarah A. Kelen, *Langland's Early Modern Identities* (Basingstoke: Palgrave Macmillan, 2007).

16. Kelen, *Langland's Early Modern Identities*, 76. "Eventually," Kelen continues, "Langland displaces Piers as the poem's center of authority, but for at least a half century, the author and his character mirror one another as authorizing predecessors invoked by sixteenth-century Protestant writers." On the appropriation of the plowman identity in early modern England, see also Mike Rodman Jones, *Radical Pastoral, 1381–1594: Appropriation and the Writing of Religious Controversy* (Burlington: Ashgate, 2011).

17. See Katharine Wilson, *Fictions of Authorship in Late Elizabethan Narratives: Euphues in Arcadia* (Oxford: Oxford University Press, 2006). For an account that theorizes the device of the persona as an index of the history of authorship, see Burt Kimmelman, *The Poetics of Authorship in the Later Middle Ages: The Emergence of the Modern Literary Persona* (New York: Peter Lang, 1996). Kimmelman emphasizes the link between what he calls "autocitation" and the emergence of literary individualism.

18. See Aaron Jaffe, *Modernism and the Culture of Celebrity* (Cambridge: Cambridge University Press, 2005).

19. This understanding of the persona shares much with Gust's concept of autofiction, which he uses to "emphasiz[e] that any literary self-presentation is a creative construction, a narrative doubling in which the fictional surrogate need not look, think, or feel like the author him/herself"; Gust, *Constructing Chaucer*, 41. Even this separation of fictional from real persons, however, retains an implicit logic of derivative reference: the autofictional persona, for Gust, is a "presentation" of a pre-existing "self," a "fictional surrogate" for the actual author. Such an

account of personae is perhaps inevitable when centered on Chaucer. My own genealogy of early modern personae, on the other hand, is intended to trace a history of textual personation that does *not* originate simply as self-reference or self-presentation.

20. See Jones, *Radical Pastoral*, and Rachel Hile, *Spenserian Satire: A Tradition of Indirection* (Manchester: Manchester University Press, 2017).

21. *Merie tales newly imprinted & made by Master Skelton Poet Laureat* (London, 1567), sig. A_2^r.

22. While Skelton thus became "indistinguishable from other jest-book heroes," Jane Griffiths suggests that his emergence as a jestbook trickster owed something to his poetry—namely, his reputation for rebellious opposition to authority; see Griffiths, *John Skelton and Poetic Authority: Defining the Liberty to Speak* (Oxford: Clarendon Press, 2006), 175.

23. Ian Munro, "Shakespeare's Jestbook: Wit, Print, Performance," *ELH* 71, no. 1 (2004), 103.

24. On Tarlton's remarkable cultural ubiquity in late sixteenth-century England, see Robert Weimann, *Shakespeare and the Popular Tradition in the Theater: Studies in the Social Dimension of Dramatic Form and Function*, ed. Robert Schwartz (Baltimore: Johns Hopkins University Press, 1978), 185–92; Alexandra Halasz, "'So beloved that men use his picture for their signs': Richard Tarlton and the Uses of Sixteenth-Century Celebrity," *Shakespeare Studies* 23 (1995): 19–38; Richard Preiss, *Clowning and Authorship in Early Modern Theatre* (Cambridge: Cambridge University Press, 2014), 110–40; and Katherine Duncan-Jones, "The Life, Death and Afterlife of Richard Tarlton," *Review of English Studies* 65, no. 268 (2014): 18–32.

25. Halasz, "Richard Tarlton," 28.

26. Gabriel Harvey, *Foure Letters, and Certain Sonnets* (London, 1592), sig. E_2^v. On Tarlton as a model for Nashe's extemporaneous style, see Karen Kettnich, "Nashe's Extemporal Vein and His Tarltonizing Wit," in *The Age of Thomas Nashe: Text, Bodies and Trespasses in Early Modern England*, ed. Stephen Guy-Bray, Joan Pong Linton, and Steve Mentz (Farnham: Ashgate, 2013), 99–114.

27. While loss rates render inferences from counts of extant titles of limited value, such counts may give some sense of the market's growth. According to John Barnard and Maureen Bell's tally of annual totals, the Short Title Catalogue gives 1,634 titles for the decade 1561–1570; for the decade 1591–1600, it gives 2,987; see *The Cambridge History of the Book in Britain: 1557–1695*, ed. John Barnard and D. F. McKenzie, with the assistance of Maureen Bell, vol. 4 of *The Cambridge History of the Book in Britain* (Cambridge: Cambridge University Press, 2002), 781–82.

28. Thomas Nashe, *The Anatomie of Absurditie*, in *The Works of Thomas Nashe*, ed. R. B. McKerrow, 5 vols. (1904–10; repr., Oxford: Basil Blackwell, 1958), 1:9.

29. William Webbe, *A Discourse of English Poetrie* (London, 1588), sig. D_1^r.

30. See Alan B. Farmer and Zachary Lesser, "What Is Print Popularity? A Map of the Elizabethan Book Trade," in *The Elizabethan Top Ten: Defining Print Popularity in Early Modern England*, ed. Andy Kesson and Emma Smith (Burlington: Ashgate, 2013), 37–39. Dividing the book trade into six categories—Religion, Politics and History, Poesy and the Arts, Science and Mathematics, School and Language Instruction, and Society and Conduct—Farmer and Lesser assess the relative popularity of these categories (and, within each category, of the genres that comprise it) by market share, reprint rate, and by first-edition weighting. According to their figures, the 1590s marked the moment when Poesy and the Arts surpassed Politics and History as the category with the second-largest market share behind Religion. Prose romance and prose fiction, for instance, commanded a combined market share of 3 percent over

the period from 1559 to 1591, but 6.7 percent in the period from 1592 to 1602. Poetry jumped from 9.1 percent to 12.7 percent, and professional plays increased from 0.3 percent to 4.0 percent. See also Lukas Erne and Tamsin Badcoe, "Shakespeare and the Popularity of Poetry Books in Print, 1583–1622," *Review of English Studies* New Series 65 (2013): 33–57. According to Erne and Badcoe, the market share of printed books of poetry between the decades 1583–1592 and 1593–1602, rose from 5.15 percent to 11.22 percent (40–41).

31. John Lyly, *"Euphues: The Anatomy of Wit" and "Euphues and His England"*, ed. Leah Scragg (Manchester: Manchester University Press, 2002), 30.

32. Halasz's study *The Marketplace of Print: Pamphlets and the Public Sphere in Early Modern England* (Cambridge: Cambridge University Press, 1997) locates Elizabethan print culture at the intersection of an emerging market economy and a nascent public sphere.

33. See Harold Love, *The Culture and Commerce of Texts: Scribal Publication in Seventeenth-Century England* (Amherst: University of Massachusetts Press, 1998), 35–46, 284–93, for an account of the different meanings *publication* might take in the circulation of manuscripts. Because copying and circulation were to a lesser or greater degree delimited by preexisting social networks, scribal circulation could allow a kind of limited publication in which texts circulated relatively widely but were not openly available—hence the reliance on manuscripts for the circulation of politically sensitive texts.

34. Michael McKeon, *The Secret History of Domesticity: Public, Private, and the Division of Knowledge* (Baltimore: Johns Hopkins University Press, 2005), 107. McKeon draws the term *social imaginary* from Charles Taylor, *Modern Social Imaginaries* (Durham: Duke University Press, 2004); coined as an expansion of Benedict Anderson's theory of the nation as "imagined community," social imaginaries include the market and the public sphere.

35. "Gentlemen Readers" was a ubiquitous form of address. Anthony Munday addressed "the well disposed Reader" in his *Zelavto. The Fovntaine of Fame. Erected in an Orchard of Amorous Aduentures* (London, 1580), sig. A_1^r, and Thomas Deloney addressed "all courteous Readers" in *The Gentle Craft* (London, 1637; Elizabethan editions not extant), sig. A_2^v. The different salutations suggest different ways of mapping the imagined communities of readers onto real social formations: by class and gender (gentlemen), for instance, or by a deliberate refusal to distinguish (*all* readers).

36. "Nobody" was frequently addressed in prefatory epistles, usually with a satirical edge. In Thomas Dekker's *Nevves from Graues-Ende: Sent to Nobody* (London, 1604), the dedicatory epistle hails "Syr Nicolas Nemo, *alias* Nobody" (sig. A_3^r). Dekker's Nobody satirizes the disappearance of patrons, but its emphasis gradually shifts toward the consumer readers who offered the only alternative to patronage. As Luke Wilson argues, the Nobody persona functioned in such instances alternately to mystify and to disclose the abstraction of economic exchange; see Wilson's chapter on the phenomenon in his *Theaters of Intention: Drama and the Law in Early Modern England* (Stanford: Stanford University Press, 2000), 216–62.

37. Jones, *Radical Pastoral*, 141. The family connection was made in a new edition of the plowman text *I Plain Piers* (1550), published as *O Read me for I am of great Antiquitie* (London, [1588?]) with a note on the title page declaring Piers to be "the Gransier of Martin mareprelitte."

38. Eric Vivier, "John Bridges, Martin Marprelate, and the Rhetoric of Satire," *English Literary Renaissance* 44, no. 1 (2014): 22.

39. See Lander's insightful analysis of the pamphlets' dialogic form in *Inventing Polemic: Religion, Print, and Literary Culture in Early Modern England* (Cambridge: Cambridge University Press, 2006), 80–110.

40. Joseph Black, "The Marprelate Controversy," in *The Oxford Handbook of English Prose, 1500–1640*, ed. Andrew Hadfield (Oxford: Oxford University Press, 2013), 550.

41. For an overview of the church's response, as well as a discussion of later imitations of and references to Martin, see Joseph Black's introduction to his superb edition of the pamphlets, *The Martin Marprelate Tracts: A Modernized and Annotated Edition* (Cambridge: Cambridge University Press, 2008), lvi–xciv.

42. See Wendy Wall, *The Imprint of Gender: Authorship and Publication in the English Renaissance* (Ithaca: Cornell University Press, 1993); Arthur Marotti, *Manuscript, Print, and the English Renaissance Lyric* (Ithaca: Cornell University Press, 1995); H. R. Woudhuysen, *Sir Philip Sidney and the Circulation of Manuscripts, 1558–1640* (Oxford: Clarendon Press, 1996); Love, *Culture and Commerce of Texts*; and Margaret Ezell, *Social Authorship and the Advent of Print* (Baltimore: Johns Hopkins University Press, 1999).

43. Philip Sidney, *The Covntesse of Pembrokes Arcadia* (London, 1590), sig. A_3^v.

44. Thus print publication, Wall suggests, was repeatedly imagined as a titillatingly erotic act of transgression—an act that both violated and, in so doing, reaffirmed social boundaries; see the chapter "Prefatorial Disclosures" in *The Imprint of Gender*.

45. See Richard A. McCabe, *"Ungainefull Arte": Poetry, Patronage, and Print in the Early Modern Era* (Oxford: Oxford University Press, 2016), 88–100; Jason Scott-Warren, *Sir John Harington and the Book as Gift* (Oxford: Oxford University Press, 2001).

46. On these and other uses of books (including, more whimsically, doodling and penmanship practice), see William H. Sherman, *Used Books: Marking Readers in Renaissance England* (Philadelphia: University of Pennsylvania Press, 2008).

47. See Zachary Lesser and Peter Stallybrass, "The First Literary *Hamlet* and the Commonplacing of Professional Plays," *Shakespeare Quarterly* 59, no. 4 (2008): 371–420.

48. Jane Griffiths, *Diverting Authorities: Experimental Glossing Practices in Manuscript and Print* (Oxford: Oxford University Press, 2014), 188. A similar blank appears in the 1590 edition of Sidney's *Arcadia*; there the tombstone for Argalus, lacking an epitaph, is printed as an empty, ornamented box. According to Joel B. Davis, handwritten versions of the epitaph (which was printed in the 1593 edition) fill the space in at least four extant copies; see Davis, *"The Countesse of Pembrokes Arcadia" and the Invention of English Literature* (New York: Palgrave Macmillan, 2011), 73–74.

49. Peter Stallybrass, afterword to *Renaissance Paratexts*, ed. Helen Smith and Louise Wilson (Cambridge: Cambridge University Press, 2013), 218.

50. On the riddling poetics of *A Hundreth Sundrie Flowres*, and its ingenious manipulation of the intersecting practices of manuscript collection, editorial compilation, and print publication, see Megan Heffernan, "Gathered by Invention: Additive Forms and Inference in Gascoigne's Poesy," *Modern Language Quarterly* 76, no. 4 (2015): 413–45.

51. Munday, *Zelavto*.

52. Andy Kesson, in an important recent revaluation of Lyly's place in early modern literary culture, counts ten books that "explicitly nam[e] Lyly's character." See Kesson, *John Lyly and Early Modern Authorship* (Manchester: Manchester University Press, 2014), 75.

53. Douglas Bruster, *Shakespeare and the Question of Culture: Early Modern Literature and the Cultural Turn* (Basingstoke: Palgrave Macmillan, 2003), 76.

54. John Lyly, *"Euphues: The Anatomy of Wit" and "Euphues and His England"*, ed. Leah Scragg (Manchester: Manchester University Press, 2003), 161, 162.

55. Ibid., 353.

56. Ibid. As Scragg points out, Mount Silixsedra does not refer to any actual place, a fact that points up Euphues's fictionality even at the moment when Lyly's narrator treats him most like a real person. Euphues, as ever, is caught in between, attributed a degree of autonomy but an autonomy located, finally, in an imaginary place.

57. David Brewer, *The Afterlife of Character, 1726–1825* (Philadelphia: University of Pennsylvania Press, 2005), 17. Brewer emphasizes the distinction between the academic canon, which privileges exclusivity of taste and enforces aesthetic and intellectual distinctions, and the social canon, with its emphasis on commonality and shared tastes. For Franco Moretti's discussion of social canons, see Moretti, "The Slaughterhouse of Literature," *Modern Language Quarterly* 61, no. 1 (2000): 207–27.

58. See Gavin Alexander, *Writing After Sidney: The Literary Response to Sir Philip Sidney, 1586–1640* (Oxford: Oxford University Press, 2006); and Jones, *Radical Pastoral*.

59. Natasha Simonova, *Early Modern Authorship and Prose Continuations: Adaptation and Ownership from Sidney to Richardson* (Basingstoke: Palgrave Macmillan, 2015). On continuation as a genre born of early modern practices of readerly compilation and collection, see Jeffrey Todd Knight, "Afterworlds: Thomas Middleton, the Book, and the Genre of Continuation," in *Formal Matters: Reading the Materials of English Renaissance Literature*, ed. Allison K. Deutermann and András Kiséry (Manchester: Manchester University Press, 2013), 77–96.

60. Simonova, *Early Modern Authorship*, 8.

61. Bruno Latour, *Reassembling the Social: An Introduction to Actor-Network-Theory* (Oxford: Oxford University Press, 2005), 46.

62. In this sense, personation is an example of what Latour calls the "figuration" of agency, the tendency (when describing action) to think of "actants" as having the accustomed individuality of "actors." See *Reassembling the Social*, 53–54.

63. Andrew Hadfield, "'Not Without Mustard': Self-Publicity and Polemic in Early Modern Literary London," in *Renaissance Transformations: The Making of English Writing 1500–1650*, ed. Margaret Healy and Thomas Healy (Edinburgh: Edinburgh University Press, 2009), 64–78. See also Marcy L. North, "Early Modern Anonymity," *Oxford Handbooks Online*, June 25, 2017, http://www.oxfordhandbooks.com/view/10.1093/oxfordhb/9780199935338.001.0001/oxfordhb-9780199935338-e-12.

64. See McCabe, *"Ungainefull Arte"*, 4–5. McCabe cites as examples Colin Clout and the Shepherd of the Ocean (Spenser and Walter Raleigh) and Corydon and Meliboeus (Thomas Watson and Thomas Walsingham) and observes that the crafting of such personae, as these examples indicate, was hardly contained to dedicatory paratexts.

65. Andrew Escobedo, *Volition's Face: Personification and the Will in Renaissance Literature* (Notre Dame: University of Notre Dame Press, 2017), 4. For an analysis (routed through semiotic and narrative theory) of personification as a trope, see Paxson, *The Poetics of Personification*. Where Escobedo sets abstract personification against the modern individual character, Elizabeth Fowler argues that individual characters emerge out of abstract "social persons"; see her *Literary Character: The Human Figure in Early English Writing* (Ithaca: Cornell University Press, 2003).

66. Escobedo, *Volition's Face*, 4, 20–21.

67. Bruster, *Shakespeare*, 79.

68. Ibid., 66, 81.

69. Ibid., 79.

70. The Making Publics project, convened at McGill from 2005 to 2010, pursued not the origins of the Habermasian public sphere but rather the multiplicity and diversity of a range of "publics," emphasizing their relevance to considerations of literature and culture, as well as politics. The project's aims are articulated, and its scope demonstrated, in a pair of essay collections: first, Bronwen Wilson and Paul Yachnin, eds., *Making Publics in Early Modern Europe: People, Things, Forms of Knowledge* (New York: Routledge, 2010); and, more recently, Yachnin and Marlene Eberhart, eds., *Forms of Association: Making Publics in Early Modern Europe* (Amherst: University of Massachusetts Press, 2015).

71. Michael Warner, *Publics and Counterpublics* (New York: Zone Books, 2002), 74, 67.

72. Nashe, *Pierce Penilesse*, 1:192.

73. Warner, *Publics*, 114.

74. Richard Helgerson, *Self-Crowned Laureates: Spenser, Jonson, Milton, and the Literary System* (Berkeley: University of California Press, 1983), 2–3.

75. Georgia Brown, *Redefining Elizabethan Literature* (Cambridge: Cambridge University Press, 2004), 5. "The 1590s," writes Brown, "have long been recognized to be one of the most important decades in English literary history, but, at the same time, the phenomenon of the 1590s has largely been ignored by criticism" (50). This project takes Brown's suggestion seriously, sharing her sense of the decade as a moment in which "the idea of literature was tentatively being elaborated" (51).

76. Helgerson acknowledges the ambiguity in calling Sidney "that most nearly laureate of amateur poets"; *Self-Crowned Laureates*, 31. For an account that identifies Sidney as the central precursor for a generation of Elizabethan and Jacobean poets, see Raphael Falco, *Conceived Presences: Literary Genealogy in Renaissance England* (Amherst: University of Massachusetts Press, 1994).

77. Brown, *Redefining Elizabethan Literature*, 47. For another insightful critique of *Self-Crowned Laureates*, see Davis, *"The Countesse of Pembrokes Arcadia"*, 10–13. Davis aims to rescue Sidney in particular from the role of "pure signifier"—his position, in Helgerson's system, as the amateur *par excellence* against whom Spenser and others define their laureate roles (11).

78. Bourdieu's theory of cultural production is developed in the essays collected in *The Field of Cultural Production: Essays on Art and Literature*, ed. Randal Johnson (New York: Columbia University Press, 1993), and revised and expanded in *The Rules of Art: Genesis and Structure of the Literary Field*, trans. Susan Emanuel (Stanford: Stanford University Press, 1996).

79. On the subfield of restricted production, see Pierre Bourdieu, "The Market of Symbolic Goods," trans. R. Swyer, in *The Field of Cultural Production*, 115–20; on relative autonomy, see Bourdieu, *Rules of Art*, 215–23.

80. This description of Bourdieu's theory of cultural production is from Michael Lucey and Tom McEnaney's introduction to a recent special issue of *Representations* on language-in-use and the literary artifact. See Lucey and McEnaney, "Introduction: Language-in-Use and Literary Fieldwork," *Representations* 137, no. 1 (2017): 3.

81. See Lori Humphrey Newcomb, *Reading Popular Romance in Early Modern England* (New York: Columbia University Press, 2002); Edward Gieskes, *Representing the Professions: Administration, Law, and Theater in Early Modern England* (Newark: University of Delaware, 2006), 227. Among other Bourdieu-influenced work on early modern literature, see especially Robert Matz, *Defending Literature in Early Modern England: Renaissance Literary Theory in Social Context* (Cambridge: Cambridge University Press, 2000); Trevor Ross, *The Making of*

the English Literary Canon: From the Middle Ages to the Late Eighteenth Century (Montreal: McGill-Queen's University Press, 1998).

82. Latour distinguishes between two kinds of objects: *intermediaries*, which "transpor[t] meaning without transformation," and *mediators*, which "transform, translate, distort, and modify the meaning or the elements they are supposed to carry." *Reassembling the Social*, 39.

83. Bourdieu, *Rules of Art*, 190.

84. Ibid., 157: "The ageing of authors, works or schools is . . . engendered in the fight between those who have already left their mark and are trying to endure, and those who cannot make their own marks in turn without consigning to the past those who have an interest in stopping time, in eternalizing the present state." In his emphasis on conflict between writers and their predecessors, Bourdieu can seem to resemble, of all critics, Harold Bloom. Of course, Bourdieu conceives of this conflict not as psychodrama ("the anxiety of influence") but as a contest over symbolic capital.

85. See Joseph Loewenstein, *The Author's Due: Printing and the Prehistory of Copyright* (Chicago: University of Chicago Press, 2002) and *Ben Jonson and Possessive Authorship* (Cambridge: Cambridge University Press, 2002). Loewenstein does not dismiss earlier accounts of authorship, such as Michel Foucault's, but he maintains that the various functions of the author-figure (including its role in rendering discourse susceptible to legal regulation and censorship) were shaped by its implication in the complex negotiations of intellectual property in the period before the emergence of modern copyright law. Under the guild regulations of the Stationers' Company, rights to copy rested with the publishers who registered a given title with the guild and thus obtained the exclusive right to print it. At times, as Loewenstein shows, a publisher's interests militated in favor of asserting a sense of authorial presence of possession. The keen interest in the uncertain authenticity of Robert Greene's several deathbed repentance pamphlets, which I examine in Chapter 1, is one example of how stationers might be led to rely on (and thus help construct) a notion of authorial possession.

86. Loewenstein, *The Author's Due*, 44. On the passage of the Statute of Anne and the discourse of authorial rights that supported it, see Mark Rose, *Authors and Owners: The Invention of Copyright* (Cambridge, Mass.: Harvard University Press, 1995), 31–48. Rose argues that the Statute shifted the discourse of authorial interests from "honor and reputation" to economic property and marked a reorientation of theories of copyright, divorcing it from censorship and consolidating it "under the rubric of property rather than regulation" (48).

87. See Marcy L. North, *The Anonymous Renaissance: Cultures of Discretion in Tudor-Stuart England* (Chicago: University of Chicago Press, 2003). On "social authorship" more broadly, see Ezell, *Social Authorship*.

88. See Kevin Pask, *The Emergence of the English Author: Scripting the Life of the Poet in Early Modern England* (Cambridge: Cambridge University Press, 1996).

89. See especially Jeffrey Masten, *Textual Intercourse: Collaboration, Authorship, and Sexualities in Renaissance Drama* (Cambridge: Cambridge University Press, 1997); and Heather Anne Hirschfeld, *Joint Enterprises: Collaborative Drama and the Institutionalization of the English Renaissance Theater* (Amherst: University of Massachusetts Press, 2004).

90. Stephen B. Dobranski, *Readers and Authorship in Early Modern England* (Cambridge: Cambridge University Press, 2005); and Simonova, *Early Modern Authorship*.

91. Reclamations of "form" and "formalism" arise periodically as responses to leading historicizing methods. Thus the ascendancy of the New Historicism was met with two collections urging a historically informed formalism: Mark David Rasmussen, ed., *Renaissance Literature*

and Its Formal Engagements (New York: Palgrave, 2002), and Stephen Cohen, ed., *Shakespeare and Historical Formalism* (Aldershot: Ashgate, 2007). More recently, Allison Deutermann and András Kiséry have responded to the rise of the history of the book with another collection, *Formal Matters: Reading the Materials of English Renaissance Literature* (Manchester: Manchester University Press, 2013).

92. David Scott Kastan, *Shakespeare and the Book* (Cambridge: Cambridge University Press, 2001), 4.

93. András Kiséry and Allison Deutermann, "The Matter of Form: Book History, Formalist Criticism, and Francis Bacon's Aphorisms," in *The Book in History, the Book as History: New Intersections of the Material Text; Essays in Honor of David Scott Kastan*, ed. Heidi Brayman Hackel, Jesse M. Lander, and Zachary Lesser (New Haven: Beinecke Rare Book and Manuscript Library, Yale University, 2016), 41.

94. Lisa Gitelman, *Always Already New: Media, History, and the Data of Culture* (Cambridge, Mass.: MIT Press, 2006), 7. Social realization for Gitelman implies much that we would consider "formal," including the "ritual collocation of people on the same mental map, sharing or engaged with popular ontologies of representation." Adrian Johns offers a similar reminder for students of "print culture," which, he argues, is "a *result* of manifold representations, practices and conflicts, rather than just the monolithic *cause* with which we are often presented." *The Nature of the Book: Print and Knowledge in the Making* (Chicago: University of Chicago Press, 1998), 20.

CHAPTER 1

1. B[arnabe] R[iche], *Greenes newes both from heauen and hell* (London, 1593), sig. A_2^r; hereafter cited parenthetically in text with the initials *GN*. The author of *Greenes Newes* is identified only as "B. R." In attributing the pamphlet to Riche, I follow its modern editor, R. B. McKerrow, who cites the text's anti-Catholic satire and references to Ireland, both typical features of Riche's writing; see in B[arnabe] R[iche] and R[ichard] B[arnfield], *Greenes Newes both from Heaven and Hell (1593) and Greenes Funeralls (1594)*, ed. R. B. McKerrow (London: Sidgwick and Jackson, 1911).

2. For a bibliography of the extant editions of Greene's works, see Kirk Melnikoff and Edward Gieskes, eds., *Writing Robert Greene: Essays on England's First Notorious Professional Writer* (Aldershot: Ashgate, 2008), 235–38.

3. The authoritative account of Greene's prodigal self-fashioning remains Richard Helgerson, *The Elizabethan Prodigals* (Berkeley: University of California Press, 1976).

4. Melnikoff and Gieskes, *Writing Robert Greene*. Subtitled "Essays on England's First Notorious Professional Writer."

5. Samuel Rowlands, *Tis Merrie when Gossips meete* (London, 1602), sig. A_3^r.

6. Henry Chettle, *Kind-Harts Dreame. Conteining fiue Apparitions, with their Inuectives against abuses raigning* (London, 1593). *Kind-Harts Dreame* was entered in the Stationers' Register on December 8, 1592; *Greenes Newes* was never registered.

7. John Dickenson, *Greene in conceipt New raised from his graue to write the tragique historie of faire Valeria of London* (London, 1598).

8. Rowlands devotes little time to Greene himself, using his name primarily as an advertising device, so I focus in this essay on the other pamphlets that resurrected him; nonetheless,

Rowlands's title suggests the degree to which the idea of Greene's haunting had seized the imagination of Elizabethan readers.

9. Melnikoff and Gieskes, *Writing Robert Greene*. This volume of essays indicates the increased interest in Greene not only as an Elizabethan playwright but as a popular print author, placing him at the center of early modern literary culture's negotiations of authorship and authority, textual property and literary value. Of particular interest in *Writing Robert Greene* are essays by Steve Mentz, who argues that Greene's fame helped consolidate the authorial name as a unitary banner for a multiplicity of works and rendered him "a public symbol for published prose fiction," and Bryan Reynolds and Henry S. Turner, who find in his precocious celebrity the conversion of the institutional prestige of Greene's Cambridge background into a specifically literary form of cultural capital. Lori Humphrey Newcomb's invaluable book-length study of the reception of *Pandosto* explores similar themes, arguing that Greene's career and reception offer glimpses into the emergence of a category of "popular" authorship over and against prestigious "literary" authorship. See Mentz, "Forming Greene: Theorizing the Early Modern Author in the *Groatsworth of Wit*," in Melnikoff and Gieskes, *Writing Robert Greene*, 115–31; Reynolds and Turner, "From *Homo Academicus* to *Poeta Publicus*: Celebrity and Transversal Knowledge in Robert Greene's *Friar Bacon and Friar Bungay* (c. 1589)," in Melnikoff and Gieskes, *Writing Robert Greene*, 39–51; and Newcomb, *Reading Popular Romance in Early Modern England* (New York: Columbia University Press, 2002).

10. See Newcomb, *Reading Popular Romance*, 70–76; Arul Kumaran, "Patronage, Print, and an Early Modern 'Pamphlet Moment,'" *Explorations in Renaissance Culture* 31, no. 1 (2005): 59–88; and Steve Mentz, *Romance for Sale in Early Modern England: The Rise of Prose Fiction* (Aldershot: Ashgate, 2006), 207–20. Of the ghost pamphlets, only Chettle's *Kind-Harts Dreame* has received significant individual attention, treated as a representation of the print marketplace and as a satire on patronage seeking; see, respectively, Alexandra Halasz, *The Marketplace of Print: Pamphlets and the Public Sphere in Early Modern England* (Cambridge: Cambridge University Press, 1997), 46–81; Arul Kumaran, "Satiric Mimicking in Henry Chettle's *Kind-Hartes Dreame*," *Studies in Philology* 109, no. 4 (2012): 429–54.

11. Although Chettle's and Riche's pamphlets, along with Thomas Nashe's *Pierce Penilesse*, are occasionally cited as evidence of an Elizabethan revival of Lucianic netherworld dialogues, Greene's presence in each (Nashe mentions him as well) suggests that the trend was inspired more by Greene's charismatic persona. Tellingly, the closest precedent for Greene's resurrection was *Tarltons Newes out of Purgatorie Onely such a iest as his iigge, fit for gentlemen to laugh at an houre, &c. Published by an old companion of his, Robin Goodfellow* (London, 1590), a ghosting of the famous stage clown Richard Tarlton. On the afterlife of this other Elizabethan celebrity, see Richard Preiss, *Clowning and Authorship in Early Modern Theatre* (Cambridge: Cambridge University Press, 2014), 110–40. On Lucianic dialogue, see Benjamin Boyce, "News from Hell: Satiritic Communications with the Nether World in English Writing of the Seventeenth and Eighteenth Centuries," *PMLA* 58, no. 2 (1943): 402–37; Lorna Hutson, *Thomas Nashe in Context* (Oxford: Oxford University Press, 1989), 127–51.

12. Chettle, *Kind-Harts Dreame*, sig. B_3^r. Hereafter cited parenthetically in text, with initials *KH*.

13. Dickenson, *Greene in conceipt*, sig. A_4^r.

14. On the rise of printed prose fiction and poetry, in particular, at the end of the sixteenth century, see Alan B. Farmer and Zachary Lesser's quantitative analysis of the early modern book trade in "What Is Print Popularity? A Map of the Elizabethan Book Trade," in

The Elizabethan Top Ten: Defining Print Popularity in Early Modern England, ed. Andy Kesson and Emma Smith (Burlington: Ashgate, 2013), 19–54, esp. 37–39.

15. Walter Ong, *Orality and Literacy: The Technologizing of the Word* (London: Methuen, 1982), 125. For a nuanced, and in certain respects sympathetic, revaluation of this line of thinking, see Harold Love's revisionist study of manuscript production in the age of print, *The Culture and Commerce of Texts: Scribal Publication in Seventeenth-Century England* (Amherst: University of Massachusetts Press, 1998), 141–48, 284–92.

16. Opponents of the idea of print culture—see especially Joseph Dane's *The Myth of Print Culture: Essays on Evidence, Textuality, and Bibliographic Method* (Toronto: University of Toronto, 2003), 10–31—typically trace its popularity to Elizabeth Eisenstein and Marshall McLuhan. But the ghost pamphlets suggest a history that begins much earlier, in the responses of early modern writers, stationers, and readers (Chettle was all three) to prevailing conditions of publication. For approaches to the topic that emphasize the cultural construction of print, see Adrian Johns, *The Nature of the Book: Print and Knowledge in the Making* (Chicago: University of Chicago Press, 1998); Jane Griffiths, *Diverting Authorities: Experimental Glossing Practices in Manuscript and Print* (Oxford: Oxford University Press, 2014); and, in study of ideas of mediation in a later period, Christina Lupton, *Knowing Books: The Consciousness of Mediation in Eighteenth-Century Britain* (Philadelphia: University of Pennsylvania Press, 2011).

17. Michael Warner, *Publics and Counterpublics* (New York: Zone Books, 2002), 67.

18. Thomas Dekker, *The Wonderfull Yeare* (London, 1603), sig. A_3^r.

19. By *fictionality* I mean not the later-emerging realistic nonreferentiality that Catherine Gallagher designates the hallmark of the modern novel but the particular logic of truth and artifice that subtends Greene's works and Elizabethan fiction more broadly. Gallagher, "The Rise of Fictionality," in *History, Geography, and Culture*, vol. 1 of *The Novel*, ed. Franco Moretti (Princeton: Princeton University Press, 2006).

20. Christine S. Lee, "The Meanings of Romance: Rethinking Early Modern Fiction," *Modern Philology* 112, no. 2 (2014): 287. As Lee demonstrates, *romance* emerged as a term for narrative prose fiction only in the seventeenth century, when it retrospectively was applied to the works of Greene, John Lyly, Thomas Lodge, Antony Munday, and others. Lacking a name, the genre in Elizabethan England depended for coherence on practical conventions.

The critical literature on sixteenth-century prose fiction has expanded dramatically in the last decade. A number of established works remain central to the field, including: Helgerson, *Elizabethan Prodigals*; Walter R. Davis, *Idea and Act in Elizabethan Fiction* (Princeton: Princeton University Press, 1969); David Margolies, *Novel and Society in Elizabethan England* (London: Croom Helm, 1985); Arthur Kinney, *Humanist Poetics: Thought, Rhetoric, and Fiction in Sixteenth-Century England* (Amherst: University of Massachusetts Press, 1986); Hutson, *Thomas Nashe in Context*; and Constance Relihan, *Fashioning Authority: The Development of Elizabethan Novelistic Discourse* (Kent: Kent State University Press, 1994). Paul Salzman's *English Prose Fiction 1558–1700: A Critical History* (Oxford: Clarendon Press, 1985) remains the best general survey of prose fiction in the sixteenth and seventeenth centuries.

Margolies's and Hutson's attention to the social and economic contexts of literary production has proven influential to recent criticism. For instance, Steve Mentz's vital account of Heliodoran romance, *Romance for Sale*, explores the form's implication in the rise of the print marketplace and the middlebrow reader. Katharine Wilson's *Fictions of Authorship in Late Elizabethan Narratives: Euphues in Arcadia* (Oxford: Clarendon Press, 2006) offers rich close readings of a range of overlooked prose narratives, including many by Greene, while Nandini

Das's *Renaissance Romance: The Transformation of English Prose Fiction, 1570–1620* (Burlington: Ashgate, 2011) explores the transformations of the genre of prose romance in the period. Preceding and perhaps helping to spark this wave of interest is Robert Maslen's brilliantly perceptive *Elizabethan Fictions: Espionage, Counter-espionage and the Duplicity of Fiction in Early Elizabethan Prose Narratives* (Oxford: Oxford University Press, 1997).

21. Maslen, *Elizabethan Fictions*, 11.

22. William Painter's *The Palace of Pleasure Beautified, adorned and well furnished, with Pleasaunt Historyes and excellent Nouelles, selected out of diuers good and commendable Authors* (London, 1566) and Geoffrey Fenton's *Certaine Tragicall Discourses written out of Frenche and Latin* (London, 1567) sparked interest in (and imitations of) Continental novellas. They also provoked the moral suspicion of writers like Roger Ascham, whose *The Scholemaster or plaine and perfite way of teachyng children* (London, 1570) inveighed against "fonde bookes, of late translated out of *Italian* into English, sold in euery shop in London, commended by honest titles the soner to corrupt honest maners" (sig. I_2^v).

23. On euphuism, see Jonas Barish, "The Prose Style of John Lyly," *ELH* 23, no. 1 (1956): 14–35.

24. Margolies, *Novel and Society in Elizabethan England*, 43. The fate of George Gascoigne's *Adventures of Master F.J.* (1573) hints at the effect of these conventions. After the first edition, which purported to record the true story of an adulterous affair, provoked scandal, Gascoigne dropped the pretense of topicality in the second, replacing English names with Italian ones and presenting the story as the translation of an Italian novella.

25. Robert Greene, *Greenes Groats-worth of witte, bought with a million of Repentance* (London, 1592), sig. B_1^r; hereafter cited parenthetically in text as *GW.*

26. Robert Greene, *Arbasto, The Anatomie of Fortune* (London, 1584), sig. E_2^r–E_2^v.

27. Greene, *Arbasto*, sig. E_2^v.

28. Greene's frame tales include *Morando* (1584), *Euphues His Censure to Philautus* (1587), *Penelopes Web* (1587), and *Perimedes the Blacke-smith* (1588). In *Perimedes* (London, 1588), the scene is simply the evening pastime of a husband and wife, the "pleasant chatte" of Perimedes and Delia "betweene them selues" (sig. B_1^v). This casual domesticity, however, is offset by its exotic setting; even a quiet evening in Alexandria puts one a long way from London. As if to underline the oddness of the mixture of the familiar and the alien, Greene preposterously informs his readers that the couple's conversations had been long ago transcribed and recently discovered in the Alexandrian annals.

29. Greene, *Arbasto*, sig. B_1^r.

30. The primary model for *Arbasto*'s frame narrative is Achilles Tatius's *Clitophon and Leucippe*, a romance that Greene presumably read in Italian translation. In Tatius's text, a traveler similarly happens upon an iconic image (a painting of Cupid), and a storyteller emerges to unfold its meaning. Compared to Clitophon, who jumps out unprompted to explain the painting's message with a story about himself, Arbasto is decidedly reluctant to speak, telling his interlocutor, "I craue not to be acquainted with such a bold guest" (sig. B_2^r). For an illuminating recent discussion of Greene's debt to Tatius, see Katharine Wilson, *Fictions of Authorship*, 87–88.

31. Greene, *Arbasto*, sig. B_3^v.

32. Wilson, *Fictions of Authorship*, 89.

33. Greene, *Arbasto*, sig. H_3^v.

34. See Tzvetan Todorov, *The Fantastic: A Structural Approach to a Literary Genre*, trans. Richard Howard, intr. Richard Scholes (Ithaca: Cornell University Press, 1975), 82–86.

Todorov argues that narrator-characters, as he terms them, can facilitate readers' identification with the characters in a text (he is particularly concerned with the genre of the fantastic) and allow a logic of authentication, whereby the narrator's credit urges readers to accept the truth of his account. Thus character narration, to borrow James Phelan's term in *Living to Tell about It: A Rhetoric and Ethics of Character Narration* (Ithaca: Cornell University Press, 2004), puts the narrative act in a particular relation to readers, a relation that can be one of trust or distrust, affection or disdain, and so forth.

35. Mikhail Bakhtin's account of addressivity reminds us that fictional narration is, like all speech and writing, a kind of utterance, a communication directed to someone: "As distinct from the signifying units of language—words and sentences—that are impersonal, belonging to nobody and addressed to nobody, the utterance has both an author . . . and an addressee." Bakhtin, "The Problem of Speech Genres," in *Speech Genres and Other Late Essays*, trans. Vern W. McGee, ed. Caryl Emerson and Michael Holquist (Austin: University of Texas Press, 1986), 95. The distance that I have described as inhering in print and in certain fictional practices can perhaps be more precisely described as attenuation, or an abstraction, of the addressivity of relevant utterances; Greene's use of Arbasto as the narrator of his own story can, by extension, be seen as an attempt to recover a more robust form of addressivity.

36. See Steve Mentz, "Magic Books: Cony-Catching and the Romance of Early Modern London," in *Rogues and Early Modern English Culture*, ed. Craig Dionne and Steve Mentz (Ann Arbor: University of Michigan Press, 2004); Linda Woodbridge, *Vagrancy, Homelessness, and English Renaissance Literature* (Champaign: University of Illinois Press, 2001). On Greene's self-fashioning in these pamphlets, see Relihan, *Fashioning Authority*, 61–70.

37. The story, too, is derivative, so much so as to draw an oblique charge of plagiarism from William Warner, who in the 1597 second edition of *Pan His Syrinx* described "one (in penning pregnenter, & a Scholler better than my selfe, on whose graue the grasse now growth green, whom otherwise, though otherwise to me guiltie, I name not) hath borrowed out of euery *Calamus* or Storie herein handled, Argument & Inuention to seueral Bookes by him published." Warner, *Syrinx, or A seauenfold historie handled with varietie of pleasant and profitable both commicall and tragicall argument* (London, 1597), sig. A_3^r.

38. Robert Greene, *Greenes Never too late. Or, A Powder of Experience: Sent to all youthfull Gentlemen* [. . .] (London, 1590), sig. B_1^r.

39. Greene, *Never Too Late*, sig. C_4^r.

40. Meredith Skura, *Tudor Autobiography: Listening for Inwardness* (Chicago: University of Chicago Press, 2008), 208.

41. See Davis, *Idea and Act*, 179; Robert W. Maslen, "Robert Greene and the Uses of Time," in Melnikoff and Gieskes, *Writing Robert Greene*, 182.

42. Das, *Renaissance Romance*, 132.

43. Greene, *Never Too Late*, sig. C_4^v.

44. The opening paragraph of the frame narrative, along similar lines, feints toward the genre of the dream vision, only to restrict it to the counterfactual: "I had flat fallen into a slumber, if I had not espied a traueller weary and desolate, to haue bended his steppes toward me" (*Never Too Late*, sig. B_1^r). Here, too, a convention of fictional framing is raised in order to be inverted.

45. Das perceptively observes that "the merging of the space of romance with the urban spaces familiar to contemporary readers . . . was a narrative move very rarely attempted by Greene's predecessors" and argues that "Greene opened up entirely new ways in which Elizabethan fiction

could conceivably enter into a conversation with reality." Das, *Renaissance Romance*, 143. My reading emphasizes the tensions between fiction and referential truth that Greene saw as resulting from this conversation.

46. Skura, *Tudor Autobiography*, 208–9; Greene, *Never Too Late*, sig. K_4^r.

47. Greene, *Francescos Fortunes: Or, The second part of Greenes Never too late* (London, 1590), sig. L_2^v.

48. For arguments in favor of Chettle, see the editor's introduction to Robert Greene, *Greene's Groatsworth of Wit: Bought with a Million of Repentance (1592)*, ed. D. Allen Carroll (Binghamton: Medieval and Renaissance Texts and Studies, 1994); John Jowett, "Johannes Factotum: Henry Chettle and *Greene's Groatsworth of Wit*," *Papers of the Bibliographical Society of America* 87, no. 4 (1993): 453–86. Brian Vickers offers an extensive critique of the Chettle attribution and uses plagiarism software to make a persuasive case for Greene's authorship in "Giving Greene His *Groatsworth*," *Papers of the Bibliographic Society of America* (forthcoming). I thank Prof. Vickers for sharing his essay with me. A shorter summary of the issues may be found in Vickers, "'Upstart Crow'? The Myth of Shakespeare's Plagiarism," *Review of English Studies*, n.s., 68, no. 284 (2016): 247–49.

49. One theory of the *Groatsworth*'s authorship, in fact, holds that Chettle essentially borrowed these matching episodes from *Never Too Late* in the process of forging it; see Warren B. Austin, "Technique of the Chettle-Greene Forgery: Supplementary Material on the Authorship of the *Groatsworth of Wit*," *Shakespeare Newsletter* 20 (1970): 43. As Vickers points out, a more plausible explanation is Greene's own habit of recycling his material; see Vickers, "Giving Greene His *Groatsworth*."

50. Greene, *Groats-worth*, sig. E_3^r.

51. W.W. Barker, "Rhetorical Romance: The 'Frivolous Toyes' of Robert Greene," in *Unfolded Tales: Essays on Renaissance Romance*, ed. George M. Logan and Gordon Teskey (Ithaca: Cornell University Press, 1989), 96.

52. Nicholas Storojenko, *Robert Greene: His Life and Works* (Moscow, 1878), trans. E. A. B. Hodgetts and repr. in *The Life and Complete Works in Prose and Verse of Robert Greene*, ed. A. B. Grosart, 13 vols. (London: privately printed, 1881–86), 1:63–64. Charles Crupi, writing more recently and more cautiously, acknowledges that the repentance pamphlets are composed in "stylized prose and conventional plots" but argues that these nonetheless "articulate questions of personal importance." Crupi, *Robert Greene* (Boston: Twayne Publishers, 1986), 35.

53. Newcomb, *Reading Popular Romance*, 55; on Greene's name as shroud, see 48–52.

54. Gabriel Harvey offered one notably divergent account, reporting in *Foure Letters, and certaine Sonnets: Especially touching Robert Greene, and other parties, by him abused* (London, 1592), a work of invective against Greene and Nashe, that Greene had died in "a surfett of pickle herringe and rennish wine" (sig. A_4^r). Nashe half-heartedly defended Greene in his reply, which came in *Strange Newes, of the Intercepting Certaine Letters*, in *The Works of Thomas Nashe*, ed. Ronald B. McKerrow, 5 vols. (1904–10, repr. Oxford: Basil Blackwell, 1958), 1:247–335, esp. 287.

55. Halasz, *Marketplace*, 38.

56. Robert Greene, *Greenes Vision: Written at the instant of his death* (London, 1592), sig. A_3^r.

57. Robert Greene, *The Repentance of Robert Greene Maister of Arts* (London, 1592), sig. A_4^r.

58. Kumaran, "Patronage, Print."

59. On Chettle's and Danter's relationship, see John Jowett, "Henry Chettle: 'Your Old Compositor,'" *Text* 15 (2003): 141–61; and on Chettle's involvement in the *Groatsworth* and

Repentance manuscripts, see Jowett, "Johannes Factotum," 466–75. After their printing partnership with William Hoskins abruptly ended in 1591, the pair apparently continued to work together, with Chettle using his connections to writers to procure manuscripts for Danter.

60. W. W. Greg and E. Boswell, *Records of the Court of the Stationers' Company 1576 to 1602: From Register B* (London: Bibliographical Society, 1930), 46.

61. This is, inevitably, speculative. Still, the record of the disagreements suggests that the relations between the parties involved were alternately, or simultaneously, cooperative and fractious. See Jowett, "Johannes Factotum," 472–74, for further speculation and background on the disputes.

62. On the relation between the early modern copyright regime, which located literary property with publishers, and the modern notion of possessive authorship, see Joseph Loewenstein, *The Author's Due: Printing and the Prehistory of Copyright* (Chicago: University of Chicago Press, 2002).

63. Greene, *Groats-worth*, sig. F_3^{v}.

64. Greene, *Repentance*, sig. D_1^{r}, D_3^{r}. Gabriel Harvey attributed to Greene a less flattering final letter to his wife, asking her merely to pay his debts to the innkeeper who provided him comfort at his death. See Harvey, *Foure Letters*, sig. B_3^{v}.

65. Two years after Greene's death, a volume of sonnets entitled *Greenes Funeralls*, published to defend its namesake from posthumous detractors, turned to the same strategy; its final two poems are a pair of psalm translations by the Irish poet Richard Stanihurst (1547–1618) that were, it reports, "used of R.G. at the instant of his death." Richard Barnfield, *Greenes Funeralls* (London, 1594), sig. C_3^{v}.

66. Greene, *Repentance*, sig. D_2^{r}.

67. This rotation suggestively echoes the rotation of voices *within* Greene's narration: the shift from the impersonal narrator telling Roberto's story to Greene himself in the *Groatsworth* and the participants in the dialogue of *Greenes Vision*. Only the *Repentance* is told entirely in Greene's voice, but even here the first-person main text is complemented by a pair of additional documents that rely on a chastely third-person voice to fill in the blanks—Burby's prefatory epistle and a concluding account of "the manner of the death and last end of *Robert Greene*"—in addition to Greene's letter to his wife and his dying prayer.

68. Dickenson, *Greene in conceipt*, sig. A_1^{r}.

69. Newcomb, *Reading Popular Romance*, 71.

70. Dickenson, *Greene in conceipt*, sig. A_3^{r}.

71. Warner, *Publics*, 96–97.

72. David Brewer, *The Afterlife of Character, 1726–1825* (Philadelphia: University of Pennsylvania Press, 2005), 14.

73. Halasz, *Marketplace*, 76–81. Halasz draws profitably on Robert Weimann's concept of the *platea*: the fluid, nonrepresentational stage space in which actors can recognize the audience, as opposed to the *locus*, which is fully invested in the drama's representational fiction. She suggests that the pamphlet's dialogic nature creates a *platea*-effect, allowing the entertaining of different forms of discursive authority.

74. Greene, *Repentance*, sig. A_4^{r}

75. *Greene in conceipt*'s narrator, for instance, mentions that he had been reading Lucian, a poet associated with both ghostly dialogues and ironic truth claims, before dreaming of Greene's ghost. Riche's hints depend—as does much of the humor in his pamphlet—on anti-Catholic satire: his Greene advises any who doubts "the truth of the matter" to compare his

story to the works of Thomas More and the Douay-Rheims Bible and to "tel me then if you do not find matter seeming more incredible the[n] any by me here alleaged" (*GN*, sig. A_4^r).

76. See Warner, *Publics*, 114ff.

77. On the related phrase "*a* per se *a*" and their shared origins in hornbook formulas of alphabetical recitation, see McKerrow's notes in Thomas Nashe, *The Works of Thomas Nashe*, ed. Ronald B. McKerrow, 5 vols. (1904–10; repr., Oxford: Basil Blackwell, 1958), 4:187, 205.

78. Dickenson, *Greene in conceipt*, sig. A_4^r.

79. Mentz, *Romance for Sale*, 211.

80. See Stephen Greenblatt, *Hamlet in Purgatory* (Princeton: Princeton University Press, 2001).

81. Preiss, *Clowning and Authorship*, 126.

82. Harvey, *Foure Letters*, sig. A_2^r.

83. Thomas Dekker, *A knights coniuring Done in earnest: discouered in iest* (London, 1607), sig. L_1^r.

84. Nashe, *Works*, 1:153.

CHAPTER 2

1. Barnabe Barnes, *Parthenophil and Parthenophe Sonnettes, madrigals, elegies, and odes* (London, 1593), sig. P_1^v.

2. Edmund Spenser, *The Shepheardes Calender*, in *The Yale Edition of the Shorter Poems of Edmund Spenser*, ed. William A. Oram et al. (New Haven: Yale University Press, 1989), 164. Hereafter, references to the *Calender* will be made parenthetically in text, by line number for verse and by page number for E. K.'s commentary.

3. On Spenser's use of Marot, see Anne Lake Prescott, *French Poets and the English Renaissance: Studies in Fame and Transformation* (New Haven: Yale University Press, 1978), 10–12; Annabel Patterson, *Pastoral and Ideology: Virgil to Valéry* (Berkeley: University of California Press, 1987), 107–32.

4. John Skelton, *Here after foloweth a lytell boke called Collyn Clout* (London, c. 1531). Skelton died in 1529; circumstantial evidence summarized in Skelton, *John Skelton: The Complete English Poems*, ed. John Scattergood (New Haven: Yale University Press, 1983), suggests a composition date in or before 1523. On the poem's popularity, see Anthony S. G. Edwards, ed., *John Skelton: The Critical Heritage* (New York: Routledge, 1981), 12. The imitation in question is a satire, published in 1541 under the title *The treatyse answerynge the boke of berdes*, which presented itself as "Compyled by Collyn clowte."

5. Kreg Segall, "Skeltonic Anxiety and Rumination in *The Shepheardes Calender*," *Studies in English Literature, 1500–1900* 47, no. 1 (2007): 29. See also Richard Helgerson, *Self-Crowned Laureates: Spenser, Jonson, Milton, and the Literary System* (Berkeley: University of California Press, 1983), 55–100; and David L. Miller's several essays on Spenserian pastoral, including "Authorship, Anonymity, and *The Shepheardes Calender*," *Modern Language Quarterly* 40, no. 3 (1979): 219–36, and "Abandoning the Quest," *ELH* 46, no. 2 (1979): 173–92.

6. Patrick Cheney, *Spenser's Famous Flight: A Renaissance Idea of a Literary Career* (Toronto: University of Toronto Press, 1993), 20.

7. On the etymology of Colin's name, see Roland Greene, "Calling Colin Clout," *Spenser Studies* 10 (1992): 233–34; Mary Ellen Lamb, *The Popular Culture of Shakespeare, Spenser and*

Jonson (New York: Routledge, 2006), 178. On Spenser's relation to Skelton, and the stakes of his appropriation of Skelton's persona, see Andrew Hadfield, *Literature, Politics, and National Identity: Reformation to Renaissance* (Cambridge: Cambridge University Press, 1994), 170–201; Segall, "Skeltonic Anxiety."

8. On lyric's relatively late incorporation into print in England, see Arthur F. Marotti, *Manuscript, Print, and the English Renaissance Lyric* (Ithaca: Cornell University Press, 1995), 209–90. More recently, Matthew Zarnowiecki, *Fair Copies: Reproducing the English Lyric from Tottel to Shakespeare* (Toronto: University of Toronto Press, 2014) has examined the ways that late sixteenth-century poetry responded to the reproduction of lyric in printed miscellanies.

9. Richard Barnfield, *Cynthia, With certaine sonnets, and the legend of Cassandra* (London, 1595), sig. C_7^v.

10. Zarnowiecki, *Fair Copies*, 5.

11. Thomas Edwards, *Cephalvs and Procris. Narcissvs* (London, 1595), sig. H_3^v.

12. See Jane Griffiths, *John Skelton and Poetic Authority: Defining the Liberty to Speak* (Oxford: Clarendon Press, 2006) 168. For a discussion of the *Calender* in the context of late sixteenth-century political and religious tensions, see David Norbrook, *Poetry and Politics in the English Renaissance* (London: Routledge, 1984), 53–90.

13. Michelle O'Callaghan, "The Duties of Societies: Literature, Friendship, and Community," in *Renaissance Transformations: The Making of English Writing 1500–1651*, ed. Margaret Healy and Thomas Healy (Edinburgh: Edinburgh University Press, 2009), 103; George Puttenham, *The Arte of English Poesie* (London, 1589), sig. F_3^v. Jennifer Richards offers an insightful account of homosocial friendship in the *Calender*, focusing on the civil conversation that Spenser strikes up with Gabriel Harvey (in the guises of Hobbinol and E. K.); see Richards, *Rhetoric and Courtliness in Early Modern Literature* (Cambridge: Cambridge University Press, 2003), 139–53.

14. For the most influential version of this argument, see Louis Montrose, "Of Gentlemen and Shepherds: The Politics of Elizabethan Pastoral Form," *ELH* 50, no. 3 (1983): 415–59. Montrose later revisited the claims of this essay, and of Alpers's response to it, framing the latter's concept of the domain against the backdrop of an emergent bourgeois domesticity; see Montrose, "Spenser's Domestic Domain: Poetry, Property, and the Early Modern Subject," in *Subject and Object in Renaissance Culture*, ed. Margreta de Grazia, Maureen Quilligan, and Peter Stallybrass (Cambridge: Cambridge University Press, 1996), 83–130.

15. Paul Alpers, "Pastoral and the Domain of Lyric in Spenser's *Shepheardes Calender*," *Representations* 12 (1985): 94.

16. Ibid.

17. The most influential proponents of the New Lyric Studies (also called "historical poetics") are Yopie Prins and Virginia Jackson, whose jointly edited volume *The Lyric Theory Reader: A Critical Anthology* (Baltimore: Johns Hopkins University Press, 2014) has codified the "lyricization" turn. Prins's *Victorian Sappho* (Princeton University Press, 1999) and Jackson's *Dickinson's Misery: A Theory of Lyric Reading* (Princeton: Princeton University Press, 2005) are the movement's seminal texts, along with a cluster of essays under the title "The New Lyric Studies" in *PMLA* 123, no.1 (2008): 181–234; more recently, a special issue devoted to historical poetics appeared in *Modern Language Quarterly*: V. Joshua Adams, Joel Callahan, and Michael Hansen, eds., "Historical Poetics," special issue, *Modern Language Quarterly* 77, no. 1 (2016). Central to the method of historical poetics is a focus on the historically specific meta-discourses surrounding poetic production.

18. Heather Dubrow, *The Challenges of Orpheus: Lyric Poetry and Early Modern England* (Baltimore: Johns Hopkins University Press, 2008). Dubrow's account valuably traces the ambiguities of lyric as a category (and of early modern lyric in particular) while insisting on its utility. Where historical poetics and its critics debate the respective importance of metadiscourse and form, Dubrow offers a third possibility: the exploration of genre through its animating myths, in this case Orpheus, Echo, Pygmalion, and David. Such myths are reflexive without standing apart from poetic production itself; in the same way, this chapter takes Colin Clout as a symbol who at once motivates lyric writing and reading and marshals an implicit reflexivity toward lyric as a category.

19. Stephanie Burt, "What Is This Thing Called Lyric?" *Modern Philology* 113, no. 3 (2016): 422–40. Burt's essay offers a useful overview of the "lyricization" turn from a critically formalist perspective.

20. Paul de Man, "Anthropomorphism and Trope in Lyric," in *The Rhetoric of Romanticism* (New York: Columbia University Press, 1984), 259.

21. A similar—though less critically suspicious—view can be found in many of the leading defenses of lyric. Jonathan Culler, for instance, insists in *Theory of the Lyric* (Cambridge, Mass.: Harvard University Press, 2015) that lyric is a primary event, not a secondary representation, and attends to the peculiar force of the present tense in so much poetry called lyric. Burt, for her part, offers this definition: "Lyric, in the term's central, durable senses, tends or aspires to replace the live, mortal, present body of one person present in one place at one time (the body of the poet or the body of the reader or the body of the singer or the body of somebody who has been addressed) with something else (impressions or inscriptions or spirits or memorials or 'poetic artifice'), by means of a variety of forms and tropes, to a variety of emotive ends (commemoration, ecstatic joy, frustration, thanksgiving, reflection, and so on)." Burt, "What Is This Thing Called Lyric?," 439.

22. Zarnowiecki, *Fair Copies*, 71.

23. See Joshua Eckhardt, *Manuscript Verse Collectors and the Politics of Anti-Courtly Love Poetry* (Oxford: Oxford University Press, 2009), which argues that the collectors of manuscript miscellanies created a genre of "anti-courtly love poetry" by juxtaposing love poetry with obscene lyrics. On the manuscript circulation of verse in the sixteenth century more broadly, see Marotti, *Manuscript, Print*, 135–208.

24. Zarnowiecki, *Fair Copies*, 4.

25. The phrase, also de Man's, is from Paul de Man, "Lyrical Voice in Contemporary Theory: Riffaterre and Jauss," in *Lyric Poetry: Beyond New Criticism*, ed. Chaviva Hosek and Patricia Parker (Ithaca: Cornell University Press, 1985), 55.

26. Alpers, "Pastoral and the Domain of Lyric," 97.

27. Greene, "Calling Colin." In "December," Greene argues, Colin achieves a voice that successfully incorporates the flexibility of dialogue. My own reading is less optimistic about Colin's integration into this dialogic model—an integration, I would suggest, that depends on the reproduction of Colin's voice as textual artifact and in turn leaves Colin further estranged from the conversational exchanges of his fellow shepherds.

28. Segall, "Skeltonic Anxiety," 43. As Segall observes, "what seems to trouble Hobbinoll most is . . . that Colin has ceased to be a member of the poetic shepherds' community."

29. Susan Snyder, *Pastoral Process: Spenser, Marvell, Milton* (Stanford: Stanford University Press, 1995), 3.

30. Louis Montrose, "'The perfecte paterne of a Poete': The Poetics of Courtship in *The Shepheardes Calender*," *Texas Studies in Literature and Language* 21, no. 1 (1979): 42.

31. Zarnowiecki, *Fair Copies*, 90.

32. William Webbe, *A Discourse of English Poetrie* (London, 1586), sig. G_2^r. Webbe's care in recording the sestina's poet and performer may have been a compensatory gesture for his uncertainty about the authorship of the *Calender*. Elsewhere he writes that he had reserved the "tytle of the rightest English Poet" for "the Author of the Sheepeheardes Kalender . . . whether it was Master *Sp.* or what rare Scholler in Pembrooke Hall soeuer, because himself and his freendes, for what respect I knowe not, would not reueale it, I force not greatly to sette downe" (sig. C_4^v).

33. *Englands Helicon Casta placent superis, pura cum veste venite, et manibus puris sumite fontis aquam* (London, 1600).

34. Catherine Nicholson, *Uncommon Tongues: Eloquence and Eccentricity in the English Renaissance* (Philadelphia: University of Pennsylvania Press, 2013), 112.

35. Wendy Wall, *The Imprint of Gender: Authorship and Publication in the English Renaissance* (Ithaca: Cornell University Press, 1993), 237.

36. As Patrick Cullen observes, the elegy "is significant not only for what it is, a lament for the death of Dido, but also for what it tells us about Colin, his obsession with death, his nostalgia for and yet increasing alienation from the pastoral world." Cullen, *Spenser, Marvell, and Renaissance Pastoral* (Cambridge, Mass.: Harvard University Press, 1970), 91. Cullen argues plausibly that Dido's death merges for Colin with Rosalind's loss; my reading emphasizes Colin's proleptic sense of his own death, a phenomenon intertwined with the sense of his elegy as a durable textual artifact.

37. Richard Halpern, *The Poetics of Primitive Accumulation: English Renaissance Culture and the Genealogy of Capital* (Ithaca: Cornell University Press, 1991), 181. E. K.'s commentary is inextricably a part of the effect of the book as a whole, which encodes the tension between orality and text, presence and distance. As Michael McCanles observes, "It is part of the fiction of *The Shepheardes Calender* that E. K.'s glosses and commentary are not part of the fiction." McCanles, "*The Shepheardes Calender* as Document and Monument," *Studies in English Literature, 1500–1900* 22, no. 1 (1982), 5.

38. Andrew Mattison, *The Unimagined in the English Renaissance: Poetry and the Limits of Mimesis* (Madison: Fairleigh Dickinson University Press, 2013), 28.

39. Michelle O'Callaghan, *The "Shepheards Nation": Jacobean Spenserians and Early Stuart Political Culture, 1612–1625* (Oxford: Clarendon Press, 2000), 5.

40. Rachel E. Hile, *Spenserian Satire: A Tradition of Indirection* (Manchester: Manchester University Press, 2017), 40–41.

41. Thomas Lodge, *Phillis honoured vvith pastorall sonnets, elegies, and amorous delights* (London, 1593), sig. A_4^v. As its title indicates, Lodge's sonnet sequence participated in the not-uncommon intermingling of pastoral and Petrarchan modes during the Elizabethan fashion for love poetry.

42. Michael Drayton, *Endimion and Phoebe. Ideas Latmus* (London, 1595), sig. G_1^v.

43. William Smith, *Chloris, or The complaint of the passionate despised shepheard* (London, 1596), sig. A_2^r.

44. Joseph Hall, *Virgidemiarum* (London, 1597), sig. A_7^r. This tribute notwithstanding, Hall's feelings about Spenser were not altogether admiring. The satire in which Hall praises Colin is an explanation to detractors (the poem is titled "His Defiance to Envy") for his choice of genre, and in the same poem he declares himself unfit for pastoral and romance, engaging in a pastiche of the latter that reads as a parody of Spenser: he must decline, Hall says, to

"scoure the rusted swords of Eluish knights, / Bathed in Pagan blood: or sheath them new / In misty morall Types" (sig. A_6^r).

45. John Marston, *The Scourge of Villanie: Three bookes of satyres* (London, 1598), sig. E_7^r.

46. Michael Drayton, *Idea the shepheards garland* (London, 1593), sig. C_3^r.

47. Richard Barnfield, *The Affectionate Shepheard* (London, 1594), sig. E_3^r.

48. Pierre Bourdieu, *The Rules of Art: Genesis and Structure of the Literary Field*, trans. Susan Emanuel (Stanford: Stanford University Press, 1996), 141, 232.

49. See Richard McCabe, "Rhyme and Reason: Poetics, Patronage, and Secrecy in Elizabethan and Jacobean Ireland," in *Literary Milieux: Essays in Text and Context, Presented to Howard Erskine-Hill*, ed. David Womersely and Richard McCabe (Newark: University of Delaware, 2008), 47.

50. Smith, *Chloris*, sig. A_2^r.

51. McCabe, "Rhyme and Reason," 47.

52. Smith, *Chloris*, sig. D_3^v.

53. Ibid., sig. A_2^v.

54. Francis Davison, *A Poeticall Rhapsody* (London, 1602), sig. N_2^v. Davison's adjective *passing* seems to play on two meanings: the primary sense of *surpassing* and a secondary reference to Colin's having passed away.

55. John Weever, *Epigrammes in the oldest cut, and newest fashion* (London, 1599), sig. G_3^r.

56. Phineas Fletcher, *Piscatorie Eclogs and other Poeticall Miscellanies* (Cambridge, 1633), sig. I_1^r.

57. Richard Niccols, *Expicedium. A funeral oration, vpon the death of the late deceased Princesse of famous memorye, Elizabeth by the grace of God, Queen of England, France and Ireland* (London, 1603), sig. B_3^r.

58. Drayton was in fact in need of patronage in 1603, due to the recent loss of the support of Lucy, Countess of Bedford. Niccols's elusive reference captures the tension of describing the conditions of the literary system in the terms of pastoral—though the poem makes Drayton's plight clear enough (particularly for those in the know), it is careful to sublimate the economic system of patronage into the moral terms of "encouragement." On Drayton's ill-fated association with the Countess of Bedford, see Barbara K. Lewalski, "Lucy, Countess of Bedford: Images of a Jacobean Courtier and Patroness," in *Politics of Discourse: The Literature and History of Seventeenth-Century England*, ed. Kevin Sharp and Steven N. Zwicker (Berkeley: University of California Press, 1987), 62–63.

59. Gabriel Harvey, "To the learned Shepheard" ("Commendatory Verses" 3), in Edmund Spenser, *The Faerie Queene*, ed. A. C. Hamilton, 2nd ed. (New York: Longman, 2007), lines 7–12.

60. Ibid., lines 14, 16.

61. George Peele, *The Araygnement of Paris a pastorall* (London, 1584). It is unclear whether Peele knew that Spenser was the author of *The Shepheardes Calender*, though he could hardly have avoided knowing that Colin was a persona for the author. Unlike later appropriations of Colin, however, which played on Colin's status as both pastoral character and author-figure, Peele's rewriting seems much more interested in the former—there is little sense that he is affiliating himself with the author of the *Calender* in the way that Drayton, Lodge, and others eventually would.

62. Peele, *Araygnement of Paris*, sig. C_2^r.

63. Colin's erstwhile companion Thenot makes the comparison explicit: "Poore *Colin*, that is ill for thee, that art as true in trust / To thy sweete smerte, as to his Nymphe *Paris* hath bin vniust." Ibid., sigs. C_2^v–C_3^r.

64. Ibid., sig. C_4^r. Venus's inclusion of an epitaph suggests the emendation of "buried" for "burned"; see George Peele, *The Arraignment of Paris*, ed. Oliphant Smeaton (London: J. M. Dent and Co., 1905), 36.

65. This evocation of writing as death may be a particularly lyric theme; see, for instance, Paul de Man's observation of "the uneasy combination of funereal monumentality with paranoid fear that characterizes the hermeneutics and the pedagogy of lyric poetry," in de Man, "Anthropomorphism and Trope," 259.

66. Scott L. Newstok, *Quoting Death in Early Modern England: The Poetics of Epitaphs Beyond the Tomb* (Basingstoke: Palgrave Macmillan, 2009), 6.

67. Bernard Lahire, *The Plural Actor*, trans. David Fernbach (Cambridge: Polity Press, 2011), 133.

68. E. C., *Emaricdulfe* (London, 1595), sig. C_7^v.

69. Barnes, *Parthenophil and Parthenophe*, sig. P_1^v.

70. Edmund Spenser, *Colin Clouts Come Home Againe*, in *Yale Edition of Shorter Poems*, lines 640–43. Hereafter citations will be made parenthetically in text.

71. Harry Berger Jr., "A Secret Discipline: *The Faerie Queene*, Book VI" [1961], reprinted in *Revisionary Play: Studies in the Spenserian Dynamics* (Berkeley: University of California Press, 1988), 239.

72. Rebecca Helfer, *Spenser's Ruins and the Art of Recollection* (Toronto: University of Toronto Press, 2012), 291.

73. For an overview of such readings and an exemplary performance of one, see Patrick Cheney's perceptive account of Colin's role in Spenser's "pastoral of progression"; Cheney, "Spenser's Pastorals: *The Shepheardes Calender* and *Colin Clouts Come Home Againe*," in *The Cambridge Companion to Spenser*, ed. Andrew Hadfield (Cambridge: Cambridge University Press, 2001), 79–105.

74. William A. Oram, "Laureate Self-Fashioning," in *Edmund Spenser in Context*, ed. Andrew Escobedo (Cambridge: Cambridge University Press, 2017), 20.

75. Edmund Spenser, *The Faerie Queene*, ed. A. C. Hamilton, 2nd ed. (New York: Longman, 2007), Book VI, canto x, stanza 10, lines 3–4. Hereafter cited parenthetically in the text. Spenser's line of course alludes to Cuddie's rhetorical question "Who knowes not Rosalend?" in the August eclogue of *The Shepheardes Calender* (line 141).

76. Andrew Hadfield, *Literature, Politics, and National Identity*, 171.

77. In referring directly to the eclogue's title, the deictic phrase "that name" unsettles Gérard Genette's influential distinction between text and paratext—the latter being a category that includes both peritexts (peripheral and ancillary components of whatever object encloses the "text," including titles) and epitexts (reviews, advertisements, and other materials that emerge in reference to the text). See Gérard Genette, *Paratexts: Thresholds of Interpretation*, trans. Jane E. Lewin (Cambridge: Cambridge University Press, 1997).

78. Helfer, *Spenser's Ruins*, 291.

79. In "Januarye," the parenthetical is instructive and possessive, emphasizing the poet's control of Colin's identity and referring to the descriptor "shepeheards boye" rather than the name; in *Colin Clout*, by contrast, the parenthetical makes clear the public visibility that Colin's name had since acquired.

80. The topical tissue of eclogue is felt in thinly veiled masks for key players in Spenser's circles and at court, most importantly Cynthia for Elizabeth and "the Shepheard of the Ocean" for Sir Walter Raleigh. Not all of the fiction refers to real situations, of course—as Donald Cheney points out, Harvey was not in Ireland at the time, though Spenser depicts Hobbinol as being present in its pastoral double. Cheney observes that the mingling of "actual autobiographical fact" with "literal falsehood" means "that we must despair of finding any single consistent frame of reference" in the poem. Donald Cheney, "Colin Clout's Homecoming: The Imaginative Travels of Edmund Spenser," *Connotations* 7, no. 2 (1997/98): 151.

81. Colin's reference to "double usury" is an oft-observed crux in the poem. In modern legal language, the term refers to interest exceeding double the legally acceptable rate. In 1604, however, the preacher George Downame defined double usury as "not onely couenanting for vsurie in money, but also impairing the thing pawned (as plate or garments) by the vse thereof," so that as interest accrued on the pawner's loan, the pawned object was itself depreciated through use. Downame's usage is evocative; it might suggest in Spenser's "dubble usurie" a fear that Colin's retelling depreciates his experiences even as it renews them. Downame, *Lectures on the XV. Psalme read in the cathedrall church of S. Paule, in London. Wherein besides many other very profitable and necessarie matters, the question of vsurie is plainely and fully decided* (London, 1604), 190.

82. Elizabeth Heale, *Autobiography and Authorship in Renaissance Verse: Chronicles of the Self* (Basingstoke: Palgrave Macmillan, 2003), 85. But see also Mattison's argument that *Colin Clout* reveals instead the "insufficiency of experience," and hence Spenser's need to imaginatively create a fictional world in order for to fulfill his ambitions; Mattison, *Unimagined*, 48.

83. Andrew Hadfield, *Edmund Spenser: A Life* (Oxford: Oxford University Press, 2012), 235.

84. Julia Reinhard Lupton, "Home-Making in Ireland: Virgil's Eclogue I and Book VI of *The Faerie Queene*," *Spenser Studies* 8 (1990): 119–41. The ambiguity of the title of *Colin Clouts Come Home Againe* is an oft-remarked feature of the eclogue. William Oram's comments in the *Yale Edition*'s introduction to the poem are representative: "If this is a poem about homecoming it is not immediately clear where 'home' lies. Spenser's courtier-audience would naturally identify home with the England the poet had left for the Irish wilds ten years earlier: coming home implies a return to the center of civility which is the court. But for Colin Clout home is Ireland"; Spenser, *Yale Edition of Shorter Poems*, 519.

85. Patricia Parker, *Inescapable Romance: Studies in the Poetics of a Mode* (Princeton: Princeton University Press, 1979), 101–13.

86. David Quint, "Archimago and Amoret: The Poem and Its Doubles," in *Worldmaking Spenser: Explorations in the Early Modern Age*, ed. Patrick Cheney and Lauren Silberman (Lexington: University of Kentucky Press, 2000), 38.

87. On court exclusivity, see Michael Schoenfeldt, "The Poetry of Conduct: Accommodation and Transgression in *The Faerie Queene*, Book 6," in *Enclosure Acts: Sexuality, Property, and Culture in Early Modern England*, ed. Richard Burt and John Michael Archer (Ithaca: Cornell University Press, 1994). On bourgeois domesticity, see Montrose, "Spenser's Domestic Domain"; Richard Rambuss, *Spenser's Secret Career* (Cambridge: Cambridge University Press, 2007). On Book 6's pastoral as pasturage commons at a moment of rising enclosure, see Benjamin Myers, "The Green and Golden World: Spenser's Rewriting of the Munster Plantation," *ELH* 76, no. 2 (2009): 473–90. For a broader reflection on aestheticizing and historicizing approaches to the episode, see Robert Stillman's measured discussion in "Spenserian

Autonomy and the Trial of New Historicism: Book Six of *The Faerie Queene*," *English Literary Renaissance* 22, no. 3 (1992): 299–314.

88. Berger, "A Secret Discipline," 236–37. Italics in original.

89. Edmund Spenser, *Amoretti and Epithalamion*, in *Yale Edition of Shorter Poems*, 584.

CHAPTER 3

1. Philip Sidney, *The Defence of Poesie* (London, 1595), sig. B_1^v.

2. Gavin Alexander, *Writing After Sidney: The Literary Response to Sir Philip Sidney, 1586–1640* (Oxford: Oxford University Press, 2006), xix.

3. Lori Humphrey Newcomb, *Reading Popular Romance in Early Modern England* (New York: Columbia University Press, 2002), 21–76.

4. Sidney, *Defence*, sig. I_3^r.

5. Gabriel Harvey, *Four Letters, and certaine Sonnets: Especially touching Robert Greene, and other parties, by him abused* (London, 1592), sig. D_2^v. "*Greenes* Arcadia" referred to *Menaphon*, a romance published in 1589; later editions of *Menaphon* beginning in 1599 have "Greenes Arcadia" as the running header.

6. Joel B. Davis, *"The Countesse of Pembrokes Arcadia" and the Invention of English Literature* (New York: Palgrave Macmillan, 2011), 144.

7. Newcomb, *Reading Popular Romance*, 26.

8. Matthew Roydon, "An Elegie, or friends passion, for his Astrophill. *Written vpon the death of the right Honorable sir Philip Sidney knight, Lord gouernor of Flushing*," in *The Phoenix Nest* [. . .] (London, 1593), sig. B_1^r.

9. H. R. Woudhuysen, *Sir Philip Sidney and the Circulation of Manuscripts, 1558–1640* (Oxford: Clarendon Press, 1996); Davis, *Invention*; Stephen B. Dobranski, *Readers and Authorship in Early Modern England* (Cambridge: Cambridge University Press, 2005), 63–96; Alexander, *Writing After Sidney*; and Natasha Simonova, *Early Modern Authorship and Prose Continuations: Adaptation and Ownership from Sidney to Richardson* (Basingstoke: Palgrave Macmillan, 2015), 29–88.

10. Simonova, *Early Modern Authorship*, 29–58.

11. Alexander, *Writing After Sidney*, xxxvi.

12. Greville wrote that "if any defect be found in the Eclogues, which although they were of *Sir Phillip Sidneis* writing, yet were they not perused by him, but left till the worke had bene finished, that then choise should haue bene made, which should haue bene taken, and in what manner brought in. At this time they haue bene chosen and disposed as the ouer-seer thought best"; in Philip Sidney, *The Covntesse of Pembrokes Arcadia* (London, 1590), sig. A_4^v. Greville's explanation is the best evidence of Sidney's wishes for the *Arcadia*. Cambridge University MS. Kk. 1.5 (Cm), the only extant manuscript of the new *Arcadia*, does not include any eclogues, but Greville—despite his willingness to remove some of the eclogues—clearly believed that Sidney intended to retain them in some form. For the argument that Greville's editing of the eclogues reflected Sidney's intentions for them, see Sukanta Chaudhuri, "The Eclogues in Sidney's *New Arcadia*," *Review of English Studies*, n.s., 35, no. 138 (1984): 185–202.

13. The poems from the old *Arcadia* that Greville omitted from or assigned to other characters in the 1590 edition were, in William Ringler's numbering, *OA* 9, 24, 31, 62, 66, 73, and 74; *OA* 9, 31, and 66 were returned to Philisides in 1593, and *OP* 5, entitled "The lad Philisides,"

was inserted then as well and assigned to Philisides. See Philip Sidney, *The Poems of Sir Philip Sidney*, ed. William A. Ringler Jr. (Oxford: Clarendon Press, 1962).

14. Richard Hillyer, *Sir Philip Sidney, Cultural Icon* (New York: Palgrave MacMillan, 2010), 41–62; G. A. Wilkes, "'Left . . . to Play the Ill Poet in My Own Part': The Literary Relationship of Sidney and Fulke Greville," *Review of English Studies* 57, no. 230 (2006): 291–309. Of particular interest is Joel B. Davis's argument that Greville used his chapter summaries to project an image of Sidney as a virtuous courtier-soldier who "rejected the effeminate lures of pastoralism to embrace a stern Stoic moral and political philosophy." Davis, "Multiple *Arcadias* and the Literary Quarrel Between Fulke Greville and the Countess of Pembroke," *Studies in Philology* 101, no. 4 (2004): 415.

15. Sidney, *Arcadia* (1590), sig. A_4^v.

16. Philip Sidney, *Astrophil and Stella*, 15.7–9. References are to sonnet and line(s). Further citations will be made in text with the initials *AS*.

17. William Ringler argues that Coredens is Edward Wotton, a diplomat who accompanied Sidney during part of his European tour and returned to England with him. Ringler *Major Poems*, 413–14. This would correspond to the mention in "On Ister bank" that "To worthy Coredens he [Languet] gave me o'er." Sidney, *The Countess of Pembroke's Arcadia (The Old Arcadia)*, ed. Jean Robertson (Oxford: Clarendon Press, 1973), 256. Edward Dyer is the other candidate; see Katherine Duncan-Jones, *Sir Philip Sidney: Courtier Poet* (New Haven: Yale University Press, 1991), 102. Edward Berry suggests a link between Mira and Queen Elizabeth in *The Making of Sir Philip Sidney* (Toronto: University of Toronto Press, 1998), 81.

18. Sidney was displaced as the Earl of Leicester's heir by the birth of Leicester's son, Robert, Baron Denbigh, in April 1581; see H. R. Woudhuysen, "Sidney, Sir Philip (1554–1586)," *Oxford Dictionary of National Biography* (Oxford: University Press, 2004; online ed.), accessed September 2014, https://doi.org/10.1093/ref:odnb/25522.

19. Annabel Patterson, *Censorship and Interpretation: The Conditions of Writing and Reading in Early Modern England* (Madison: University of Wisconsin Press, 1984), 32–51; Blair Worden, *The Sound of Virtue: Philip Sidney's "Arcadia" and Elizabethan Politics* (New Haven: Yale University Press, 1997). Modern readings of the *Arcadia* as a covert political commentary go back to Edwin Greenlaw, "Sidney's *Arcadia* as an Example of Elizabethan Allegory," in *Anniversary Papers by Colleagues and Pupils of George Lyman Kittredge* (Boston and London: Ginn and Company, 1913), 327–37.

20. Both keys date to the early decades of the seventeenth century; Oxinden was given his copy of the *Arcadia* by his father in 1628. Oxinden's key, which assigns historical analogues to ten of the romance's main characters, is written on a blank page at the end of a copy of the 1598 edition of the *Arcadia* available at the Beinecke Rare Book and Manuscript Library, Yale University (call number Ig Si14 + 590c). Castillion's key, under the heading "The Interpretation of the chiefeste names in s[r] Phil. Sydnes Arcadia," can be found in his manuscript letterbook, also at the Beinecke (call number Osborn fb69). Although Castillion's key is primarily concerned with the etymologies of Sidney' character-names, he also ventures topical identifications for the princes and princesses. The two keys are in agreement on the identities of the two princesses, whom Oxinden and Castillion both believe to be Penelope Devereux, Lady Rich, and her sister Dorothy, the Countess of Northumberland. Only Oxinden includes Philisides, whom he identifies as "S[r]. Philip Sydney himselfe." On Oxinden's key and his other annotations, see William Dean, "Henry Oxinden's Key (1628) to *The Countess of Pembroke's Arcadia*: Some Facts and Conjectures," *Sidney Newsletter and Journal* 12, no. 2 (1993): 14–21.

21. Dobranski, *Readers*, 63–96. Dobranski points out that the representation of Basilius's kingship must have seemed uncannily pertinent to readers in the middle of the seventeenth century.

22. Arthur Marotti, "'Love Is Not Love': Elizabethan Sonnet Sequences and the Social Order," *ELH* 49, no. 2 (1982): 396–428. See also Ann Rosalind Jones and Peter Stallybrass, "The Politics of *Astrophil and Stella*," *Studies in English Literature, 1500–1900* 24, no. 1 (1984): 53–68.

23. Jonathan Crewe, *Hidden Designs: The Critical Profession and Renaissance Literature* (London: Methuen, 1986), 81. Crewe's own interpretation of the sequence demonstrates the temptation to overread: he speculates that the sonnets encode an incestuous affair between Philip and Mary Sidney.

24. Sidney, *Poems*, 490. Ringler notes that Thomas Lant's engravings of Sidney's funeral processions depict his armor as decorated with stars.

25. See Duncan-Jones' commentary on sonnet 28 in Philip Sidney, *The Major Works, including "Astrophil and Stella"*, ed. Katherine Duncan-Jones (Oxford: Oxford University Press, 2002), 361.

26. Woudhuysen, *Circulation*, 246. The tight network stands in contrast to the wider circulation of manuscript poetry by some other poets, most notably John Donne, many of whose poems exist in numerous versions because they had been transcribed (and in the process revised) so often. The wider dissemination of Donne's poetry may have had to do with the self-advertising function of much manuscript poetry: perhaps a stronger imperative for Donne, an aspiring courtier, than for the solidly aristocratic Sidney. On Donne's manuscript circulation, see Gary A. Stringer, "The Composition and Dissemination of Donne's Writings," in *The Oxford Handbook of John Donne*, ed. Jeanne Shami, Dennis Flynn, and M. Thomas Hester (Oxford: Oxford University Press, 2011), 12–25; Arthur F. Marotti, *John Donne: Coterie Poet* (Madison: University of Wisconsin Press, 1986).

27. Woudhuysen, *Circulation*, 297.

28. Patricia Fumerton's brilliant comparison of Elizabethan sonnet sequences and portrait miniatures gets at this dynamic of revelation and concealment: a "game of secrecy," she suggests, in which the poet "builds up around his private love rooms of increasingly public 'selves.' One's intimacy with the poet, as with the miniature owner, determined how far one could pass within, and only the initiate could reach the inner sanctum." Fumerton, "'Secret' Arts: Elizabethan Miniatures and Sonnets," *Representations* 15 (1986), 75.

29. Philip Sidney, *The Countess of Pembroke's Arcadia (The Old Arcadia)*, ed. Jean Robertson (Oxford: Clarendon Press, 1973), 3. All further citations of the old *Arcadia* will be from this edition and will be made parenthetically in text and identified with the initials *OA* followed by the page number. The earliest existing version of the dedication is in Ponsonby's 1590 edition of the new *Arcadia*. Scholars agree that the dedication was composed for the old *Arcadia*, though it is unclear whether it would have been unique to Mary's gifted copy or transcribed with the rest of the text in other manuscript copies. See Woudhuysen, *Circulation*, 306.

30. Wendy Wall, *The Imprint of Gender: Authorship and Publication in the English Renaissance* (Ithaca: Cornell University Press, 1993), 154.

31. Woudhuysen, *Circulation*, 309–10. "At least seven and perhaps as many as fourteen copies were made from Sidney's working version of the *Old Arcadia* during a period which might have been as brief as the twenty or so months between the spring of 1581 and the end of 1582," Woudhuysen finds, concluding that Sidney must have "wanted the *Old Arcadia* widely

published in manuscript." In his edition of Sidney's *Poems*, Ringler argues that the ten "surviving copies" of the manuscript "indicate the existence at one time of at least five others," and possibly more; Sidney, *Poems*, lx.

32. Greville's letter is transcribed in Sidney, *Poems*, 530. William Ponsonby had alerted Greville of the unnamed stationer's intent to publish the *Arcadia*, and Walsingham's intervention was evidently successful. Ponsonby would soon benefit himself, receiving the title to the *Arcadia* for its publication four years later. For an account of the letter and the preempting of the 1586 *Arcadia*, see Woudhuysen, *Circulation*, 224–26.

33. See Kathryn Schwarz, *Tough Love: Amazon Encounters in the English Renaissance* (Durham: Duke University Press, 2000), 175–201; Julie Crawford, "Sidney's Sapphics and the Role of Interpretive Communities," *ELH* 69, no. 4 (2002): 979–1007. Also see Helen Hackett's brief treatment in *Women and Romance Fiction in the English Renaissance* (Cambridge: Cambridge University Press, 2000), 111–15.

34. Philip Sidney, *The Covntesse of Pembrokes Arcadia* (London, 1590), sig. T_{1}^{r}. The same passage appears in the second edition; Sidney, *The Covntesse of Pembrokes Arcadia* (London, 1593), sig. M_{1}^{r}.

35. Ibid., sig. Kk_{4}^{r}.

36. Sidney, *Defence*, sig. B_{1}^{v}.

37. On Sidney's reputation at the time of his death, see Dominic Baker-Smith, "'Great Expectation': Sidney's Death and the Poets," in *Sir Philip Sidney: 1586 and the Creation of a Legend*, ed. Jan van Dorsten, Dominic Baker-Smith, and Arthur Kinney (Leiden: Brill, 1986), 83–103; Kevin Pask, *The Emergence of the English Author: Scripting the Life of the Poet in Early Modern England* (Cambridge: Cambridge University Press, 1996), 53–82. On Sidney's debt to European intellectual circles, and especially to the influence of Philip Melanchthon, see Robert Stillman, *Philip Sidney and the Poetics of Renaissance Cosmopolitanism* (Aldershot: Ashgate, 2008).

38. Pask, *Emergence*, 54.

39. For Spenser's account of this group, see his letter to Gabriel Harvey, dated October 5, 1579, and published in Gabriel Harvey and Edmund Spenser, *Two Other very commendable Letters, of the same mens writing* (London, 1580). Spenser identifies Sidney and Dyer as the group's leaders ("they have me, I thanke them, in some vse of familiarity," he bragged), writing that they had "proclaimed . . . a generall surceasing and silence of balde Rymers, and also of the verie beste to: in steade whereof, they haue by authoritie of their whole Senate, prescribed certaine Lawes and rules of Quantities of English sillables, for English Verse" (sig. G_{3}^{v}). Noting that there are no contemporary references to it, Howard Maynadier argued that the group was at most casual and occasional, and not a formal academy; see Maynadier, "The Areopagus of Sidney and Spenser," *Modern Language Review* 4, no. 3 (1909): 289–301. Spenser's boasting of his friendship with Sidney and Dyer suggests the possibility of exaggeration; both Spenser and Harvey would have had much to gain from publishing accounts of their closeness to the revered courtiers. "In those texts of Spenser (and Harvey)," writes Kevin Pask, "we can recover the cultural fantasy of imagined proximity to Sidney which reveals desired solutions to the socioliterary dilemma of Elizabethan poetry"; Pask, *Emergence*, 88.

40. Thomas Howell, *H. His Deuises, for his owne exercise, and his Friends pleasure* (London, 1581), sig. E_{4}^{v}.

41. On the several mentions of Sidney's writings in the Latin collections—exceptions in anthologies focused mostly on Sidney's other achievements—see Martin Garrett, ed., *Sidney: The Critical Heritage* (London: Routledge, 1996), 2.

42. Angel Day, *Vpon the life and death of the most worthy, and thrise renowmed knight, Sir Phillip Sidney* (London, [1586–87?]), sig. A_3^v.

43. George Whetstone, *Sir Phillip Sidney, his honorable life, his valiant death, and true vertues* (London, 1587); on Whetstone's confusion over the authorship of *The Shepheardes Calender*, see Garrett, *Critical Heritage*, 110.

44. Whetstone, *Sir Phillip Sidney*, sig. B_2^v.

45. Abraham Fraunce, *The Arcadian rhetorike: or The praecepts of rhetorike*. London, 1588. Both Sidney and Fraunce attended Shrewsbury School, and Sidney supported Fraunce while the latter studied at Oxford. Afterward, he appears to have continued to benefit from the patronage of Sidney and the Pembrokes, dedicating a series of books to Mary Sidney. See William Barker, "Fraunce [France], Abraham," in *Oxford Dictionary of National Biography* (Oxford: Oxford University Press, 2004), online ed., accessed July 2011, https://doi.org/10.1093/ref:odnb/10133.

46. Newcomb, *Reading Popular Romance*, 64. Newcomb points out that Fraunce's manual may solve the mystery of Sidney's apparent influence on romances by Greene and Lodge, writers who lacked any close connection to Sidney, before the publication of the *Arcadia*.

47. See Allessandra Petrina, "Polyglottia and the Vindication of English Poetry: Abraham Fraunce's *Arcadian Rhetorike*," *Neophilologus* 83, no. 2 (1999): 317–29, on the desire to elevate English letters to the level of Homer, Virgil, and Tasso—and to add Sidney in particular to their rank. On the vernacular rhetorical manuals and the emulative, oppositional, ambivalent relation of English to classical eloquence, see Jenny C. Mann, *Outlaw Rhetoric: Figuring Vernacular Eloquence in Shakespeare's England* (Ithaca: Cornell University Press, 2012).

48. Davis, *Invention*, 126.

49. On the social ambition that the vernacular rhetorical manuals courted, see Frank Whigham, *Ambition and Privilege: The Social Tropes of Elizabethan Courtesy Theory* (Berkeley: University of California Press, 1984). Whigham's book focuses on courtesy literature rather than rhetorical manuals specifically, but there was substantial overlap between the two categories: George Puttenham's *The Arte of English Poesie* (1589), Whigham's signal example, was among other things an inventory of rhetorical tropes.

50. Philip Sidney, *Syr P.S. His Astrophel and Stella Wherein the excellence of sweete poesie is concluded* (London, 1591), sig. A_3^r.

51. Ibid., sig. A_3^v. The Latin is a quotation from Ovid's *Amores* 3.2.44: "The time for applause is here—the golden procession is coming." Ovid, *Heroides; Amores*, trans. Grant Showerman, rev. G. P. Goold (Cambridge: Harvard University Press, 1977).

52. Sidney, *Syr P.S. His Astrophel and Stella*, sig. A_3^v.

53. Newcomb, *Reading Popular Romance*, 45.

54. Ibid., 30.

55. Sidney, *Arcadia* (1593), sig. $¶_4^r$.

56. Joshua Phillips, *English Fictions of Communal Identity, 1485–1603* (Farnham: Ashgate, 2010), 187.

57. Davis, *Invention*, 146. For Davis, the fashioning of the 1593 edition reflected Mary Sidney's neo-Stoic politics. On Mary's emergence, after her brother's death, as a literary figure in her own right, see Margaret P. Hannay, *Philip's Phoenix: Mary Sidney, Countess of Pembroke* (Oxford: Oxford University Press, 1990), 59–83.

58. Sidney, *Arcadia* (1593), sig. $¶_4^v$.

59. Ibid.

60. Sidney, *Arcadia* (1590), sig. A_4^v.

61. For the dialogue between Philisides and Geron, see Sidney, *Arcadia* (1593), sigs. V_2^r–V_3^v; for the echo poem, see Sidney, *Arcadia* (1590), sigs. Ii_3^r–Ii_2^v, and *Arcadia* (1593), sigs. V_4^v–V_5^v; for "On Ister Bank," see *Arcadia* (1590), sigs. N_2^r–N_5^r, and *Arcadia* (1593), sigs. Kk_5^v–Ll_1^v.

62. See Fraunce, *Rhetorike*, sig. D_8^v.

63. On the several continuations of Sidney's broken narrative, including William Alexander's, see Gavin Alexander, *Writing After Sidney*, 268–82; Simonova, *Early Modern Authorship*, 49–56.

64. For Bourdieu, cultural fields are to be understood as networks of "objective relations . . . between positions" in which positions are given meaning by "the structure and distribution of those kinds of capital (or of power) whose possession governs the obtaining of specific profits (such as literary prestige) put into play in the field." Position-takings, then, are the works, acts, and statements by which agents lay claim to particular positions—to particular configurations of symbolic capital in the form of authority or prestige—within the field. Pierre Bourdieu, *The Rules of Art: Genesis and Structure of the Literary Field*, trans. Susan Emanuel (Stanford: Stanford University Press, 1996), 231.

65. Pierre Bourdieu, "The Field of Cultural Production, or: The Economic World Reversed," trans. Richard Nice, in *The Field of Cultural Production: Essays on Art and Literature*, ed. Randal Johnson (New York: Columbia University Press, 1993), 39. He later offers another, more substantial definition of the field of restricted production: "The field of production *per se* owes its own structure to the opposition between the *field of restricted production* as a system producing cultural goods (and the instruments for appropriating these goods) objectively destined for a public of producers of cultural goods, and the *field of large-scale cultural production*, specifically organized with a view to the production of cultural goods destined for non-producers of cultural goods, 'the public at large'" (115).

66. *Exequiæ Illustrissimi Equitis, D. Philippi Sidnaei, Grattisimae Memoriae ac Nomini Ipensæ* (Oxford, 1587), sig. E_1^v, repr. in Colaianne and Godshalk, eds., *Elegies for Sir Philip Sidney*, translation mine. It is unclear how Latewar had access to Sidney's writings; the explanation may be his apparent friendship with Samuel Daniel, who was a student at Oxford at the same time. On Latewar, see Karl Josef Holtgen, "Richard Latewar: Elizabethan Poet and Divine," *Anglia: Zeitschrift fur Englische Philologie* 89 (1971): 417–38.

67. *Exequiæ Illustrissimi Equitis*, sigs. E_1^v, translation mine.

68. Roydon, "Elegie," sig. B_2^v. Thomas Nashe's praise for the poem in 1589 documents its circulation for at least some time before that date.

69. Barnabe Barnes, *Parthenophil and Parthenophe Sonnettes, madrigals, elegies and odes* (London, 1593), sig. P_1^r.

70. Edmund Spenser, *The Ruines of Time*, lines 673–75, in *The Yale Edition of the Shorter Poems of Edmund Spenser*, ed. William A. Oram et al. (New Haven: Yale University Press, 1989).

71. John Dickenson, *The Shepheardes Complaint. A passionate Eclogue, written in English Hexameters* (London, [1592–93?]); Dickenson, *Arisbas, Euphues amidst his slumbers: Or Cupids Iourney to Hell* (London, 1594). *The Shepheardes Complaint* is typically dated to 1596, but as Gavin Alexander points out, references to the text in *Arisbas* suggest that it was published in 1592 or 1593; see Alexander, *Writing After Sidney*, 265.

72. Dickenson, *Arisbas*, sig. A_3^v.

73. Alexander, *Writing After Sidney*, 268.

74. Dickenson, *Arisbas*, sig. G_3^r.

75. Ibid., sig. G_3^v.

76. Ibid., sig. G_4^r.

77. Dickenson, *Shepheardes Complaint*, sig. B_3^v.

78. Ibid., sig. A_2^v.

79. Dickenson, *Arisbas*, sig. A_3^v.

80. Ibid., sig. A_4^r.

81. Ibid., sig. E_3^r,

82. Roydon, "Elegie," sig. B_2^r.

83. Edmund Spenser, *The Faerie Queene*, ed. A.C. Hamilton, 2nd ed. (New York: Longman, 2007), Book VI, canto x, stanza 16, line 4. Roydon's use of the construction to celebrate Astrophil may have suggested Spenser's application of it to his own persona as well.

84. Richard A. McCabe, *"Ungainefull Arte": Poetry, Patronage, and Print in the Early Modern Era* (Oxford: Oxford University Press, 2016), 247.

85. Spenser, *Yale Edition of Shorter Poems*, 230.

86. On representations of Spenser's relationship with Sidney, see Pask, *Emergence*, 83–112. Pask argues that while the relationship between the two was originally framed as one of patronage, accounts increasingly turned it "into one of 'intimate friendship' or familiarity between two *poets* rather than between patron and client" (83). In the seventeenth and eighteenth centuries, Pask shows, Spenser's ascendant cultural authority led to narratives in which Sidney came under his literary tutelage.

87. Edmund Spenser, "Astrophel," in *Colin Clouts come home againe* (London: T. C. for William Ponsonby, 1595), sig. F_1^r. Citations from this volume will hereafter be cited in text, identified by the initials *CC* and by signature.

88. Although scholars generally agree that the poem is Spenser's, there have been arguments in favor of assigning it to Mary Sidney. See especially Hannay, *Philip's Phoenix*, 63–68; Lisa M. Klein, "Spenser's *Astrophel* and the Sidney Legend," *Sidney Newsletter and Journal* 12, no. 2 (1993): 42–55.

89. Bryskett's "The Mourning Muse of Thestylis," as Dennis Kay points out, was entered in the Stationers' Register on August 22, 1587; see Kay, *Melodious Tears: The English Funeral Elegy from Spenser to Milton* (Oxford: Clarendon Press, 1990), 54.

90. Paul Alpers, *What Is Pastoral?* (Chicago: University of Chicago Press, 1996), 81.

91. Lycon, Frederic B. Tromly points out, is an anagram for Colin; see Tromly, "Lodowick Bryskett's Elegies on Sidney in Spenser's *Astrophel* Volume," *Review of English Studies*, n.s., 37, no. 147 (1986), 386. The name may also simply refer to Bryskett himself, sharing as it does a first letter with his given name.

92. On the identities of the poets, see William Oram's notes in Spenser, *Yale Edition of Shorter Poems*, 540–42. Oram suggests that Harpalus is George Turberville; Corydon, either Edward Dyer or Abraham Fraunce; Alcyon, Sir Arthur Gorges; Palin, George Peele; Alcon, Thomas Lodge; Palemon, Thomas Churchyard; and Aetion, Michael Drayton. In the eclogue's roster of poets, William Alabaster and Samuel Daniel are identified by last name rather than by pseudonym.

93. On pastoral as an escape or withdrawal into a "green world," see Harry Berger Jr., "The Renaissance Imagination: Second World and Green World," in *Second World and Green World: Studies in Renaissance Fiction-Making* (Berkeley: University of California Press, 1988), 3–40.

94. Dickenson, *Arisbas*, sigs. E_3^r–E_3^v.

95. Alexander, *Writing After Sidney*, 268.

96. Falco perceptively argues that late Elizabethan writers, most influentially Spenser, fashioned Sidney after his death as the "primary genealogical authority" for English literature. Raphael Falco, *Conceived Presences: Literary Genealogy in Renaissance England* (Amherst: University of Massachusetts Press, 1994), 67.

97. Garth Bond, "'Rare poemes aske rare friends': Ben Jonson, Coterie Poet," *Modern Philology* 107, no. 3 (2010): 380–99.

98. On restricted production and autonomization, see Bourdieu, "The Market for Symbolic Goods," trans. R. Swyer, in *Field of Cultural Production*, 113–20.

99. Alexander, *Writing After Sidney*, 334.

100. Thomas Nashe, *Have with You to Saffron-Walden* (1596), in *The Works of Thomas Nashe*, ed. R. B. McKerrow, 5 vols. (1904; repr., Oxford: Basil Blackwell, 1958), 3:116. For the name-dropping that provoked Nashe's mockery, see Gabriel Harvey, *Pierces Supererogation or A New Prayse of the Old Asse. A Preparative to certaine Larger Discourses, intitutled Nashes S. Fame* (London, 1593), sigs. F_1^r–F_1^v.

CHAPTER 4

1. Philip Sidney, *The Defence of Poesie* (London, 1595), sig. I_3^r.

2. Thomas Nashe, *The Anatomie of Absurditie*, in *The Works of Thomas Nashe*, ed. Ronald B. McKerrow, 5 vols. (1904–10, repr. Oxford: Basil Blackwell, 1958), 1:9. All citations of Nashe's writings will refer to McKerrow's edition, and will be made parenthetically in text, with the abbreviation *TN*.

3. Gabriel Harvey, *Pierces Supererogation or A New Prayse of the Old Asse. A Preparative to certaine Larger Discourses, intituled Nashes S. Fame.* (London, 1593), sigs. Dd_2^v–Dd_3^r.

4. Charles Nicholl, *A Cup of News: The Life of Thomas Nashe* (London: Routledge, 1984), 99.

5. G. R. Hibbard, *Thomas Nashe: A Critical Introduction* (Cambridge, Mass.: Harvard University Press, 1962), 50.

6. Laurie Ellinghausen, *Labor and Writing in Early Modern England, 1567–1667* (Aldershot: Ashgate, 2008), 37–38.

7. Jennifer Richards, *Rhetoric and Courtliness in Early Modern Literature* (Cambridge: Cambridge University Press, 2003), 117; Mike Rodman Jones, *Radical Pastoral, 1381–1594: Appropriation and the Writing of Religious Controversy* (Burlington: Ashgate, 2011), 152–60.

8. Lorna Hutson, *Thomas Nashe in Context* (Oxford: Oxford University Press, 1989), 180.

9. Whereas Hutson and Jonathan Crewe, among others, position Nashe as in different ways subversive—Hutson by aligning Nashe's rhetoric with Bakhtinian dialogism, and Crewe by reading his prose as a deconstruction of the possibility of stable communication—critics like Arthur Kinney frame him as a as a staunch defender of classical genres against the advancing decay of his own era. See Crewe, *Unredeemed Rhetoric: Thomas Nashe and the Scandal of Authorship* (Baltimore: Johns Hopkins University Press, 1982); Kinney, *Humanist Poetics: Thought, Rhetoric, and Fiction in Sixteenth-Century England* (Amherst: University of Massachusetts Press, 1986), 304–62.

10. Alexandra Halasz, *The Marketplace of Print: Pamphlets and the Public Sphere in Early Modern England* (Cambridge: Cambridge University Press, 1997), 87.

11. Richard Harvey, *A Theologicall Discourse of the Lamb of God and His Enemies* (London, 1590), sig. a_2^v. As McKerrow notes, the epistle "occurs in but few copies of the *Lamb of God*, having probably been added after the original publication of the work," an inference supported by its appearance, between signatures A and B, as signature *a*. Nashe, *Workes*, 5:176.

12. Harvey, *Theologicall Discourse*, sig. a_2^v.

13. If Richard Harvey's attack on Nashe was the proximate cause of the latter's quarrel with Gabriel Harvey, the quarrel's roots arguably went back much further. According to one theory, John Lyly (like Nashe an anti-Martinist pamphleteer in 1588–89) had suggested to Edward de Vere, Earl of Oxford, during the latter's flare-up with Philip Sidney a decade earlier, that a poem of Gabriel Harvey's had been intended as an insult against him—an act of sabotage that Harvey never forgave. See R. B. McKerrow's account of the quarrel in his magisterial edition of Nashe's works: Nashe, *Works* 5:65–110. As McKerrow points out, that Harvey's quarrel with Nashe originated in the accusation of his insulting de Vere meant that the quarrel was an offspring of de Vere's well-known tensions with Philip Sidney in 1579 and 1580.

14. *Draff* refers to dregs or lees, often specifically "the refuse or grains of malt after brewing or distilling." *Oxford English Dictionary*, s.v. "draff (n.)," definition (a), accessed September 26, 2018, http://www.oed.com/view/Entry/57394.

15. Bernard Capp, "Harvey, Richard (*bap.* 1560, *d.* 1630)," in *Oxford Dictionary of National Biography* (Oxford: Oxford University Press, 2004; online ed.), accessed February 16, 2015, http://www.oxforddnb.com/view/article/12527.

16. Halasz, *Marketplace*, 82–89.

17. Ben Jonson, *The workes of Benjamin Jonson. The second Volume* (London, 1641), sig. N_2^v. Jonson's comments on his fellow readers soon turn into a rant: "There are never wanting that dare preferre the worst *Preachers*, the worst *Pleaders*, the worst *Poets*; not that the better have left to write, or speake better, but that they that heare them judge worse . . . Nay, if it were put to the question of the Water-rimers [John Taylor's] workes against *Spencers*, I doubt not, but they would find more *Suffrages*; because the most favour common vices, out of a Prerogative the vulgar have, to lose their judgements, and the like that which is naught" (sig. N_3^r). Like Webbe and Nashe, Jonson attributes the erasure of distinctions not to the absence of good poets but to the failure of readers to adequately value them. Later in the book, Jonson returns to the question of judgment: "To judge of Poets is only the facultie of Poets; and not of all Poets, but the best. . . . But, some will say, *Criticks* are a kind of Tinkers; that make more faults, then they mend ordinarily. . . . But the office of a true *Critick*, or *Censor*, is, not to throw by a letter any where, or damne an innocent Syllabe, but lay the words together, and amend them; judge sincerely of the Author, and his matter, which is the signe of a solid and perfect learning in a man" (sig. R_3^r). If Jonson's sober authority differs markedly from Nashe's exuberant irreverence, it has much in common with Gabriel Harvey's stern declaration that "Judgement is the wisest reader of bookes."

18. William Webbe, *A Discourse of English Poetrie* (London, 1588), sig. A_4^r.

19. The decline of patronage was, of course, a familiar topos in the period: a major theme, for instance, of Spenser's "The Tears of the Muses" (1591). According to Kevin Pask, "The amount of patronage may not have declined, but the number of writers competing for it certainly increased." Pask, *The Emergence of the English Author: Scripting the Life of the Poet in Early Modern England* (Cambridge: Cambridge University Press, 1996), 85. Alexandra Halasz points out that the profoundly influential pedagogue Richard Mulcaster worried about a surplus

of educated men occurring simultaneously with a shortage of employment opportunities. Halasz, *Marketplace*, 83–84. The literary consequences of this frustration have been traced by Richard Helgerson in *The Elizabethan Prodigals* (Berkeley: University of California Press, 1977) and more recently by Jeff Dolven in *Scenes of Instruction in Renaissance Romance* (Chicago: University of Chicago Press, 2007). For an overview of the patronage system, its interactions with the print marketplace, and the rhetoric of patronal solicitation, see Richard A. McCabe, *"Ungainefull Arte": Poetry, Patronage, and Print in the Early Modern Era* (Oxford: Oxford University Press, 2016).

20. Certainly the market provided little incentive for writers to spend more time writing better work. Rather than being paid royalties based on sales, writers generally received only a small payment (the typical fee for a short pamphlet seems to have been forty shillings) upon transfer of the manuscript, after which rights to the copy (and to future profits) belonged exclusively to the publisher. See Peter Blayney, "The Publication of Playbooks," in *A New History of Early English Drama*, ed. John D. Cox and David Scott Kastan (New York: Columbia University Press, 1997), 395–96.

21. McCabe, *"Ungainefull Arte"*, 225.

22. This circularity provides a striking example for Pierre Bourdieu's anti-Kantian argument that the concept of aesthetic taste is a "universalization of the dispositions associated with a particular social and economic condition." Bourdieu, *Distinction: A Social Critique of the Judgement of Taste*, trans. Richard Nice (Cambridge, Mass.: Harvard University Press, 1984), 493.

23. Nashe was probably unable to see the irony that trailed this argument: if the plight of England's young humanist writers was partly a function of declining patronage, it was also a function of the "pedagogical reproduction of learned men," which created an oversupply that began to dilute the cultural value of learning. See Halasz, *Marketplace*, 87. For Halasz, the Nashe-Harvey quarrel was in many respects a response to the resulting uncertainty about the authority of the humanist orator.

24. Few would have disagreed with Nashe's praise of the widely revered Sidney, but the point was not the content of the judgment; rather, it was that Nashe was the one offering it.

25. Arthur Marotti, *Manuscript, Print, and the English Renaissance Lyric* (Ithaca: Cornell University Press, 1995), 314.

26. Pierre Bourdieu, "The Field of Cultural Production, or: The Economic World Reversed," trans. Richard Nice, in *The Field of Cultural Production: Essays on Art and Literature*, ed. Randal Johnson (New York: Columbia University Press, 1993), 42.

27. Toward the end of the pamphlet, Nashe observes his fellow English readers' voracious desire for news, explaining why Pierce spends the second half of the pamphlet interrogating the Knight of the Post about devils, hell, and the supernatural: "I bring *Pierce Penilesse* to question with the diuel, as a young nouice would talke with a great trauailer; who, carrieng an Englishmans appetite to enquire of of news, will be sure to make what vse of him he maie, and not leaue anie thing vnaskt, that he can resolue him of" (*TN*, 1:240).

28. See Nashe, *Works*, 4:93, McKerrow's note.

29. See Melissa Hull Geil, "Reproducing Paper Monsters in Thomas Nashe," in *The Age of Thomas Nashe: Text, Bodies and Trespasses in Early Modern England*, ed. Stephen Guy-Bray, Joan Pong Linton, and Steve Mentz (Farnham: Ashgate, 2013), 77–98.

30. Jones, *Radical Pastoral*, 154. As Jones points out, the Marprelate pamphleteers had sought to frame "Plain Piers" as Martin's "Gransier" (141).

31. David Landreth, *The Face of Mammon: The Matter of Money in English Renaissance Literature* (Oxford: Oxford University Press, 2012), 186–87. Pierce's near nonexistence, his proximity to what Landreth calls "the minimal," is a version of the devil's invisible ubiquity and, in this sense, an accommodation to the anonymous, dispersed public for which Nashe wrote. The paradox of self-annihilation and self-dispersal that occupies Landreth is also the subject of Tamsin Theresa Badcoe's "'As many Ciphers without an I': Self-Reflexive Violence in the Work of Thomas Nashe," *Modern Philology* 111, no. 3 (2014): 384–407, which revealingly links depictions of bodily violence in Nashe's self-representations to an awareness of the dispersal entailed by print dissemination.

32. David J. Baker, *On Demand: Writing for the Market in Early Modern England* (Stanford: Stanford University Press, 2010), 35–61.

33. Crewe, *Unredeemed Rhetoric*, 46.

34. Hutson, *Thomas Nashe*, 175.

35. Georgia Brown, *Redefining Elizabethan Literature* (Cambridge: Cambridge University Press, 2004), 95.

36. The most thorough analysis of the market for early modern printed books is Alan B. Farmer and Zachary Lesser's "What Is Print Popularity? A Map of the Elizabethan Book Trade," in *The Elizabethan Top Ten: Defining Print Popularity in Early Modern England*, ed. Andy Kesson and Emma Smith (Burlington: Ashgate, 2013), 19–54. Farmer and Lesser show that religious books commanded a plurality of the market share in speculative book trade, approximately 40%, between 1559 and 1602. By comparison, "Poesy and the Arts," another of the six categories into which they divide all *Short-Title Catalogue* entries from the period, commanded a market share of 19.2%. See also Blayney, "The Publication of Playbooks."

37. Farmer and Lesser's analysis of the book trade makes clear that history constituted another significant rival in the market. Their category of "History and Politics," which includes "law, news, travel and political geography, military arts and sciences, trade and economics, political theory, and most other books that treat world events," comprised a market share of 20.9 percent from 1559 to 1602, just ahead of "Poesy and the Arts." Yet Farmer and Lesser point out that by the time Pierce mocked the "Chronigraphers" in the print marketplace, Poesy and the Arts was in the process of surpassing History and Politics in market share. Farmer and Lesser, "What Is Print Popularity?" 29, 31, 37.

38. Pierre Bourdieu, *The Rules of Art: Genesis and Structure of the Literary Field*, trans. Susan Emanuel (Stanford: Stanford University Press, 1996), 224. Elsewhere, Bourdieu makes clear that the regulation of the field's boundaries and the internal struggle for prestige and authority are one and the same: "The field of cultural production is the site of struggles in which what is at stake is the power to impose the dominant definition of the writer and therefore delimit the population of those entitled to take part in the struggle to define the writer." Bourdieu, "The Field of Cultural Production," 42.

39. McKerrow writes that the attack on Richard Harvey "bear[s] strong traces of having been an afterthought." Nashe, *Works*, 5:78. Yet the emergence of the attack at the end of a passage that progressively collapses Pierce into Nashe suggests that it is in fact the natural conclusion of Pierce's discussion of poetry and publication.

40. Pierce's discussion of pride is fascinating as a moment where moral and protosociological discourses come apart, a vice in one domain turning into a virtue (at least in certain respects) in the other. It stands also as a challenge to readings that would take Pierce as a

naïve fool—here the moral discourse is subverted not by a satiric mode that takes Pierce as its object but by Pierce himself, arguing earnestly.

41. McKerrow, in his exhaustive (and astonishingly learned) commentary on Nashe's works, offers a dry assessment of the line: "I have no idea what this means" (Nashe, *Works*, 4:120).

42. One of the odd twists of *Pierce Penilesse* is that although Nashe's persona is, according to the logic of the framing narrative, the voice of the supplication presented by a narrator who is presumed to be Nashe himself, Pierce remains the central figure even after the text of the supplication has ended. In the dialogue on the supernatural that follows, the Knight of the Post addresses himself not to "Tom" but to "Persie" (*TN*, 1:219). By this point, Nashe seems either to have been displaced by Pierce or to have become him.

43. Henry Chettle, *Kind-Harts Dreame. Conteining fiue Apparitions, with their Inuectives against abuses raigning* (London, 1593), sig. E_1^r.

44. Ibid., sig. E_1^v.

45. As McKerrow explains, Greene had provoked Harvey with a passage in his satire *A Quip for an Upstart Courtier* (1592) that apparently mocked Harvey and his brothers. (Greene soon thought better of it and contrived to have the passage removed, and it is no longer extant.) The timeline of the pamphlets is remarkably compressed: *A Quip* was entered in the Stationers' Register on July 20, 1592; *Pierce Penilesse* on August 8; *Foure Letters* on December 4; and *Kind-Harts Dreame* on December 8. Harvey seems to have encountered *Pierce Penilesse*, with its attack on his brother Richard, relatively late in the composition of *Foure Letters*, for the abuse of Nashe gives the impression of being a late addition to a text intended primarily to rebuke Greene. See McKerrow's invaluable overview of the quarrel in Nashe, *Works*, 5:65–110.

46. In addition to McKerrow's discussion, there are useful surveys of the controversy in Nicholl, *A Cup of News*, and Stephen Hilliard, *The Singularity of Thomas Nashe* (Lincoln: University of Nebraska Press, 1986).

47. See Brown, *Redefining Elizabethan Literature*, 76.

48. Edward Arber, ed., *Transcript of the Registers of the Company of Stationers of London 1554–1640*, 5 vols. (London, 1875), 3:677. One of the ban's cruel twists was that it scrupulously preserved Harvey's academic title even as it lumps him with Nashe. As I will argue, Harvey worked strenuously to insist on his difference from an opponent with whom he sensed he had a great deal in common.

49. Harvey, *Pierces Supererogation*, sig. Z_4^r; hereafter cited in the text as *PS*.

50. Gabriel Harvey, *Foure Letters, and certaine Sonnets: Especially touching Robert Greene, and other parties, by him abused* (London, 1592), sig. D_2^v; hereafter cited parenthetically in text as *FL*.

51. McKerrow's words. Nashe, *Works*, 5:71. Harvey also took the degree of doctor of civil law from Oxford in 1585.

52. See Bourdieu's discussion of *habitus* in *Distinction*, 169–75. For a more involved discussion of the similar mentalities that resulted from Nashe's and Harvey's shared Cambridge backgrounds, see Maria Teresa Micaela Prendergast, *Railing, Reviling, and Invective in English Literary Culture, 1588–1617: The Anti-Poetics of Theater and Print* (Farnham: Ashgate, 2012), 75–101.

53. This is not to say that there were no differences in the content of their opinions. Their evaluations of particular poets—Barnabe Barnes is a prominent example—were occasionally at odds. The two also staked out opposing territory in the debates over Petrus Ramus's theories of rhetoric and logic, which were then gaining popularity at Cambridge; Harvey was a committed Ramist, while Nashe mocked the school in the *Anatomie*.

54. McKerrow writes: "There must have been some inherent opposition between the two: each must have represented to the other the class or the type which he most detested: there must, I think, have been a conflict of principles as well as of persons." Nashe, *Works*, 5:66.

55. Halasz, *Marketplace*, 82–113; Brown, *Redefining Elizabethan Literature*, 1, 75–81.

56. The authoritative source on Petrus Ramus and his "method" is Walter Ong, *Ramus, Method and the Decay of Dialogue: From the Art of Discourse to the Art of Reason* (Cambridge, Mass.: Harvard University Press, 1958). On Harvey's Ramism, see Kendrick W. Prewitt, "Gabriel Harvey and the Practice of Method," *Studies in English Literature, 1500–1900* 39, no. 1 (1999): 19–39; Gerard Passannante, "The Art of Reading Earthquakes: On Harvey's Wit, Ramus's Method, and the Renaissance of Lucretius," *Renaissance Quarterly* 61, no. 3 (2008): 792–832.

57. On Ramism and selective reading, see Passannante, "Reading Earthquakes," 805–7.

58. For Harvey's discussion of Nashe's disturbing singularity, see *PS*, sigs. Aa_2^v–Aa_3^v. Stephen Hilliard discusses the ambiguity of Nashe's singularity: "To be singular was to be different and original, estimable characteristics in literature and on the streets of London to the point that they threatened to become disruptive to the traditional social order." Hilliard, *Singularity*, 3.

59. Prendergast, *Railing*, 79. Prendergast suggests that Harvey and Nashe both triangulate their relation to the university, creating "homosocial bonds with peers via the mediations of the *alma mater*," which finds its other in the "mechanical fecundities of the printing press" (87). She writes: "Certainly, if we follow Eve Sedgwick's commentary that the Girardian triangle gestures to an underlying homoerotic current between male rivals, then one might see in Harvey's and Nashe's vituperations a strong fascination for, even obsession with, each other" (99).

60. Passannante, "Reading Earthquakes," 795.

61. Hilliard, *Singularity*, 65.

62. On this disappointment, see Jason Scott-Warren, "Harvey, Gabriel (1552/3–1631)," in *Oxford Dictionary of National Biography* (Oxford: Oxford University Press, 2004; online ed.), accessed September 3, 2014, http://www.oxforddnb.com/view/article/12517.

63. *Supererogation* carries the theological (and, especially, Catholic) meaning of "the performance of good works beyond what God commands or requires," and Harvey may have intended an implication of theological travesty; more generally, the word refers to any form of superfluity. *Oxford English Dictionary*, online ed., s.v., "supererogation (n.)," accessed September 3, 2014, http://www.oed.com/view/Entry/194275.

64. Nashe did not invent the word *omnigatherum*—the first usage cited by the *Oxford English Dictionary* dates to 1430—but it does provide an interesting link between Harvey and Nashe: in *Foure Letters*, Harvey uses it in a stream of invective against Robert Greene: "a Louer, a Souldier, a Trauailer, Merchaunt, a Broker, an Artificer, a Botcher, a Petti-fogger, a Player, a Coosener, a Rayler, a beggar, an Omnigatherum, a Gay nothing" (*FL*, sig. D_2^r). Harvey uses it to describe a class of contemporary writer that included Nashe as well as Greene, a class indexed as socially inferior to the refined and retiring elite. Nashe, for his part, restores the word to its original meaning—an assembled crowd—and takes this revision a step further in fashioning the omnigatherum as a reading audience, an *omnes* gathered only virtually. But in leaving in play the sense of social derogation that Harvey invested in the term, Nashe betrays just how complicated the negotiations of value in his critical position were.

65. Little work has been done on the legal satire embedded in *Haue with You*, but it is clear that Nashe—who at one point found himself in debtors' prison—was interested at least in poking fun at lawyers' jargon.

66. *Parthenophil and Parthenophe*, a sonnet sequence, was published in 1593 by Wolfe. Barnes's contributions to *Pierces Supererogation* can be found in sigs. $***_{1}^{v}$–$***_{3}^{v}$, directly before a second title page begins signature A.

67. Hutson, *Thomas Nashe*, 211.

68. Thomas Dekker, *Newes from hell brought by the Diuells carrier* (London, 1606), sig. A_{3}^{r}.

69. Dekker, *Newes from hell*, sig. B_{2}^{v}. Not only an expression of affection for Nashe through Pierce, the passage is arguably also a sly insult at Dekker's fellow repliers, perhaps alluded to in the form of the devil's failed scholars.

70. *The Returne of the knight of the poste from Hell, with the diuels aunswere to the supplication of Pierce Penilesse, with some relation of the last treasons* (London, 1606), sig. A_{3}^{r}.

71. Dekker, *Newes from hell*, sig. A_{4}^{v}. The twin answers, he added, proved the devil a liar, "because hee's found in two Tales, about one matter." Much of the anonymously authored *Returne* was focused on other topics than Pierce, devoting substantial space, for instance, to a report from London's streets in the wake of the exposure of the Gunpowder Plot.

72. Neil Rhodes, *Elizabethan Grotesque* (London: Routledge and Kegan Paul, 1980), 59. Rhodes places Middleton as the foremost heir of Nashe's combination of intensely physical prose and his proto-journalistic interest in social realism.

73. Thomas Middleton, *The blacke booke* (London, 1604), sig. D_{1}^{v}.

74. Jeffrey Todd Knight, "Afterworlds: Thomas Middleton, the Book, and the Genre of Continuation," in *Formal Matters: Reading the Materials of English Renaissance Literature*, ed. Allison K. Deutermann and András Kiséry (Manchester: Manchester University Press, 2013), 89.

75. Dekker, *Newes from hell*, sigs. C_{2}^{r}–C_{2}^{v}.

CODA

1. Matthew Roydon, "An Elegie, or friends passion, for his Astrophill. *Written vpon the death of the right Honorable sir Philip Sidney knight, Lord gouernor of Flushing*," in *The Phoenix Nest* [. . .] (London, 1593), sigs. B_{1}^{r}, B_{2}^{v}; John Dickenson, *Arisbas, Euphues amidst his slumbers: Or Cupids Iourney to Hell* (London, 1594), sig. E_{3}^{r}.

2. Michel Foucault, "What Is an Author?" in *Textual Strategies: Perspectives in Post-Structuralist Criticism*, ed. Josué V. Harari (Ithaca: Cornell University Press, 1979), 147.

3. Alexandra Gillespie, *Print Culture and the Medieval Author: Chaucer, Lydgate, and Their Books 1473–1557* (Oxford: Oxford University Press, 2006), 5.

4. A. J. Minnis, *Medieval Theory of Authorship: Scholastic Literary Attitudes in the Later Middle Ages* (London: Scolar Press, 1984), 12. In a different context, Boris Maslov's account of "the historical ontology" of the author similarly emphasizes the concept's role in framing the past. Developing an analogy between lawgivers (Moses) and poets (Homer), Maslov argues that references to authorial individuality work "to introduce stability into an inherently dynamic tradition." Maslov, *Pindar and the Emergence of Literature* (Cambridge: Cambridge University Press, 2015), 54.

5. Roger Chartier, *The Order of Books: Readers, Authors, and Libraries in Europe Between the Fourteenth and Eighteenth Centuries*, trans. Lydia G. Cochrane (Stanford: Stanford University Press, 1994), 58.

6. Robert Greene, *Greenes Vision: Written at the instant of his death* (London: 1592), sigs. B_{4}^{v}–C_{1}^{r}.

7. Ibid., sig. H_1^r.

8. Joseph Loewenstein, *Ben Jonson and Possessive Authorship* (Cambridge: Cambridge University Press, 2002), 1–2.

9. Anthony Munday, *The famous and renovvned historie of Primaleon of Greece, sonne to the great and mighty Prince Palmerin d'Oliua, Emperour of Constantinople* (London, 1619), sig. O_2^v. Although it was first published in 1596, the only extant copy of that edition is incomplete; the earliest extant text to contain the poem, "Beautie sate bathing," is the 1619 combined edition, which contains all the three "books" of *Primaleon*.

10. *Englands Helicon* (London, 1600), sigs. D_3^v–D_4^r. The lack of an extant copy of the first edition of the second part of *Primaleon* leaves open the possibility that the poem was inserted into Munday's romance after being printed in *Englands Helicon*. Nonetheless, because the name "Shepheard Tonie" apparently refers to Munday's first name, it seems likely that Ling had taken the poem from Munday's book.

11. Ibid., sig. Bb_4^r.

12. On this division, and on Tottel's reorganization of the miscellany between the first and second editions, see J. Christopher Warner, *The Making and Marketing of Tottel's Miscellany, 1557: Songs and Sonnets in the Summer of the Martyrs' Fires* (Farnham: Ashgate, 2013), 10–11, 38–40.

13. Matthew Zarnowiecki, *Fair Copies: Reproducing the English Lyric from Tottel to Shakespeare* (Toronto: University of Toronto Press, 2014), 39.

14. *The Paradyse of Daynty Deuises aptly furnished, with sundry pithie and learned inuentions* (London, 1576), sig. A_2^r.

15. *The Phoenix Nest. Built vp with the most rare and refined workes of Noble men, worthy Knights, gallant Gentlemen, Masters of Arts, and braue Schollers* (London, 1593), sig. A_1^r.

16. *Songes and sonettes, written by the right honorable Lorde Henry Haward late Earle of Surrey, and other* (London, 1557), sig. A_1^v. The seminal article on the reluctance that aristocratic poets professed toward print is J. W. Saunders, "The Stigma of Print: A Note on the Social Bases of Tudor Poetry," *Essays in Criticism* 1, no. 2 (1951): 139–64. See also Wendy Wall's analysis in the context of gender, voyeurism, and self-display in Wall, "Disclosures in Print: The 'Violent Enlargement' of the Renaissance Voyeuristic Text," *Studies in English Literature, 1500–1900* 29 (1989): 35–59.

17. If the authors were insulated, of course, the risk that the poetry itself would lose social distinction in the process of publication remained. Adam Smyth describes this as "the inevitable tension at the heart of the miscellanies: a tension between cultivating a sense of the socially eminent . . . and debasing that eminence through its transfer to the public." Smyth, "'Such a general itching after book-learning': Popular Readers of 'the most eminent Wits,'" *Yearbook of English Studies* 33 (2003): 267. The benefits of this advertising strategy were such that even anthologies *not* based on manuscript miscellanies claimed to be. Eric Nebeker has pointed the dependence of early print miscellanies on broadside ballads, which already had a print audience and which could help fill out a book for print. This less prestigious source material may have heightened the need for the anthologies to present themselves as cousins of the aristocratic manuscript miscellanies. See Nebeker, "Broadside Ballads, Miscellanies, and the Lyric in Print," *ELH* 76, no. 4 (2009): 989–1013.

18. Elizabeth Heale, *Autobiography and Authorship in Renaissance Verse: Chronicles of the Self* (Basingstoke: Palgrave Macmillan, 2003), 11.

19. See *Englands Helicon*, ed. Hugh Macdonald (Cambridge, Mass.: Harvard University Press, 1962), xx.

20. Marcy L. North, *The Anonymous Renaissance: Cultures of Discretion in Tudor-Stuart England* (Chicago: University of Chicago Press, 2003), 77. North's discussion situates the *Englands Helicon*, and its cancel slips, in the context of Renaissance practices of anonymity.

21. The editorial responsibility for the volume is itself an interesting story. It was long believed to be the work of the gentleman John Bodenham, who had sponsored a series of other collections. In a prefatory sonnet to Bodenham, a certain A. B. had described the book as "thy *Helicon*." See *England's Helicon 1600, 1614*, ed. Hyder Edward Rollins (Cambridge, Mass.: Harvard University Press, 1935), 1:3. But the preface to the reader was written by an L. N., believed to be the bookseller and publisher Nicholas Ling; scholars now assign primary editorial responsibility to Ling and understand Bodenham to have been a general sponsor for the project. See Rollins's discussion of the issue in *Englands Helicon, 1600, 1614*, 2:41–63.

22. See *Englands Helicon* (1962), xxi.

23. *Englands Helicon* (1600), sig. A_4^r.

24. Loewenstein, *The Author's Due: Printing and the Prehistory of Copyright* (Chicago: University of Chicago Press, 2002), 131. The preface exemplifies Loewenstein's suggestion that possessive authorship emerged as a back-formation of proprietary competition among publishers. On the importance of Ling's account of authorial rights, see also Loewenstein, *Jonson and Possessive Authorship*, 64, 148–51.

25. *Englands Helicon* (1600), sig. A_4^r.

26. *Englands Helicon* (1600), sig. A_4^v.

27. *Englands Helicon* (1600), sigs. D_4^r, E_1^r.

28. Robert Burton, *The Anatomy of Melancholy, What It Is. With All the Kindes, Causes, Symptomes, Prognostickes, and Severall Cures of It* (Oxford, 1621), sig. A_7^r.

29. Robert Burton, *The Anatomy of Melancholy, What It Is. With All the Kindes, Causes, Symptomes, Prognostickes, and Severall Cures of It* (Oxford, 1624), sig. B_2^r.

30. Burton, *Anatomy* (1621), sig. A_3^r.

31. Ibid., sig. A_3^v.

32. For an especially lucid discussion of Democritus's "medial position" between detachment and implication, see Christopher Tilmouth, "Burton's 'Turning Picture': Argument and Anxiety in *The Anatomy of Melancholy*," *Review of English Studies*, n.s., 56, no. 226 (2005): 524–49. On Democritus's place in the history of self-defeating satirical personae, beginning with Horatian and Juvenalian satire and including Erasmus's *Praise of Folly*, see James S. Tillman, "The Satirist Satirized: Burton's Democritus Jr.," *Studies in the Literary Imagination* 10, no. 2 (1977): 89–96.

33. I quote here from the third edition of Burton's *The Anatomy of Melancholy What it is, With All the Kinds, Causes, Symptomes, Prognostickes, & Seuerall Cures of It* (Oxford, 1628), sig. K_2^r. The passage is largely the same as in the first edition (Burton, *Anatomy* [1621], sig. E_7^v), but the third edition introduces the intriguing middle clause "what it is . . . him that is so indeede."

34. Drew Daniel, *The Melancholy Assemblage: Affect and Epistemology in the English Renaissance* (New York: Fordham University Press, 2013), 172. Daniel suggests that the critical focus on Burton's ambiguous self-presentation has crowded out an attention to the experience of reading the *Anatomy* beyond "Democritus Junior to the Reader"; in the *Anatomy* proper, individual intention matters less than the dialectical interplay of the ideas that the text accumulates.

35. Burton, *Anatomy* (1621), sig. A_5^r.

36. Democritus natu minimus [pseud.], *England Know thy Drivers, and their Driver: or, Democritus Natu Minimus* (London, 1647), sig. A_2^r. The two pamphlets by "Democritus Junior"

are *Mercvrius Diabolicus, Or Hells Intelligencer* (London, 1647) and *Wit's Progresse Wherein are launc't the various crimes, Are incident to these sad times* (London, 1647). Eleven years later, "Democritus Secundus" offered a miscellany of stories and aphorisms in *Comes Facundus in Via. The Fellow-Traveller* (London, 1658).

37. Quoted in Douglas Bush, *English Literature in the Earlier Seventeenth Century: 1600–1660* (New York: Oxford University Press, 1945), 280.

38. *Authorialism* is Benedetti's term for the aesthetic ideology, one in her argument central to late modern art and literature, that takes the status of being "authored" as the main criterion of artistic legitimacy even as it rejects (in a symptomatic disavowal) the categories of authorial genius and intention. Literature responds, Benedetti suggests, by engaging in reflexive fictions of authorial constraint or estrangement, as when Calvino or Borges credit fictional authors with their own writing. See Carla Benedetti, *The Empty Cage: Inquiry into the Mysterious Disappearance of the Author*, trans. William J. Hartley (Ithaca: Cornell University Press, 2005).

39. Tim Parks, *The Novel: A Survival Guide* (Oxford: Oxford University Press, 2015), 34–35.

40. Michel Houellebecq, *Submission*, trans. Lorin Stein (New York: Farrar, Straus and Giroux, 2015), 5.

41. Rita Felski, *The Limits of Critique* (Chicago: University of Chicago Press, 2015), 179–80.

42. Blakey Vermeule, *Why Do We Care About Literary Characters?* (Baltimore: Johns Hopkins University Press, 2010), x.

43. Ibid., 17.

44. This is the title of a newspaper article and a romance novel; see Emily Jupp, "What Would Jane Austen Do?" *Independent*, January 28, 2012, http://www.independent.co.uk/arts-entertainment/books/features/what-would-jane-austen-do-7815084.html; and Laurie Brown, *What Would Jane Austen Do?* (Naperville: Sourcebooks Casablanca, 2009). The intense personal attachments Austen elicits—and has since the nineteenth-century—have earned her most devoted readers their own label: Janeites. On Janeitism and the suspicion with which academic readers have tended to approach it, see Deidre Lynch, "The Cult of Jane," in *Jane Austen in Context*, ed. Janet Todd (Cambridge: Cambridge University Press, 2005), 111–20.

BIBLIOGRAPHY

PRIMARY WORKS

Arber, Edward, ed. *Transcript of the Registers of the Company of Stationers of London 1554–1640*. 5 vols. London, 1875.

Ascham, Roger. *The Scholemaster or plaine and perfite way of teachyng children*. London, 1570.

Barnes, Barnabe. *Parthenophil and Parthenophe Sonnettes, madrigals, elegies and odes*. London, 1593.

Barnfield, Richard. *The Affectionate Shepheard*. London, 1594.

———. *Cynthia, With certaine sonnets, and the legend of Cassandra*. London, 1595.

———. *Greenes funeralls*. London, 1594.

Burton, Robert. *The Anatomy of Melancholy, What It Is. With All the Kindes, Causes, Symptomes, Prognostickes, and Severall Cures of It*. Oxford, 1621.

———. *The Anatomy of Melancholy, What It Is. With All the Kindes, Causes, Symptomes, Prognostickes, and Severall Cures of It*. Oxford, 1624.

———. *The Anatomy of Melancholy What it is, With All the Kinds, Causes, Symptomes, Prognostickes, & Seuerall Cures of It*. Oxford, 1628.

Chaucer, Geoffrey. *The Canterbury Tales*. In *The Riverside Chaucer*. Edited by Larry D. Benson. 3rd ed, 3–328. Boston: Houghton Mifflin, 1987.

Chettle, Henry. *Kind-Harts Dreame. Conteining fiue Apparitions, with their Inuectives against abuses raigning*. London, 1593.

Cornwallis, William. *Essayes*. London, 1600.

Davison, Francis. *A Poeticall Rhapsody*. London, 1602.

Day, Angel. *Vpon the life and death of the most worthy, and thrise renowmed knight, Sir Phillip Sidney*. London, [1586–87?].

Dekker, Thomas. *A knights coniuring Done in earnest: discouered in iest*. London, 1607.

———. *Nevves from Graues-Ende: Sent to Nobody*. London, 1604.

———. *Newes from hell brought by the Diuells carrier*. London, 1606.

———. *The Wonderfull Yeare*. London, 1603.

Deloney, Thomas. *The Gentle Craft*. London, 1637.

Democritus Junior [pseud.]. *Mercvrius Diabolicus, Or Hells Intelligencer*. London, 1647.

———. *Wit's Progresse Wherein are launc't the various crimes, Are incident to these sad times*. London, 1647.

Democritus natu minimus [pseud.]. *England Know thy Drivers, and their Driver: or, Democritus Natu Minimus*. London, 1647.

Democritus secundus [pseud.]. *Comes Facundus in Via. The Fellow-Traveller*. London, 1658.

Dickenson, John. *Arisbas, Euphues amidst his slumbers: Or Cupids Iourney to Hell*. London, 1594.

———. *Greene in conceipt New raised from his graue to write the tragique historie of faire Valeria of London*. London, 1598.

———. *The Shepheardes Complaint. A passionate Eclogue, written in English Hexameters* London, [1592–93?].

Downame, George. *Lectures on the XV. Psalme read in the cathedrall church of S. Paule, in London. Wherein besides many other very profitable and necessarie matters, the question of vsurie is plainely and fully decided*. London, 1604.

Drayton, Michael. *Idea the shepheards garland*. London, 1593.

———. *Poly-Olbion*. London, 1612.

E. C. *Emaricdulfe*. London, 1595.

Edwards, Thomas. *Cephalvs and Procris. Narcissvs*. London, 1595.

Elegies for Sir Philip Sidney. Edited by A. J. Colaianne and W. L. Godshalk. Delmar: Scholars' Facsimiles and Reprints, 1980.

Englands Helicon. Edited by Hugh Macdonald. Cambridge, Mass.: Harvard University Press, 1962.

England's Helicon 1600, 1614. Edited by Hyder Edward Rollins. 2 vols. Cambridge, Mass.: Harvard University Press, 1935.

Englands Helicon Casta placent superis, pura cum veste venite, et manibus puris sumite fontis aquam. London, 1600.

Exequiæ Illustrissimi Equitis, D. Philippi Sidnaei, Grattisimae Memoriae ac Nomini Ipensæ. Oxford, 1587.

Fenton, Geoffrey. *Certaine Tragicall Discourses written out of Frenche and Latin*. London, 1567.

Filmer, Robert. *Quaestio quodlibetica, or, A discourse whether it may bee lawfull to take use for money*. London, 1653.

The First and best Part of Scoggins Iests Full of witty mirth and pleasant shifts. London, 1626.

Fletcher, Phineas. *Piscatorie Eclogs and other Poeticall Miscellanies*. Cambridge, 1633.

Fraunce, Abraham. *The Arcadian rhetorike: or The praecepts of rhetorike*. London, 1588.

Gascoigne, George. *A Hundreth Sundrie Flowres*. Edited by G. W. Pigman III. Oxford: Clarendon Press, 2000.

Greene, Robert. *Arbasto, The Anatomie of Fortune*. London, 1584.

———. *Euphues his censure to Philautus wherein is presented a philosophicall combat betweene Hector and Achylles* [. . .]. London, 1587.

———. *Francescos Fortunes: Or, The second part of Greenes Never too late*. London, 1590.

———. *Greene's Groatsworth of Wit: Bought with a Million of Repentance (1592)*. Edited by D. Allen Carroll. Binghamton: Medieval and Renaissance Texts and Studies, 1994.

———. *Greenes Groats-worth of witte, bought with a million of Repentance*. London, 1592.

———. *Greenes Never too late. Or, A Powder of Experience: Sent to all youthfull Gentlemen* [. . .]. London, 1590.

———. *Greenes Vision: Written at the instant of his death*. London, 1592.

———. *Menaphon Camillas alarum to slumbering Euphues*. London, 1589.

———. *Perimedes the Blacke-Smith, A golden methode, how to vse the minde in pleasant and profitable exercise*. London, 1588.

———. *A Quip for an Vpstart Courtier: Or, A quaint dispute betvveen Veluet breeches and Cloth-breeches. Wherein is plainely set downe the disorders in all Estates and Trades*. London, 1592.

———. *The Repentance of Robert Greene Maister of Arts*. London, 1592.

Greg, W. W., and E. Boswell. *Records of the Court of the Stationers' Company 1576 to 1602: From Register B.* London: Bibliographical Society, 1930.

Hall, Joseph. *Virgidemiarum.* London, 1597.

Harvey, Gabriel. *Foure Letters, and certaine Sonnets: Especially touching Robert Greene, and other parties, by him abused.* London, 1592.

———. *Pierces Supererogation or A New Prayse of the Old Asse. A Preparative to certaine Larger Discourses, intituled Nashes S. Fame.* London, 1593.

———. "To the learned Shepheard" ("Commendatory Verses" 3). In Spenser, *Faerie Queene,* 722.

Harvey, Gabriel and Edmund Spenser. *Two Other very commendable Letters, of the same mens writing.* London, 1580.

Harvey, Richard. *A Theologicall Discourse of the Lamb of God and His Enemies.* London, 1590.

Houellebecq, Michel. *Submission.* Translated by Lorin Stein. New York: Farrar, Straus and Giroux, 2015.

Howell, Thomas. *H. His Deuises, for his owne exercise, and his Friends pleasure.* London, 1581.

Jonson, Ben. *The workes of Benjamin Jonson. The second Volume.* London, 1641.

Kemp, William. *Kemps nine daies wonder. Performed in a daunce from London to Norwich.* London, 1600.

Lodge, Thomas. *Euphues shadow, the battaile of the sences Wherein youthfull folly is set downe in his right figure, and vaine fancies are prooued to produce many offences.* London, 1592.

———. *Rosalynde. Euphues golden legacie: found after his death in his cell at Silexedra.* London, 1590.

———. *Phillis honoured vvith pastorall sonnets, elegies, and amorous delights.* London, 1593.

Lydgate, John. *The Siege of Thebes.* Edited by Robert R. Edwards. Kalamazoo: Medieval Institute Publications, 2001.

Lyly, John. *"Euphues: The Anatomy of Wit" and "Euphues and His England".* Edited by Leah Scragg. Manchester: Manchester University Press, 2003.

———. *Euphues. The Anatomy of Wyt. Very pleasant for all Gentlemen to reade, and most necessary to remember.* London, 1578.

Marot, Clément. *Eglogue sur le trepas de ma dame Louise de Savoye.* In *Les oeuvres de Clément Marot, de Cahors,* sigs. F_5^v–G_1^v. Lyon, 1538.

Marston, John. *The Scourge of Villanie: Three bookes of satyres.* London, 1598.

Merie tales Newly Imprinted & made by Master Skelton Poet Laureat. London, 1567.

Middleton, Thomas. *The blacke booke.* London, 1604.

Munday, Anthony. *The famous and renovvned historie of Primaleon of Greece, sonne to the great and mighty Prince Palmerin d'Oliua, Emperour of Constantinople.* London, 1619.

———. *Zelavto. The Fovntaine of Fame. Erected in an Orchard of Amorous Aduentures.* London, 1580.

Nashe, Thomas. *The Anatomie of Absurditie.* 1589. In *Works,* 1:1–49.

———. *Have with you to Saffron-walden. Or, Gabriell Harueys Hunt is vp.* 1596. In *Works,* 3:1–139.

———. *Pierce Penilesse his Supplication to the Diuell.* 1592. In *Works,* 1:137–245.

———. *Strange Newes, of the Intercepting Certaine Letters.* 1592–93. In *Works,* 1:247–335.

———. *The Works of Thomas Nashe.* Edited by R. B. McKerrow. 5 vols. 1904–10. Reprint, Oxford: Basil Blackwell, 1958.

Niccols, Richard. *Expicedium. A funeral oration, vpon the death of the late deceased Princesse of famous memorye, Elizabeth by the grace of God, Queen of England, France and Ireland.* London, 1603.

O Read me for I am of great Antiquitie. London, [1588?].

Ovid, *Heroides; Amores* Translated by Grant Showerman, revised by G. P. Goold. Cambridge: Harvard University Press, 1977.

Painter, William. The *Palace of Pleasure Beautified, adorned and well furnished, with Pleasaunt Historyes and excellent Nouelles, selected out of diuers good and commendable Authors* London, 1566.

The Paradyse of Daynty Deuises aptly furnished, with sundry pithie and learned inuentions. London, 1576.

Peele, George. *The Araygnement of Paris a pastorall*. London, 1584.

———. *The Arraignment of Paris*. Edited by Oliphant Smeaton. London: J. M. Dent and Co., 1905.

The Phoenix Nest. Built vp with the most rare and refined workes of Noble men, worthy Knights, gallant Gentlemen, Masters of Arts, and braue Schollers. London, 1593.

Pierce the Ploughmans Crede. London, 1553.

Puttenham, George. *The Arte of English Poesie*. London, 1589.

The returne of the knight of the poste from Hell, with the diuels aunswere to the supplication of Pierce Penilesse, with some relation of the last treasons. London, 1606.

R[iche], B[arnabe]. *Greenes newes both from heauen and hell*. London: 1593.

R[iche], B[arnabe], and R[ichard] B[arnfield]. *Greenes Newes both from Heaven and Hell (1593) and Greenes Funeralls (1594)*. Edited by R. B. McKerrow. London: Sidgwick and Jackson, 1911.

Rowlands, Samuel. *Greenes Ghost Haunting Conie-Catchers*. London, 1602.

———. *Tis Merrie when Gossips meete*. London, 1602.

Roydon, Matthew. "An Elegie, or friends passion, for his Astrophill. *Written vpon the death of the right Honorable sir Philip Sidney knight, Lord gouernor of Flushing*." In *The Phoenix Nest* [. . .], sigs. B_1^r–B_4^v. London, 1593.

Sidney, Philip. *Astrophil and Stella*. In *Poems*, 163–237.

———. *The Countess of Pembroke's Arcadia (The Old Arcadia)*. Edited by Jean Robertson. Oxford: Clarendon Press, 1973.

———. *The Covntesse of Pembrokes Arcadia*. London, 1590.

———. *The Covntesse of Pembrokes Arcadia*. London, 1593.

———. *The Covntesse of Pembrokes Arcadia*. London, 1598.

———. *The Defence of Poesie*. London, 1595.

———. *The Major Works, including "Astrophil and Stella"*. Edited by Katherine Duncan-Jones. Oxford: Oxford University Press, 2002.

———. *The Poems of Sir Philip Sidney*. Edited by William A. Ringler Jr. Oxford: Clarendon Press, 1962.

———. *Syr P.S. His Astrophel and Stella Wherein the excellence of sweete poesie is concluded*. London, 1591.

Skelton, John. *Here after foloweth a lytell boke called Collyn Clout*. London, c. 1531.

———. *John Skelton: The Complete English Poems*. Edited by John Scattergood. New Haven: Yale University Press, 1983.

Smith, William. *Chloris, or The complaint of the passionate despised shepheard*. London, 1596.

Songes and Sonettes, written by the right honorable Lorde Henry Haward late Earle of Surrey, and other. London, 1557.

Spenser, Edmund. *Amoretti and Epithalamion*. In *Yale Edition of Shorter Poems*, 585–679.

———. *Colin Clouts come home againe.* London: T. C. for William Ponsonby, 1595.
———. *Colin Clouts Come Home Againe.* In *Yale Edition of Shorter Poems*, 517–81.
———. *The Faerie Queene.* Edited by A. C. Hamilton. 2nd ed. New York: Longman, 2007.
———. *The Shepheardes Calender.* 1579. In *Yale Edition of Shorter Poems*, 1–213.
———. *The Yale Edition of the Shorter Poems of Edmund Spenser.* Edited by William A. Oram, Einar Bjorvand, Ronald Bond, Thomas H. Cain, Alexander Dunlop, and Richard Schell. New Haven: Yale University Press, 1989.
Tarltons Iests. London, 1613.
Tarltons newes out of purgatorie Onely such a iest as his iigge, fit for gentlemen to laugh at an houre, &c. Published by an old companion of his, Robin Goodfellow. London, 1590.
The treatyse answerynge the boke of berdes. London, [1641?].
Warner, William. *Pan his Syrinx, or Pipe, Compact of Seven Reedes.* London, 1584.
———. *Syrinx, or A seauenfold historie handled with varietie of pleasant and profitable both commicall and tragicall argument.* London, 1597.
Webbe, William. *A Discourse of English Poetrie.* London, 1586.
Weever, John. *Epigrammes in the oldest cut, and newest fashion.* London, 1599.
Whetstone, George. *Sir Phillip Sidney, his honorable life, his valiant death, and true vertues.* London, 1587.

SECONDARY WORKS

Adams, V. Joshua, Joel Callahan, and Michael Hansen, eds. "Historical Poetics." Special issue, *Modern Language Quarterly* 77, no. 1 (2016).
Alexander, Gavin. *Writing After Sidney: The Literary Response to Sir Philip Sidney, 1586–1640.* Oxford: Oxford University Press, 2006.
Alpers, Paul. "Pastoral and the Domain of Lyric in Spenser's *Shepheardes Calender.*" *Representations* 12 (1985): 83–100.
———. *What Is Pastoral?* Chicago: University of Chicago Press, 1996.
Anderson, Benedict. *Imagined Communities: Reflections on the Origin and Spread of Nationalism.* London: Verso, 1983.
Austin, Warren B. "Technique of the Chettle-Greene Forgery: Supplementary Material on the Authorship of the *Groatsworth of Wit.*" *Shakespeare Newsletter* 20 (1970): 43.
Badcoe, Tamsin Theresa. "'As many Ciphers without an I': Self-Reflexive Violence in the Work of Thomas Nashe." *Modern Philology* 111, no. 3 (2014): 384–407.
Baker, David J. *On Demand: Writing for the Market in Early Modern England.* Stanford: Stanford University Press, 2010.
Baker-Smith, Dominic. "'Great Expectation': Sidney's Death and the Poets." In *Sir Philip Sidney: 1586 and the Creation of a Legend*, edited by Jan van Dorsten, Dominic Baker-Smith, and Arthur Kinney, 83–103. Leiden: Brill, 1986.
Bakhtin, Mikhail. "The Problem of Speech Genres." In *Speech Genres and Other Late Essays*, translated by Vern W. McGee and edited by Caryl Emerson and Michael Holquist, 60–102. Austin: University of Texas Press, 1986.
Barbour, Reid. *Deciphering Elizabethan Fiction.* Newark: University of Delaware Press, 1993.
Barish, Jonas. "The Prose Style of John Lyly." *ELH* 23, no. 1 (1956): 14–35.

Barker, W. W. "Rhetorical Romance: The 'Frivolous Toyes' of Robert Greene." In *Unfolded Tales: Essays on Renaissance Romance*, edited by George M. Logan and Gordon Teskey. Ithaca: Cornell University Press, 1989.

Barker, William. "Fraunce [France], Abraham." In *Oxford Dictionary of National Biography*. Oxford: Oxford University Press, 2004; online ed. Accessed July 2011. https://doi.org/10.1093/ref:odnb/10133.

Barnard, John, and D. F. McKenzie, eds. *The Cambridge History of the Book in Britain, 1557–1695*. With the assistance of Maureen Bell. Vol. 4 of *The Cambridge History of the Book in Britain*. Cambridge: Cambridge University Press, 2002.

Benedetti, Carla. *The Empty Cage: Inquiry into the Mysterious Disappearance of the Author*. Translated by William J. Hartley. Ithaca: Cornell University Press, 2005.

Berger, Harry, Jr. "A Secret Discipline: *The Faerie Queene*, Book VI." In *Revisionary Play: Studies in the Spenserian Dynamics*. Berkeley: University of California Press, 1988.

———. "The Renaissance Imagination: Second World and Green World." In *Second World and Green World: Studies in Renaissance Fiction-Making*, 3–40. Berkeley: University of California Press, 1988.

Berry, Edward. *The Making of Sir Philip Sidney*. Toronto: University of Toronto Press, 1998.

Black, Joseph. "The Marprelate Controversy." In *The Oxford Handbook of English Prose, 1500–1640*, edited by Andrew Hadfield, 544–59. Oxford: Oxford University Press, 2013.

———, ed. *The Martin Marprelate Tracts: A Modernized and Annotated Edition*. Cambridge: Cambridge University Press, 2008.

Blayney, Peter. "The Publication of Playbooks." In *A New History of Early English Drama*, edited by John D. Cox and David Scott Kastan. New York: Columbia University Press, 1997.

Bond, Garth. "'Rare poemes aske rare friends': Ben Jonson, Coterie Poet." *Modern Philology* 107, no. 3 (2010): 380–99.

Booth, Wayne. *The Rhetoric of Fiction*. Chicago: University of Chicago Press, 1961.

Bourdieu, Pierre. *Distinction: A Social Critique of the Judgment of Taste*. Translated by Richard Nice. Cambridge, Mass.: Harvard University Press, 1984.

———. *The Field of Cultural Production: Essays on Art and Literature*. Edited by Randal Johnson. New York: Columbia University Press, 1993.

———. "The Field of Cultural Production, or: The Economic World Reversed." Translated by Richard Nice. In *The Field of Cultural Production*, 29–73.

———. "The Market of Symbolic Goods." Translated by R. Swyer. In *The Field of Cultural Production*, 112–41.

———. *The Rules of Art: Genesis and Structure of the Literary Field*. Translated by Susan Emanuel. Stanford: Stanford University Press, 1996.

Boyce, Benjamin. "News from Hell: Satiritic Communications with the Nether World in English Writing of the Seventeenth and Eighteenth Centuries." *PMLA* 58, no. 2 (1943): 402–37.

Brewer, David. *The Afterlife of Character, 1726–1815*. Philadelphia: University of Pennsylvania Press, 2005.

Brown, Georgia. *Redefining Elizabethan Literature*. Cambridge: Cambridge University Press, 2004.

Bruster, Douglas. *Shakespeare and the Question of Culture: Early Modern Literature and the Cultural Turn*. Basingstoke: Palgrave Macmillan, 2003.

Burt, Stephanie. "What Is This Thing Called Lyric?" *Modern Philology* 113, no. 3 (2016): 422–40.
Bush, Douglas. *English Literature in the Earlier Seventeenth Century: 1600–1660*. New York: Oxford University Press, 1945.
Capp, Bernard. "Harvey, Richard (bap. 1560, d. 1630)." In *Oxford Dictionary of National Biography*. Oxford: Oxford University Press, 2004; online ed. Accessed February 16, 2015. http://www.oxforddnb.com/view/article/12527.
Chartier, Roger. *The Order of Books: Readers, Authors, and Libraries in Europe Between the Fourteenth and Eighteenth Centuries*. Translated by Lydia G. Cochrane. Stanford: Stanford University Press, 1994.
Chaudhuri, Sukanta. "The Eclogues in Sidney's *New Arcadia*." *Review of English Studies*, n.s., 35, no. 138 (1984): 185–202.
Cheney, Donald. "Colin Clout's Homecoming: The Imaginative Travels of Edmund Spenser." *Connotations* 7, no. 2 (1997/98): 146–58.
Cheney, Patrick. *Spenser's Famous Flight: A Renaissance Idea of a Literary Career*. Toronto: University of Toronto Press, 1993.
———. "Spenser's Pastorals: *The Shepheardes Calender* and *Colin Clouts Come Home Againe*." In *The Cambridge Companion to Spenser*, edited by Andrew Hadfield. Cambridge: Cambridge University Press, 2001.
Cohen, Stephen, ed. *Shakespeare and Historical Formalism*. Aldershot: Ashgate, 2007.
Crawford, Julie. "Sidney's Sapphics and the Role of Interpretive Communities." *ELH* 69, no. 4 (2002): 979–1007.
Crewe, Jonathan. *Hidden Designs: The Critical Profession and Renaissance Literature*. London: Methuen, 1986.
———. *Unredeemed Rhetoric: Thomas Nashe and the Scandal of Authorship*. Baltimore: Johns Hopkins University Press, 1982.
Crupi, Charles. *Robert Greene*. Boston: Twayne Publishers, 1986.
Cullen, Patrick. *Spenser, Marvell, and Renaissance Pastoral*. Cambridge, Mass.: Harvard University Press, 1970.
Culler, Jonathan. *Theory of the Lyric*. Cambridge, Mass.: Harvard University Press, 2015.
Cummings, R. W., ed. *Edmund Spenser: The Critical Heritage*. London: Routledge, 1996.
Dane, Joseph. *The Myth of Print Culture: Essays on Evidence, Textuality, and Bibliographical Method*. Toronto: University of Toronto Press, 2003.
Daniel, Drew. *The Melancholy Assemblage: Affect and Epistemology in the English Renaissance*. New York: Fordham University Press, 2013.
Das, Nandini. *Renaissance Romance: The Transformation of English Prose Fiction, 1570–1620*. Burlington: Ashgate, 2011.
Davis, Joel B. *"The Countesse of Pembrokes Arcadia" and the Invention of English Literature*. New York: Palgrave Macmillan, 2011.
———. "Multiple *Arcadias* and the Literary Quarrel Between Fulke Greville and the Countess of Pembroke." *Studies in Philology* 101, no. 4 (2004): 401–30.
Davis, Walter R. *Idea and Act in Elizabethan Fiction*. Princeton: Princeton University Press, 1969.
de Man, Paul. "Anthropomorphism and Trope in Lyric." In *The Rhetoric of Romanticism*, 239–62.
———. "Autobiography as De-Facement." In *The Rhetoric of Romanticism*, 67–82.
———. "Lyrical Voice in Contemporary Theory: Riffaterre and Jauss." In *Lyric Poetry: Beyond New Criticism*, edited by Chaviva Hosek and Patricia Parker, 55–72. Ithaca: Cornell University Press, 1985.

———. *The Rhetoric of Romanticism*. New York: Columbia University Press, 1984.

Dean, William. "Henry Oxinden's Key (1628) to *The Countess of Pembroke's Arcadia*: Some Facts and Conjectures." *Sidney Newsletter and Journal* 12, no. 2 (1993): 14–21.

Deutermann, Allison, and András Kiséry, eds. *Formal Matters: Reading the Materials of English Renaissance Literature*. Manchester: Manchester University Press, 2013.

Dionne, Craig, and Steve Mentz, eds. *Rogues and Early Modern English Culture*. Ann Arbor: University of Michigan Press, 2004.

Dobranski, Stephen B. *Readers and Authorship in Early Modern England*. Cambridge: Cambridge University Press, 2005.

Dolven, Jeff. *Scenes of Instruction in Renaissance Romance*. Chicago: University of Chicago Press, 2007.

Donaldson, E. Talbot. *Speaking of Chaucer*. New York: W. W. Norton, 1970.

Dubrow, Heather. *The Challenges of Orpheus: Lyric Poetry and Early Modern England*. Baltimore: Johns Hopkins University Press, 2008.

Duncan-Jones, Katherine. "The Life, Death and Afterlife of Richard Tarlton." *Review of English Studies* 65, no. 268 (2014): 18–32.

———. *Sir Philip Sidney: Courtier Poet*. New Haven: Yale University Press, 1991.

Durling, Robert. *The Figure of the Poet in Renaissance Epic*. Cambridge, Mass.: Harvard University Press, 1965.

Eckhardt, Joshua. *Manuscript Verse Collectors and the Politics of Anti-Courtly Love Poetry*. Oxford: Oxford University Press, 2009.

Edwards, Anthony S. G., ed. *John Skelton: The Critical Heritage*. New York: Routledge, 1981.

Ellinghausen, Laurie. *Labor and Writing in Early Modern England, 1567–1667*. Aldershot: Ashgate, 2008.

Elliot, Robert. *The Literary Persona*. Chicago: University of Chicago Press, 1982.

Enterline, Lynn. *Shakespeare's Schoolroom: Rhetoric, Discipline, Emotion*. Philadelphia: University of Pennsylvania Press, 2011.

Erne, Lukas and Tamsin Badcoe. "Shakespeare and the Popularity of Poetry Books in Print, 1583–1622." *Review of English Studies* New Series 65 (2013): 33–57.

Escobedo, Andrew. *Volition's Face: Personification and the Will in Renaissance Literature*. Notre Dame: University of Notre Dame Press, 2017.

Ezell, Margaret. *Social Authorship and the Advent of Print*. Baltimore: Johns Hopkins University Press, 1999.

Falco, Raphael. *Conceived Presences: Literary Genealogy in Renaissance England*. Amherst: University of Massachusetts Press, 1994.

Farmer, Alan B., and Zachary Lesser. "What Is Print Popularity? A Map of the Elizabethan Book Trade." In *The Elizabethan Top Ten: Defining Print Popularity in Early Modern England*, edited by Andy Kesson and Emma Smith, 19–54. Burlington: Ashgate, 2013.

Felski, Rita. *The Limits of Critique*. Chicago: University of Chicago Press, 2015.

Foucault, Michel. "What Is an Author?" In *Textual Strategies: Perspectives in Post-Structuralist Criticism*, edited by Josué V. Harari, 141–60. Ithaca: Cornell University Press, 1979.

Fowler, Elizabeth. *Literary Character: The Human Figure in Early English Writing*. Ithaca: Cornell University Press, 2003.

Fumerton, Patricia. "'Secret' Arts: Elizabethan Miniatures and Sonnets." *Representations* 15 (1986): 57–95.

Gallagher, Catherine. "The Rise of Fictionality." In *History, Geography, and Culture*. Vol. 1 of *The Novel*, edited by Franco Moretti, 336–63. Princeton: Princeton University Press, 2006.

Garrett, Martin, ed. *Sidney: The Critical Heritage*. London: Routledge, 1996.

Geil, Melissa Hull. "Reproducing Paper Monsters in Thomas Nashe." In *The Age of Thomas Nashe: Text, Bodies and Trespasses in Early Modern England*, edited by Stephen Guy-Bray, Joan Pong Linton, and Steve Mentz, 77–98. Farnham: Ashgate, 2013.

Genette, Gérard. *Paratexts: Thresholds of Interpretation*. Translated by Jane E. Lewin. Cambridge: Cambridge University Press, 1997.

Gieskes, Edward. *Representing the Professions: Administration, Law, and Theater in Early Modern England*. Newark: University of Delaware Press, 2006.

Gillespie, Alexandra. *Print Culture and the Medieval Author: Chaucer, Lydgate, and Their Books 1473–1557*. Oxford: Oxford University Press, 2006.

Gitelman, Lisa. *Always Already New: Media, History, and the Data of Culture*. Cambridge, Mass.: MIT Press, 2006.

Greenblatt, Stephen. *Hamlet in Purgatory*. Princeton: Princeton University Press, 2001.

Greene, Roland. "Calling Colin Clout." *Spenser Studies* 10 (1992): 229–44.

Greenlaw, Edwin. "Sidney's *Arcadia* as an Example of Elizabethan Allegory." In *Anniversary Papers by Colleagues and Pupils of George Lyman Kittredge*, 327–37. Boston and London: Ginn and Company, 1913.

Griffiths, Jane. *Diverting Authorities: Experimental Glossing Practices in Manuscript and Print*. Oxford: Oxford University Press, 2014.

———. *John Skelton and Poetic Authority: Defining the Liberty to Speak*. Oxford: Clarendon Press, 2006.

Gust, Geoffrey W. *Constructing Chaucer: Author and Autofiction in the Critical Tradition*. Basingstoke: Palgrave Macmillan, 2009.

Habermas, Jürgen. *The Structural Transformation of the Public Sphere: An Inquiry into a Category of Bourgeois Society*. Translated by Thomas Burger. Cambridge: Polity Press, 1989.

Hackett, Helen. *Women and Romance Fiction in the English Renaissance*. Cambridge: Cambridge University Press, 2000.

Hadfield, Andrew. *Edmund Spenser: A Life*. Oxford: Oxford University Press, 2012.

———. *Literature, Politics, and National Identity: Reformation to Renaissance*. Cambridge: Cambridge University Press, 1994.

———. "'Not Without Mustard': Self-Publicity and Polemic in Early Modern Literary London." In *Renaissance Transformations: The Making of English Writing 1500–1650*, edited by Margaret Healy and Thomas Healy, 64–78. Edinburgh: Edinburgh University Press, 2009.

Hager, Alan. *Dazzling Images: The Masks of Sir Philip Sidney*. Newark: University of Delaware Press, 1991.

Halasz, Alexandra. *The Marketplace of Print: Pamphlets and the Public Sphere in Early Modern England*. Cambridge: Cambridge University Press, 1997.

———. "'So beloved that men use his picture for their signs': Richard Tarlton and the Uses of Sixteenth-Century Celebrity." *Shakespeare Studies* 23 (1995): 19–38.

Halpern, Richard. *The Poetics of Primitive Accumulation: English Renaissance Culture and the Genealogy of Capital*. Ithaca: Cornell University Press, 1991.

Hannay, Margaret P. *Philip's Phoenix: Mary Sidney, Countess of Pembroke*. Oxford: Oxford University Press, 1990.

Heale, Elizabeth. *Autobiography and Authorship in Renaissance Verse: Chronicles of the Self.* Basingstoke: Palgrave Macmillan, 2003.

Heffernan, Megan. "Gathered by Invention: Additive Forms and Inference in Gascoigne's Poesy." *Modern Language Quarterly* 76, no. 4 (2015): 413–45.

Helfer, Rebecca. *Spenser's Ruins and the Art of Recollection.* Toronto: University of Toronto Press, 2012.

Helgerson, Richard. *The Elizabethan Prodigals.* Berkeley: University of California Press, 1976.

———. *Self-Crowned Laureates: Spenser, Jonson, Milton, and the Literary System.* Berkeley: University of California Press, 1983.

Hibbard, G. R. *Thomas Nashe: A Critical Introduction.* Cambridge, Mass.: Harvard University Press, 1962.

Hile, Rachel E. *Spenserian Satire: A Tradition of Indirection.* Manchester: Manchester University Press, 2017.

Hilliard, Stephen. *The Singularity of Thomas Nashe.* Lincoln: University of Nebraska Press, 1986.

Hillyer, Richard. *Sir Philip Sidney, Cultural Icon.* New York: Palgrave Macmillan, 2010.

Hirschfeld, Heather Anne. *Joint Enterprises: Collaborative Drama and the Institutionalization of the English Renaissance Theater.* Amherst: University of Massachusetts Press, 2004.

Holtgen, Karl Josef. "Richard Latewar: Elizabethan Poet and Divine." *Anglia: Zeitschrift fur Englische Philologie* 89 (1971): 417–38.

Hutson, Lorna. *Thomas Nashe in Context.* Oxford: Oxford University Press, 1989.

Jackson, Virginia. *Dickinson's Misery: A Theory of Lyric Reading.* Princeton: Princeton University Press, 2005.

Jaffe, Aaron. *Modernism and the Culture of Celebrity.* Cambridge: Cambridge University Press, 2005.

Johns, Adrian. *The Nature of the Book: Print and Knowledge in the Making.* Chicago: University of Chicago Press, 1998.

Jones, Ann Rosalind, and Peter Stallybrass. "The Politics of *Astrophil and Stella.*" *Studies in English Literature, 1500–1900* 24, no. 1 (1984): 53–68.

Jones, Mike Rodman. *Radical Pastoral, 1381–1594: Appropriation and the Writing of Religious Controversy.* Burlington: Ashgate, 2011.

Jowett, John. "Henry Chettle: 'Your Old Compositor.'" *Text* 15 (2003): 141–61.

———. "Johannes Factotum: Henry Chettle and *Greene's Groatsworth of Wit.*" *Papers of the Bibliographical Society of America* 87, no. 4 (1993): 453–86.

Jupp, Emily. "What Would Jane Austen Do?" *Independent*, January 28, 2012. http://www.independent.co.uk/arts-entertainment/books/features/what-would-jane-austen-do-7815084.html.

Kastan, David Scott. *Shakespeare and the Book.* Cambridge: Cambridge University Press, 2001.

Kay, Dennis. *Melodious Tears: The English Funeral Elegy from Spenser to Milton.* Oxford: Clarendon Press, 1990.

Kelen, Sarah A. *Langland's Early Modern Identities.* Basingstoke: Palgrave Macmillan, 2007.

Kesson, Andy. *John Lyly and Early Modern Authorship.* Manchester: Manchester University Press, 2014.

Kettnich, Karen. "Nashe's Extemporal Vein and His Tarltonizing Wit." In *The Age of Thomas Nashe: Text, Bodies and Trespasses in Early Modern England*, edited by Stephen Guy-Bray, Joan Pong Linton, and Steve Mentz, 99–114. Farnham: Ashgate, 2013.

Kimmelman, Burt. *The Poetics of Authorship in the Later Middle Ages: The Emergence of the Modern Literary Persona*. New York: Peter Lang, 1996.

Kinney, Arthur. *Humanist Poetics: Thought, Rhetoric, and Fiction in Sixteenth-Century England*. Amherst: University of Massachusetts Press, 1986.

Kiséry, András, and Allison Deutermann. "The Matter of Form: Book History, Formalist Criticism, and Francis Bacon's Aphorisms." In *The Book in History, the Book as History: New Intersections of the Material Text; Essays in Honor of David Scott Kastan*, edited by Heidi Brayman Hackel, Jesse M. Lander, and Zachary Lesser, 29–63. New Haven: Beinecke Rare Book and Manuscript Library, Yale University, 2016.

Klein, Lisa. "Spenser's *Astrophel* and the Sidney Legend." *Sidney Newsletter and Journal* 12, no. 2 (1993): 42–55.

Knight, Jeffrey Todd. "Afterworlds: Thomas Middleton, the Book, and the Genre of Continuation." In *Formal Matters: Reading the Materials of English Renaissance Literature*, edited by Allison K. Deutermann and András Kiséry, 77–96. Manchester: Manchester University Press, 2013.

Kumaran, Arul. "Patronage, Print, and an Early Modern 'Pamphlet Moment.'" *Explorations in Renaissance Culture* 31, no. 1 (2005): 59–88.

———. "Satiric Mimicking in Henry Chettle's *Kind-Hartes Dreame*." *Studies in Philology* 109, no. 4 (2012): 429–54.

Lahire, Bernard. *The Plural Actor*. Translated by David Fernbach. Cambridge: Polity Press, 2011.

Lamb, Mary Ellen. *The Popular Culture of Shakespeare, Spenser and Jonson*. New York: Routledge, 2006.

Lander, Jesse. *Inventing Polemic: Religion, Print, and Literary Culture in Early Modern England*. Cambridge: Cambridge University Press, 2006.

Landreth, David. *The Face of Mammon: The Matter of Money in English Renaissance Literature*. Oxford: Oxford University Press, 2012.

Latour, Bruno. *Reassembling the Social: An Introduction to Actor-Network-Theory*. Oxford: Oxford University Press, 2005.

Lee, Christine S. "The Meanings of Romance: Rethinking Early Modern Fiction." *Modern Philology* 112, no. 2 (2014): 287–311.

Lerer, Seth. *Chaucer and His Readers: Imagining the Author in Late-Medieval England*. Princeton: Princeton University Press, 1993.

Lesser, Zachary. *Renaissance Drama and the Politics of Publication: Readings in the English Book Trade*. Cambridge: Cambridge University Press, 2004.

Lesser, Zachary, and Peter Stallybrass. "The First Literary *Hamlet* and the Commonplacing of Professional Plays." *Shakespeare Quarterly* 59, no. 4 (2008): 371–420.

Lewalski, Barbara K. "Lucy, Countess of Bedford: Images of a Jacobean Courtier and Patroness." In *Politics of Discourse: The Literature and History of Seventeenth-Century England*, edited by Kevin Sharp and Steven N. Zwicker, 52–77. Berkeley: University of California Press, 1987.

Loewenstein, Joseph. *The Author's Due: Printing and the Prehistory of Copyright*. Chicago: University of Chicago Press, 2002.

———. *Ben Jonson and Possessive Authorship*. Cambridge: Cambridge University Press, 2002.

Love, Harold. *The Culture and Commerce of Texts: Scribal Publication in Seventeenth-Century England*. Amherst: University of Massachusetts Press, 1998.

Lucey, Michael, and Tom McEnaney. "Introduction: Language-in-Use and Literary Fieldwork." *Representations* 137, no. 1 (2017): 1–22.

Lupton, Christina. *Knowing Books: The Consciousness of Mediation in Eighteenth-Century Britain.* Philadelphia: University of Pennsylvania Press, 2011.

Lupton, Julia Reinhard. "Home-Making in Ireland: Virgil's Eclogue I and Book VI of *The Faerie Queene.*" *Spenser Studies* 8 (1990): 119–41.

Lynch, Deidre. "The Cult of Jane." In *Jane Austen in Context*, edited by Janet Todd, 111–20. Cambridge: Cambridge University Press, 2005.

Mann, Jenny C. *Outlaw Rhetoric: Figuring Vernacular Eloquence in Shakespeare's England.* Ithaca: Cornell University Press, 2012.

Margolies, David. *Novel and Society in Elizabethan England.* London: Croom Helm, 1985.

Marotti, Arthur F. *John Donne: Coterie Poet.* Madison: University of Wisconsin Press, 1986.

———. "'Love Is Not Love': Elizabethan Sonnet Sequences and the Social Order." *ELH* 49, no. 2 (1982): 396–428.

———. *Manuscript, Print, and the English Renaissance Lyric.* Ithaca: Cornell University Press, 1995.

Maslen, Robert W. *Elizabethan Fictions: Espionage, Counter-espionage and the Duplicity of Fiction in Early Elizabethan Prose Narratives.* Oxford: Oxford University Press, 1997.

———. "Robert Greene and the Uses of Time." In *Writing Robert Greene: Essays on England's First Notorious Professional Writer*, edited by Kirk Melnikoff and Edward Gieskes, 157–88. Aldershot: Ashgate, 2008.

Maslov, Boris. *Pindar and the Emergence of Literature.* Cambridge: Cambridge University Press, 2015.

Masten, Jeffrey. *Textual Intercourse: Collaboration, Authorship, and Sexualities in Renaissance Drama.* Cambridge: Cambridge University Press, 1997.

Mattison, Andrew. *The Unimagined in the English Renaissance: Poetry and the Limits of Mimesis.* Madison: Fairleigh Dickinson University Press, 2013.

Matz, Robert. *Defending Literature in Early Modern England: Renaissance Literary Theory in Social Context.* Cambridge: Cambridge University Press, 2000.

Maynadier, Howard. "The Areopagus of Sidney and Spenser." *Modern Language Review* 4, no. 3 (1909): 289–301.

McCabe, Richard. "Rhyme and Reason: Poetics, Patronage, and Secrecy in Elizabethan and Jacobean Ireland." In *Literary Milieux: Essays in Text and Context, Presented to Howard Erskine-Hill*, edited by David Womersely and Richard McCabe, 30–51. Newark: University of Delaware, 2008.

———. *"Ungainefull Arte": Poetry Patronage, and Print in the Early Modern Era.* Oxford: Oxford University Press, 2016.

McCanles, Michael. "*The Shepheardes Calender* as Document and Monument." *Studies in English Literature, 1500–1900* 22, no. 1 (1982): 5–19.

McKeon, Michael. *The Secret History of Domesticity: Public, Private, and the Division of Knowledge.* Baltimore: Johns Hopkins University Press, 2005.

Melnikoff, Kirk, and Edward Gieskes, eds. *Writing Robert Greene: Essays on England's First Notorious Professional Writer.* Aldershot: Ashgate, 2008.

Mentz, Steve. "Forming Greene: Theorizing the Early Modern Author in the *Groatsworth of Wit.*" In *Writing Robert Greene: Essays on England's First Notorious Professional Writer*, edited by Kirk Melnikoff and Edward Gieskes, 115–31. Aldershot: Ashgate, 2008.

———. "Magic Books: Cony-Catching and the Romance of Early Modern London." In *Rogues and Early Modern English Culture*, edited by Craig Dionne and Steve Mentz, 240–58. Ann Arbor: University of Michigan Press, 2004.

———. *Romance for Sale in Early Modern England: The Rise of Prose Fiction*. Aldershot: Ashgate, 2006.

———. "Selling Sidney: William Ponsonby, Thomas Nashe, and the Boundaries of Elizabethan Print and Manuscript Cultures." *Text* 13 (2000): 151–74.

Miller, David L. "Abandoning the Quest." *ELH* 46, no. 2 (1979): 173–92.

———. "Authorship, Anonymity, and *The Shepheardes Calender*." *Modern Language Quarterly* 40, no. 3 (1979): 219–36.

Minnis, A. J. *Medieval Theory of Authorship: Scholastic Literary Attitudes in the Later Middle Ages*. London: Scolar Press, 1984.

Montrose, Louis. "Of Gentlemen and Shepherds: The Politics of Elizabethan Pastoral Form." *ELH* 50, no. 3 (1983): 415–59.

———. "The perfecte paterne of a Poete: The Poetics of Courtship in *The Shepheardes Calender*." *Texas Studies in Literature and Language* 21, no. 1 (1979): 34–67.

———. "Spenser's Domestic Domain: Poetry, Property, and the Early Modern Subject." In *Subject and Object in Renaissance Culture*, edited by Margreta de Grazia, Maureen Quilligan, and Peter Stallybrass, 83–130. Cambridge: Cambridge University Press, 1996.

Moretti, Franco. "The Slaughterhouse of Literature." *Modern Language Quarterly* 61, no. 1 (2000): 207–27.

Munro, Ian. "Shakespeare's Jestbook: Wit, Print, Performance." *ELH* 71, no. 1 (2004): 89–113.

Myers, Benjamin P. "The Green and Golden World: Spenser's Rewriting of the Munster Plantation." *ELH* 76, no. 2 (2009): 473–90.

Nebeker, Eric. "Broadside Ballads, Miscellanies, and the Lyric in Print." *ELH* 76, no. 4 (2009): 989–1013.

"The New Lyric Studies." *PMLA* 123, no. 1 (2008): 181–234.

Newcomb, Lori Humphrey. *Reading Popular Romance in Early Modern England*. New York: Columbia University Press, 2002.

Newstok, Scott L. *Quoting Death in Early Modern England: The Poetics of Epitaphs Beyond the Tomb*. Basingstoke: Palgrave Macmillan, 2009.

Nicholl, Charles. *A Cup of News: The Life of Thomas Nashe*. London: Routledge, 1984.

Nicholson, Catherine. *Uncommon Tongues: Eloquence and Eccentricity in the English Renaissance*. Philadelphia: University of Pennsylvania Press, 2013.

Norbrook, David. *Poetry and Politics in the English Renaissance*. London: Routledge, 1984.

North, Marcy L. *The Anonymous Renaissance: Cultures of Discretion in Tudor-Stuart England*. Chicago: University of Chicago Press, 2003.

———. "Early Modern Anonymity." *Oxford Handbooks Online*. November 2015, accessed June 25, 2017. http://www.oxfordhandbooks.com/view/10.1093/oxfordhb/9780199935338.001.0001/oxfordhb-9780199935338-e-12.

O'Callaghan, Michelle. "The Duties of Societies: Literature, Friendship, and Community." In *Renaissance Transformations: The Making of English Writing 1500–1650*, edited by Margaret Healy and Thomas Healy, 97–111. Edinburgh: Edinburgh University Press, 2009.

———. *The "Shepheards Nation": Jacobean Spenserians and Early Stuart Political Culture, 1612–1625*. Oxford: Clarendon Press, 2000.

Ong, Walter. *Orality and Literacy: The Technologizing of the Word*. London: Methuen, 1982.

———. *Ramus, Method and the Decay of Dialogue: From the Art of Discourse to the Art of Reason.* Cambridge, Mass.: Harvard University Press, 1958.
Oram, William. "Laureate Self-Fashioning." In *Edmund Spenser in Context*, edited by Andrew Escobedo, 14–22. Cambridge: Cambridge University Press, 2017.
Owens, Judith. *Enabling Engagements: Edmund Spenser and the Poetics of Patronage.* Montreal: McGill-Queens University Press, 2002.
Paige, Nicholas. *Before Fiction: The Ancien Régime of the Novel.* Philadelphia: University of Pennsylvania Press, 2011.
Parker, Patricia. *Inescapable Romance: Studies in the Poetics of a Mode.* Princeton: Princeton University Press, 1979.
Parks, Tim. *The Novel: A Survival Guide.* Oxford: Oxford University Press, 2015.
Pask, Kevin. *The Emergence of the English Author: Scripting the Life of the Poet in Early Modern England.* Cambridge: Cambridge University Press, 1996.
Passannante, Gerard. "The Art of Reading Earthquakes: On Harvey's Wit, Ramus's Method, and the Renaissance of Lucretius." *Renaissance Quarterly* 61, no. 3 (2008): 792–832.
Patterson, Annabel. *Censorship and Interpretation: The Conditions of Reading and Writing in Early Modern England.* Madison: University of Wisconsin Press, 1984.
———. *Pastoral and Ideology: Virgil to Valéry.* Berkeley: University of California Press, 1987.
Paxson, James J. *The Poetics of Personification.* Cambridge: Cambridge University Press, 1994.
Petrina, Allessandra. "Polyglottia and the Vindication of English Poetry: Abraham Fraunce's *Arcadian Rhetorike.*" *Neophilologus* 83, no. 2 (1999): 317–29.
Phelan, James. *Living to Tell About It: A Rhetoric and Ethics of Character Narration.* Ithaca: Cornell University Press, 2004.
Phillips, Joshua. *English Fictions of Communal Identity, 1485–1603.* Farnham: Ashgate, 2010.
Preiss, Richard. *Clowning and Authorship in Early Modern Theatre.* Cambridge: Cambridge University Press, 2014.
Prendergast, Maria Teresa Micaela. *Railing, Reviling, and Invective in English Literary Culture, 1588–1617: The Anti-Poetics of Theater and Print.* Farnham: Ashgate, 2012.
Prescott, Anne Lake. *French Poets and the English Renaissance: Studies in Fame and Transformation.* New Haven and London: Yale University Press, 1978.
Prewitt, Kendrick W. "Gabriel Harvey and the Practice of Method." *Studies in English Literature, 1500–1900* 39, no. 1 (1999): 19–39.
Prins, Yopie. *Victorian Sappho.* Princeton: Princeton University Press, 1999.
Prins, Yopie, and Virginia Jackson, eds. *The Lyric Theory Reader: A Critical Anthology.* Baltimore: Johns Hopkins University Press, 2014.
Quint, David. "Archimago and Amoret: The Poem and Its Doubles." In *Worldmaking Spenser: Explorations in the Early Modern Age*, ed. Patrick Cheney and Lauren Silberman, 32–42. Lexington: University of Kentucky Press, 2000.
Rambuss, Richard. *Spenser's Secret Career.* Cambridge: Cambridge University Press, 2007.
Rasmussen, Mark David, ed. *Renaissance Literature and Its Formal Engagements.* New York: Palgrave, 2002.
Relihan, Constance. *Fashioning Authority: The Development of Elizabethan Novelistic Discourse.* Kent: Kent State University Press, 1994.
Reynolds, Bryan, and Henry S. Turner. "From *Homo Academicus* to *Poeta Publicus*: Celebrity and Transversal Knowledge in Robert Greene's *Friar Bacon and Friar Bungay* (c. 1589)."

In *Writing Robert Greene: Essays on England's First Notorious Professional Writer*, edited by Kirk Melnikoff and Edward Gieskes, 39–51. Aldershot: Ashgate, 2008.

Rhodes, Neil. *Elizabethan Grotesque*. London: Routledge and Kegan Paul, 1980.

Richards, Jennifer. *Rhetoric and Courtliness in Early Modern Literature*. Cambridge: Cambridge University Press, 2003.

Rose, Mark. *Authors and Owners: The Invention of Copyright*. Cambridge, Mass.: Harvard University Press, 1995.

Ross, Trevor. *The Making of the English Literary Canon: From the Middle Ages to the Late Eighteenth Century*. Montreal: McGill-Queen's University Press, 1998.

Salzman, Paul. *English Prose Fiction 1558–1700: A Critical History*. Oxford: Clarendon Press, 1985.

Saunders, J. W. "The Stigma of Print: A Note on the Social Bases of Tudor Poetry." *Essays in Criticism* 1, no. 2 (1951): 139–64.

Schoenfeldt, Michael. "The Poetry of Conduct: Accommodation and Transgression in *The Faerie Queene*, Book 6." In *Enclosure Acts: Sexuality, Property, and Culture in Early Modern England*, edited by Richard Burt and John Michael Archer, 151–69. Ithaca: Cornell University Press, 1994.

Schwarz, Kathryn. *Tough Love: Amazon Encounters in the English Renaissance*. Durham: Duke University Press, 2000.

Scott-Warren, Jason. "Harvey, Gabriel (1552/3–1631)." In *Oxford Dictionary of National Biography*. Oxford University Press, 2004; online ed. Accessed September 3, 2014. http://www.oxforddnb.com/view/10.1093/ref:odnb/9780198614128.001.0001/odnb-9780198614128-e-12517.

———. *Sir John Harington and the Book as Gift*. Oxford: Oxford University Press, 2001.

Segall, Kreg. "Skeltonic Anxiety and Rumination in *The Shepheardes Calender*." *Studies in English Literature, 1500–1900* 47, no. 1 (2007): 29–56.

Sherman, William H. *Used Books: Marking Readers in Renaissance England*. Philadelphia: University of Pennsylvania Press, 2008.

Simonova, Natasha. *Early Modern Authorship and Prose Continuations: Adaptation and Ownership from Sidney to Richardson*. Basingstoke: Palgrave Macmillan, 2015.

Skura, Meredith. *Tudor Autobiography: Listening for Inwardness*. Chicago: University of Chicago Press, 2008.

Smyth, Adam. "'Such a general itching after book-learning': Popular Readers of 'the most eminent Wits.'" *Yearbook of English Studies* 33 (2003): 262–72.

Snyder, Susan. *Pastoral Process: Spenser, Marvell, Milton*. Stanford: Stanford University Press, 1995.

Stallybrass, Peter. Afterword to *Renaissance Paratexts*, edited by Helen Smith and Louise Wilson, 204–19. Cambridge: Cambridge University Press, 2013.

Stillman, Robert. *Philip Sidney and the Poetics of Renaissance Cosmopolitanism*. Aldershot: Ashgate, 2008.

———. "Spenserian Autonomy and the Trial of New Historicism: Book Six of *The Faerie Queene*." *English Literary Renaissance* 22, no. 3 (1992): 299–314.

Storojenko, Nicholas. *Robert Greene: His Life and Works*. Moscow, 1878. Translated by E. A. B. Hodgetts and reprinted in vol. 1 of *The Life and Complete Works in Prose and Verse of Robert Greene*, edited by A. B. Grosart. 15 vols. London: privately printed, 1881–86.

Stringer, Gary A. "The Composition and Dissemination of Donne's Writings." In *The Oxford Handbook of John Donne*, edited by Jeanne Shami, Dennis Flynn, and M. Thomas Hester, 12–25. Oxford: Oxford University Press, 2011.

Taylor, Charles. *Modern Social Imaginaries*. Durham: Duke University Press, 2004.

Tillman, James S. "The Satirist Satirized: Burton's Democritus Jr." *Studies in the Literary Imagination* 10, no. 2 (1977): 89–96.

Tilmouth, Christopher. "Burton's 'Turning Picture': Argument and Anxiety in *The Anatomy of Melancholy*." *Review of English Studies*, n.s., 56, no. 226 (2005): 524–49.

Todorov, Tzvetan. *The Fantastic: A Structural Approach to a Literary Genre*. Translated by Richard Howard, with an introduction by Richard Scholes. Ithaca: Cornell University Press, 1975.

Tromly, Frederic B. "Lodowick Bryskett's Elegies on Sidney in Spenser's *Astrophel* Volume." *Review of English Studies*, n.s., 37, no. 147 (1986): 384–88.

Vermeule, Blakey. *Why Do We Care About Literary Characters?* Baltimore: Johns Hopkins University Press, 2010.

Vickers, Brian. "Giving Greene His *Groatsworth*." *Papers of the Bibliographic Society of America* (forthcoming).

———. "'Upstart Crow'? The Myth of Shakespeare's Plagiarism." *Review of English Studies*, n.s., 68, no. 284 (2016): 244–67.

Vivier, Eric. "John Bridges, Martin Marprelate, and the Rhetoric of Satire." *English Literary Renaissance* 44, no. 1 (2014): 3–5.

Wall, Wendy. "Disclosures in Print: The 'Violent Enlargement' of the Renaissance Voyeuristic Text." *Studies in English Literature, 1500–1900* 29 (1989): 35–59.

———. *The Imprint of Gender: Authorship and Publication in the English Renaissance*. Ithaca: Cornell University Press, 1993.

Warner, J. Christopher. *The Making and Marketing of Tottel's Miscellany, 1557: Songs and Sonnets in the Summer of the Martyrs' Fires*. Farnham: Ashgate, 2013.

Warner, Michael. *Publics and Counterpublics*. New York: Zone Books, 2002.

Weimann, Robert. *Shakespeare and the Popular Tradition in the Theater: Studies in the Social Dimension of Dramatic Form and Function*. Edited and translated by Robert Schwartz. Baltimore: Johns Hopkins University Press, 1978.

Whigham, Frank. *Ambition and Privilege: The Social Tropes of Elizabethan Courtesy Theory*. Berkeley: University of California Press, 1984.

Wilkes, G. A. "'Left . . . to Play the Ill Poet in My Own Part': The Literary Relationship of Sidney and Fulke Greville." *Review of English Studies* 57, no. 230 (2006): 291–309.

Wilson, Bronwen, and Paul Yachnin, eds. *Making Publics in Early Modern Europe: People, Things, Forms of Knowledge*. New York: Routledge, 2010.

Wilson, Katharine. *Fictions of Authorship in Late Elizabethan Narratives: Euphues in Arcadia*. Oxford: Clarendon Press, 2006.

Wilson, Luke. *Theaters of Intention: Drama and the Law in Early Modern England*. Stanford: Stanford University Press, 2000.

Woodbridge, Linda. *Vagrancy, Homelessness, and English Renaissance Literature*. Champaign: University of Illinois Press, 2001.

Worden, Blair. *The Sound of Virtue: Philip Sidney's "Arcadia" and Elizabethan Politics*. New Haven: Yale University Press, 1997.

Woudhuysen, H. R. "Sidney, Sir Philip (1554–1586)." In *Oxford Dictionary of National Biography*. Oxford: University Press, 2004; online ed. Accessed September 2014. https://doi.org/10.1093/ref:odnb/25522.

———. *Sir Philip Sidney and the Circulation of Manuscripts, 1558–1640*. Oxford: Clarendon Press, 1996.

Yachnin, Paul, and Marlene Eberhart, eds. *Forms of Association: Making Publics in Early Modern Europe*. Amherst: University of Massachusetts Press, 2015.

Yates, Frances. *Astraea: The Imperial Theme in the Sixteenth Century*. London: Routledge and Kegan Paul, 1975.

Zarnowiecki, Matthew. *Fair Copies: Reproducing the English Lyric from Tottel to Shakespeare*. Toronto: University of Toronto Press, 2014.

INDEX

ACKNOWLEDGMENTS

I am profoundly grateful to the many people whose generosity has shaped the preceding pages.

This book began as a conversation with David Scott Kastan in a New Haven coffee shop in October 2011. Since then, he has been the project's wisest reader, its most incisive critic, its strongest champion. David believed in the book even when my own confidence flagged, and his imagination helped me to see what it might become. My debts to David, as a scholar, teacher, mentor, and friend, are innumerable.

At Yale University, Lawrence Manley and Catherine Nicholson were rigorous, generous, and patient advisors; they were also brilliant models of learning and critical acuity. David Quint and John Rogers read an early version of the manuscript and offered invaluable comments. A Folger Institute colloquium led by Barbara K. Lewalski, "Constructing and Representing Authorship in Early Modern England," proved a vital testing ground for the project early in its development. Many friends and colleagues have read the manuscript in part or whole, or worked through its ideas with me in conversation. I am grateful to Carla Baricz, Andrew Brown, Merve Emre, Len Gutkin, Matthew Harrison, Brad Holden, Andrew Hui, Andrew Kau, Tom Koenigs, Michael Komorowski, Ross Macdonald, Tom Olsen, Tessie Prakas, Aaron Pratt, Rebecca Rush, Debapriya Sarkar, Joe Stadolnik, Justin Sider, and Emily Vasiliauskas—and to more whom I fear I have forgotten here. Matt Hunter deserves special mention: he has read these pages and reread them, and his advice has helped me through many an impasse. The manuscript benefited from the expert guidance of Jerry Singerman and Lily Palladino at the University of Pennsylvania Press, and from the thoughtful responses of two anonymous readers for the Press, whose advice greatly strengthened the book in the final stages of its revision. Over the last several years, I have taught at the State University of New York at New Paltz, at Wesleyan University, and now at the State University of New York at Geneseo; I am grateful to my colleagues for welcoming me so warmly and making these institutions such congenial intellectual homes.

Earlier versions of Chapters 1 and 3 have appeared, respectively, in *Modern Language Quarterly* and *English Literary Renaissance*. I thank the editors and readers at both journals for their constructive suggestions. I have presented parts of the book at the conventions of the Renaissance Society of America and the Sixteenth Century Society, where they were sharpened by the generous and insightful questions of audiences and copresenters. I am especially grateful to have been able to present a version of Chapter 2, at the invitation of Emily Vasiliauskas, to the Class of 1960 Scholars at Williams College.

My deepest thanks go to my family: my siblings, Claire, Andy, Dan, and Martin; my stepmother, Joanie; and my father, Steve, the best example of a scholar and a person one could have. I write in loving memory of my late mother Nancy, my first and wisest teacher.

The last word, of course, goes to Anne. Her love made this book possible and reminds me daily that there is a world beyond it.